# *Bloom's Modern Critical Views*

African-American
  Poets: Volume I
African-American
  Poets: Volume II
Aldous Huxley
Alfred, Lord Tennyson
Alice Munro
Alice Walker
American Women
 ·Poets: 1650–1950
Amy Tan
Anton Chekhov
Arthur Miller
Asian-American
  Writers
August Wilson
The Bible
The Brontës
Carson McCullers
Charles Dickens
Christopher Marlowe
Contemporary Poets
Cormac McCarthy
C.S. Lewis
Dante Aligheri
David Mamet
Derek Walcott
Don DeLillo
Doris Lessing
Edgar Allan Poe
Émile Zola
Emily Dickinson
Ernest Hemingway
Eudora Welty
Eugene O'Neill
F. Scott Fitzgerald
Flannery O'Connor
Franz Kafka
Gabriel García
  Márquez

Geoffrey Chaucer
George Orwell
G.K. Chesterton
Gwendolyn Brooks
Hans Christian
  Andersen
Henry David Thoreau
Herman Melville
Hermann Hesse
H.G. Wells
Hispanic-American
  Writers
Homer
Honoré de Balzac
Jamaica Kincaid
James Joyce
Jane Austen
Jay Wright
J.D. Salinger
Jean-Paul Sartre
John Irving
John Keats
John Milton
John Steinbeck
José Saramago
J.R.R. Tolkien
Julio Cortázar
Kate Chopin
Kurt Vonnegut
Langston Hughes
Leo Tolstoy
Marcel Proust
Margaret Atwood
Mark Twain
Mary Wollstonecraft
  Shelley
Maya Angelou
Miguel de Cervantes
Milan Kundera
Nathaniel Hawthorne

Norman Mailer
Octavio Paz
Paul Auster
Philip Roth
Ralph Ellison
Ralph Waldo Emerson
Ray Bradbury
Richard Wright
Robert Browning
Robert Frost
Robert Hayden
Robert Louis
  Stevenson
Salman Rushdie
Stephen Crane
Stephen King
Sylvia Plath
Tennessee Williams
Thomas Hardy
Thomas Pynchon
Tom Wolfe
Toni Morrison
Tony Kushner
Truman Capote
Walt Whitman
W.E.B. Du Bois
William Blake
William Faulkner
William Gaddis
William Shakespeare,
  The Comedies
William Shakespeare,
  The Histories
William Shakespeare,
  The Tragedies
William Wordsworth
Zora Neale Hurston

*Bloom's Modern Critical Views*

# ALICE MUNRO

*Edited and with an introduction by*
Harold Bloom
Sterling Professor of the Humanities
Yale University

BLOOM'S
LITERARY CRITICISM
*An imprint of Infobase Publishing*

Bloom's Literary Criticism
An imprint of Infobase Publishing
132 West 31st Street
New York NY 10001

**Library of Congress Cataloging-in-Publication Data**
Alice Munro / edited and with an introduction by Harold Bloom.
    p. cm. — (Bloom's modern critical views)
  Includes bibliographical references and index.
  ISBN 978-1-60413-587-9
  1. Munro, Alice—Criticism and interpretation.    I. Bloom, Harold.    II. Title.
  III. Series.
  PR9199.3.M8Z53 2009
  813'.54—dc22

                                        2009014161

Bloom's Literary Criticism books are available at special discounts when purchased in bulk quantities for businesses, associations, institutions, or sales promotions. Please call our Special Sales Department in New York at (212) 967-8800 or (800) 322-8755.

You can find Chelsea House on the World Wide Web at
http://www.chelseahouse.com.

Contributing editor: Pamela Loos
Cover designed by Takeshi Takahashi

Printed in the United States of America
IBT IBT 10 9 8 7 6 5 4 3 2 1

This book is printed on acid-free paper.

All links and Web addresses were checked and verified to be correct at the time of publication. Because of the dynamic nature of the Web, some addresses and links may have changed since publication and may no longer be valid.

# Contents

Editor's Note      vii

Introduction     1
   *Harold Bloom*

*Dance of the Happy Shades*: Reading the Signs of Invasion     5
   *Magdalene Redekop*

"Every Last Thing . . . Everlasting":
   Alice Munro and the Limits of Narrative     29
   *Katherine J. Mayberry*

The Art of Alice Munro: Memory, Identity,
   and the Aesthetics of Connection     41
   *Georgeann Murphy*

"It's What I Believe": Patterns of
   Complicity in *The Progress of Love*     57
   *Ajay Heble*

"It Was about Vanishing":
   A Glimpse of Alice Munro's Stories     81
   *Mark Levene*

Getting Loose: Women and Narration in
   Alice Munro's *Friend of My Youth*     103
   *Deborah Heller*

Searching Bluebeard's Chambers:
    Grimm, Gothic, and Bible Mysteries in
    Alice Munro's "The Love of a Good Woman"          123
    *Judith McCombs*

Short Fiction with Attitude: The Lives of Boys
    and Men in the *Lives of Girls and Women*          143
    *Janet Beer*

Rewriting the Frontier: Wilderness and Social
    Code in the Fiction of Alice Munro                153
    *Rowland Smith*

Intimate Dislocations: Alice Munro,
    *Hateship, Friendship, Courtship, Loveship, Marriage*          167
    *Coral Ann Howells*

Chronology          193

Contributors          195

Bibliography          197

Acknowledgments          201

Index          203

# Editor's Note

My introduction praises Alice Munro for narrative exuberance and her accurate sense of what divides women and men. Nevertheless, I ponder her self-imposed limitations of scope and temperament.

In a brilliant pioneering study, Magdalene Redekop outlines the precise patterns of compassion and ironic distancing in Munro's first book of stories.

Katherine J. Mayberry examines some of the ways that Munro's storytellers discover the limits of narration, while Georgeann Murphy meditates on issues of memory, and Ajay Heble finds in Munro a "poetics of surprise."

"Survival over victory" is stressed as the choice of Munro's womenfolk by Mark Levene, after which Deborah Heller returns us to Munro's irony and Judith McCombs investigates mythic origins, including some biblical ones.

Janet Beer turns to the subsidiary role of male characters in Munro, while Rowland Smith invokes the frontier code that Munro revises.

In this volume's final essay, Coral Ann Howells melds spatial dislocations with Munro's visions of the complex relations of women with men.

HAROLD BLOOM

# Introduction

I read through Alice Munro's *Selected Stories* (1996) when that splendid volume appeared and have just reread all of it a dozen years later. Her more recent work is unknown to me, but the 545 pages of her culling from seven books of stories are more than enough to suggest her permanence as a writer. She joins the major artists of short fiction of the twentieth century: Landolfi, Calvino, Hardy, Kipling, Maugham, Saki (H.H. Munro), Frank O'Connor, Elizabeth Bowen, Edna O'Brien, Mann, Walser, Andreyev, Bunin, Dinesen, Schulz, Peretz, Singer, Agnon, Arenas, Cortázar, Gordimer, Wharton, Anderson, Katherine Anne Porter, Welty, Flannery O'Connor, Nabokov, Malamud, Ozick, Abish, Barthelme, and others. I omit the greatest: Henry James, Chekhov, D.H. Lawrence, Kafka, Babel, Borges, Joyce, Faulkner, Hemingway, Scott Fitzgerald. Those ten stand apart, but Alice Munro is in good company in the era of the short story.

She is not a fantasist or a visionary and scarcely a symbolist. Alice Munro's art is strictly mimetic yet what it imitates is the tangled yarn of that border area where our drives live us. Her sense of a concluded human life avoids retrospection. No one mounts to paradise on her stairway of surprise, and no one consequential (to the reader) drives into perdition. Ordinary unhappiness, which in others is not colorful to us, is an achievement for most of her women and many of her men. She is, with Katherine Anne Porter and Edna O'Brien, one of the wise women of the Post-Freudian Evening Land in its long decline.

That said, her narrative exuberance seems contrary to her realization "that love is not kind or honest and does not contribute to happiness in any

1

reliable way" (*Selected Stories*, p. 236). D.H. Lawrence's helpful admonition—to trust the tale, not the teller—has little relevance to her stories, since their art is to tell themselves. There is a limitation but only in comparison to such as Joyce, Lawrence, Hemingway, Babel: we do not feel life itself composing the narrative. But Turgenev and Tolstoy are miracles at representation, as are Joyce and Lawrence. Munro keeps within her circumference, knowing that to generalize, unless you are Tolstoy, is aesthetic idiocy. She inhabits her bookshop of the heart and generously offers her women, in particular, as volumes for sale. Munro's fictive marriages are world-without-end bargains (Shakespeare's rending phrase in *Love's Labour's Lost*) and she studies, not their nostalgias, but their surprising endurances. When they fail, somehow *they* fail and not their wives and husbands whose resurgent wills ebb in the domain of the drives.

2

Do Munro's stories blend into one another? A friend ventures that reproach, and it is true that I have no particular favorites among the twenty-eight published together in 1996. Her tonalities may be too consistent, her characters not sufficiently distinguished from one another to allow a tale as memorable as Hemingway's "Hills Like White Elephants" or Porter's "Flowering Judas." She seems to sacrifice singularities to her integral sense of the differences between women and men.

Yet that accurate sense is of enormous human and aesthetic value, and to clearly convey it demands a subtler art than I might expect Munro to have mastered. Her stories have a touch of the triumphant slyness of Shakespearean comedy, from which Jane Austen and Virginia Woolf derived so much. Again, my citations are too grand: Munro has little of Austen's or Woolf's uncanny, understated intricacy of phrasemaking in the service of a comic vision. Their ironies, like Shakespeare's, can be too large to be seen (as G.K. Chesterton said of Chaucer). Munro's ironies are palpable and enable her storytelling to apprehend "those old marriages, where love and grudges could be growing underground, so confused and stubborn, it must have seemed they had forever" (the end of "The Progress of Love," p. 288).

Munro, immensely skilled and wisely compassionate as she is, lacks the fine madness of great literary art. One could not say of her characters what Eudora Welty remarked of Lawrence's that they "don't really speak their words—not conversationally, not to one another—they are *not* speaking in the street, but are playing like fountains or radiating like the moon or storming like the sea, or their silence as the silence of wicked rocks." But Munro's people are the immanences of our daily lives whereas Lawrence's speak for our daemonic otherness that transcends the everyday whether it wants to or not.

A prophet and a polemicist, Lawrence nevertheless expanded the limits of art. Munro is happy to remain within the horizons of Chekhov and Turgenev, Hemingway and Joyce, and her naturalism is so firm and rich as to preclude any necessity for defense. Scattered in her prose are observations true beyond context, particularly relating not so much to what men find attractive in young women but to the elements such women *believe* are the stimuli to attraction. Munro blurs the line between the objective and the subjective, and between the small and the large, in order to discover what, if anything, will suffice for a more abundant life.

MAGDALENE REDEKOP

# Dance of the Happy Shades:
## *Reading the Signs of Invasion*

**"Walker Brothers Cowboy": Playing "I Spy"**
The first story in Alice Munro's first collection of stories begins with a prologue that compares paternal and maternal images of reproduction. A playful tone is set in the first sentence: "After supper my father says, 'Want to go down and see if the Lake's still there?'" The sentence immediately following, however, exposes the dark underside of the mocking surface:

> We leave my mother sewing under the dining-room light, making clothes for me against the opening of school. She has ripped up for this purpose an old suit and an old plaid wool dress of hers, and she has to cut and match very cleverly and also make me stand and turn for endless fittings, sweaty, itching from the hot wool, ungrateful. (DHS, 1)

The daughter resents being a dressmaker's dummy; like the daughter in "Red Dress—1946," she is humiliated by the exposure of her body during fittings: "I felt like a great raw lump, clumsy and goose-pimpled" (DHS, 148). If the daughter is like a lump of clay ("with me, her creation;" DHS, 5) the mother in "Walker Brothers Cowboy" is like a parody of the biblical God who fashions Adam out of clay. The mother herself, however, is virtually bodiless. She is nothing but a pair of sewing hands that work on

From *Mothers and Other Clowns: The Stories of Alice Munro*, pp. 37–59. © 1992 by Magdalene Redekop.

5

thriftily with patterns and plaids of the past to construct something for the daughter's future.

We remain aware of these caring hands as we listen to the father explaining to his daughter about the origins of the Great Lakes: "Like that—and he shows me his hand with his spread fingers pressing the rock-hard ground where we are sitting" (DHS, 3). It is not, in the father's account, a divine hand that made these lakes but rather "fingers of ice" that gouged out the deep places. Unlike those fingers, moreover, the father's hand snakes "hardly any impression" since he is working with rock, not with fabric or clay. This gesture, like the mother's sewing, is an absurd and failed miming of the action of the Father in *Genesis*. The difference is that the maternal action requires the body of the daughter. What the father will give his daughter in this story is not totally unlike the mother's reproductions. The difference is that while the mother sews a dress for her, the father shows her, by example, how to construct a mask. Both parents ensure, however, that the daughter's idea of reproduction will be one based on thrift. The father's mask is also made from a borrowed pattern.

Cowboy songs are a product of the American frontier. This Canadianized "cowboy," however, does not make his own laws as he travels but is more obviously bound to the economy of his country. There is no melodrama of the wild west here. The major danger is the boredom that threatens the pedlar's day. The horse, that brute energy or matter which is dominated by the heroic cowboy, is conspicuous by its absence and replaced by the car. Although this machine suggests domination of nature, the proper noun *Walker* mutes that image and the solitary romantic cowboy is acknowledged as part of a company, a male collective of "Brothers."

The father can cheerfully say "I" because he is a member of the company. He knows, from the beginning that "I" is a pose, a disguise. The father's "salesman's spiel"—the mask of the "Walker Brothers Cowboy"—becomes associated, by Munro's choice of title, with the story itself. *Spiel* is the German word for play and the father puts his very identity into this play. The absence of the mother on this field trip thus shows that her identity is not so easily put into play. In the midst of the radical instability of the father's sense of self, there is a paradoxical stability. When they arrive at Nora's yard, Nora does not at first recognize him. When she does, she says: "Oh, my Lord God . . . it's you" (DHS, 10), to which the father responds with typical self-mockery: "It was, the last time I looked in the mirror" (DHS, 10). The father's clowning will offer the daughter a means of survival but his gift to his daughter has a cutting edge; if she adopts his method (and she has no choice if she writes herself into playful existence) then she seems to be denying the mother's world. The daughter who writes will find herself caught, willy-nilly, between the maternal and paternal responses to self-representation. The narrating daughter is embarrassed by the mother's efforts to be more than herself, to be a "lady" and she prefers the father's pose as less than himself—a boy. The mother's idea of self-reproduction is ironically more bound than is the father's, by the patriarchal order. She is trapped inside the sign "lady" which balances the word "Lord" (raised as a fleeting echo by Nora's exclamation). The mother conspires, furthermore, to keep herself there.

When we do become aware of the mother's body in this story it is not her body but the body of a lady: "She walks serenely like a lady shopping, like a *lady* shopping, past the housewives in loose beltless dresses torn under the arms" (DHS, 5). Her voice, the "voice so high, proud and ringing" is the voiceless voice of a lady. The daughter loathes even her own name when this voice speaks it in public. Although Nora later says the names in turn (DHS, 12), they are never inscribed in the story. Ben Jordan, the father, has the power to rename himself, however playfully, while the daughter sees her nameless mother and herself as "objects of universal ridicule. Even the dirty words chalked on the sidewalk are laughing at us" (DHS, 5). They cannot be resisting readers of the text on the sidewalk unless they have some sense of a self that is doing the reading. Mother and daughter will remain as objects of ridicule, unless they can find a way to construct themselves as subjects.

This mother who is confined to the body of a lady has no sense of humour. Her husband's talk of piles and boils hints at the comic protuberances that characterize what Bakhtin calls the "grotesque body." Since the body of the woman is the "major battleground in the hysterical repression of the 'grotesque form'" (White, 1989, 165), the mother's bourgeois response is predictable. The "pedlar's song" is "Not a very funny song, in my mother's opinion" (DHS, 4). "Sometimes," says the daughter, "trying to make my mother laugh he pretends to be himself in a farm kitchen, spreading out his sample case" and the mother does "laugh finally, unwillingly" (DHS, 8). Laughter requires distance and the mother cannot pretend to be herself when she is so firmly encased in the costume of the lady. Like Addie in *Lives*, she has an "innocence," a "way of not knowing when people [are] laughing" (LGW, 81). The narrating daughter yearns to escape the mother, to escape the evidence of the cruelty that her mother does to herself in the name of the Father. The father, in his "salesman's outfit," offers a "rising hope of adventure" (DHS, 6).

The adventure that does occur is a practical joke that acts as the central text within the text of the story, evoking multiple responses that expose the distribution of power. The adventure is less important, in itself, than are the reproductions of that adventure, the responses to the joke. These are played out against a grey background. The children play the game "*I Spy*" but "it is hard to find many colours" (DHS, 9). The daughter's own first hand account is a spare reporting of what her eyes spy while her father waits at the door of the house and someone empties a chamberpot from an upstairs window. The little brother "laughs and laughs" but the daughter is silent. She sees a window "slammed down, the blind drawn" and notes that "we never did see a hand or face." The silence of the father and the menacing hand behind the blind help to distance the daughter from her brother's naive response: "'Pee, pee,' sings my brother ecstatically. 'Somebody dumped down pee!'" To which the father replies: "'Just don't tell your mother that. . . . She isn't liable to see the joke'" (DHS, 10).

"Just don't tell" is a phrase echoed in "Images" where the father instructs the daughter: "'But don't say anything about it at home. Don't mention it to your Momma or Mary, either one'" (DHS, 42). "Walker Brothers Cowboy" is full of "things not to be mentioned" (DHS, 18). In this story (as in "Images") the text of the story itself is an unmentionable joke hidden from the mother, a guilty secret shared with the father. We share the daughter's pain about the mother since she cannot "see the joke," since she cannot read what we are reading. The victim of the practical joke is literally the father but by this silence a substitution takes place and the scapegoat is seen to be the mother, who is the "object of ridicule." We are sensitized to this by the fact that the "other" woman—the father's old flame—usurps the mother's place. The father is a comedian in need of an audience and that is precisely what Nora provides.

The approach to the house and to the character of Nora will be recapitulated in a different form in the later story "Lichen" (PL, 32–55). Like Stella in that story, Nora is overweight. Her "arms are heavy, and every bit of her skin you can see is covered with little dark freckles like measles" (DHS, 12). Like Stella, Nora dresses flamboyantly. The body, rendered highly visible, is matched by the high visibility of the dress which is flowered lavishly. "'It's the first time I knew there was such a thing as green poppies,' my father says, looking at her dress" (DHS, 12). His boyish wonder echoes that of Stephen in *Portrait of the Artist as a Young Man*: "But you could not have a green rose. But perhaps somewhere in the world you could" (Joyce, 1916, 12). Nora's denial is significant: "'You would be surprised all the things you never knew. . . . They're not poppies anyway, they're just flowers'" (DHS, 12–13). The father here presumes to label the fabric (choosing an image associated with male heroism) and Nora's resistance takes back the acts of fabrication and naming.

Shortly after arrival at Nora's house, the father constructs a narrative joke out of the practical joke:

> But after a while he turns to a familiar incident. He tells about the
> chamberpot that was emptied out the window. "Picture me there,"

he says, "hollering my heartiest. *Oh, lady, it's your Walker Brothers man, anybody home?*" He does himself hollering, grinning absurdly, waiting, looking up in pleased expectation and then—oh, ducking covering his head with his arms, looking as if he begged for mercy (when he never did anything like that, I was watching), and Nora laughs, almost as hard as my brother did at the time. (DHS, 15)

Nora is right when she protests: "That's not a word true!" and yet the exaggeration, the distortion, the mocking self-presentation is a release. Release comes from the multiplication of pictures produced by the father's imperative: "Picture me." What we picture, in fact, is a convention of clowning. The cowboy steps aside to make room for a Charlie Chaplin act.

Francis Sparshott refers to Charlie Chaplin's characterizations as having a "quality of pure mime, an illumination of an action from within" (Sparshott, 1988, 336). This adaptation of the "movement traditions of circus clowns" is one of a "variety of movement arts" that are "neither acting nor dance but belong to this alternative tradition of mime, an enhanced and poeticized presentation, neither of personality nor of body movement, but precisely of action as taking on an exemplary nature of its own" (Sparshott, 1988, 336). At the end of *Lives of Girls and Women*, Bobby Sherriff's gesture will offer another example of Munro's interest in such movements. Like many kinds of body language, such gestures are "*thrown away*" (Sparshott, 1988, 331) and Munro's fiction recovers them. The miming of the father in "Walker Brothers Cowboy" is of particular significance because he claims to be miming or "doing" himself. Miming, however, is not impersonating, as Sparshott notes (1988, 335). The very absurdity of the father's claim serves to draw attention to the mime itself and to his immediate audience and the particulars of this visit. "One can mime oneself walking as one walked on a specific occasion or as one walks in specific circumstances," Sparshott notes, "so long as the occasion or the circumstances do not at present obtain" (1988, 334). The father's act of doing himself shows up the absurdity of our illusions about autonomous identity, exposing the reality that we make ourselves up out of an assortment of conventions. It also makes visible the presence of Nora who, in turn, makes his mime visible by her laughter.

Subsequent stories by Munro will show just how important the father's example of mimicry is to the daughter's work as an artist. When Ralph Gillespie in "Who Do You Think You Are?" does Milton Homer and Rose does Ralph doing Milton Homer we are seeing complex variations on this father doing himself. The problems enter when you consider *doing* the mother who cannot *do* herself. Nora, the mock mother, plays a mediating role in the daughter's response to this problem. The song, "Walker Brothers Cowboy" which, to the mother, was "[n]ot a very funny song" is to Nora hysterically funny: "she laughs so much that in places he has to stop and wait for her to get over laughing so he can go on, because she makes him laugh too" (DHS, 15). Nora is open to comedy. She is a match for the father because she can pretend to be herself *doing* her own mother. We sense the father's need for her nurturing as we enter her maternal space and we remain conscious of the infantilized mother who is the object of her mothering.

Two dead metaphors of the mother are enclosed in Nora's house, like mocking icons set up for Nora to imitate. The first is the body of Nora's own Momma: "Blind! . . . Her eyes are closed, the eyelids sunk away down, showing no shape of the eyeball, just hollows. From one hollow comes a drop of silver liquid, a medicine, or a miraculous tear" (DHS, 12). The blind mother "falls asleep, her head on the side, her mouth open." The open mouth does not speak and the eyes do not see. This maternal blindness is not transcended by paradox. Unlike Milton and Homer, but like Milton Homer, this mother is no seer. In contrast to this image is the "picture on the wall of Mary, Jesus's mother . . . in shades of bright blue and pink with a spiked band of light around her head" (DHS, 14). This picture, unlike the blind Momma, does make claims to authority. The image of the virgin birth, however, is belied by the multiplicity of phallic spikes.

It is Nora who is able to confront the limits of her own power. When the father invites her to visit and gives directions, "Nora does not repeat these directions." Instead, she writes her own text on the machine, a text which we cannot see: "She touches the fender, making an unintelligible mark in the dust there" (DHS, 17). Don't look to Nora for help. Implicitly she warns us all "never to count on" the extra sense of the mother (PL, 105). In the act of writing her unintelligible mark in the dust, Nora gestures her abdication, her retreat into her house. Like an inversion of Ibsen's Nora, she plans her own exit and writes herself out from inside the story. This exercise of choice, anticipating that of Meda in "Meneseteung," is what gives her potential power. Her very abdication, moreover, makes available to the daughter, as reader in the text, a possibility for resistance. Hope comes not from the "rising hope of adventure," not from desire for some nebulous ideal (a cowboy's futuristic dream) but rather from the opacities themselves, from awareness of the very act of imaging. "I was watching" (DHS, 15) is the crucial phrase and "I Spy" is the game. I spy something that is green.

The awareness of this act of imaging, however, comes with a sense of the inadequacy of the images. Nora remains other—unabsorbed into the images that surround her—and the landscape left behind "changes into something you will never know" (DHS, 18). This is not the blurry and romantic view seen from a horse but rather the miniaturized and severely framed view seen in the rearview mirror of a car. The concluding image of the story is that of the children facing backwards in the car while the father drives them forwards towards the house in which their mother lies, having her headache. The inversion is complete. We have been turned inside out if we began by assuming that children look to the future and adults look to the past. The narrator, of course, looks in both directions and that is why she is a writer.

At some deep level, the daughter is aware that what they are driving towards and what they are driving away from are the same thing in this sense: both are something that you do not know. Nora began as an ideal reader for the father's text—the text being the song "Walker Brothers Cowboy" which is situated within the story "Walker Brothers Cowboy." By her act of making a mark (an alternative text) that we cannot read, she absents herself from the story. She does not, however, by this gesture become a non-reader. She becomes, rather, the reader of texts that we do not see. The other in "other woman" and the other in mother come together behind a blind spot which cuts the daughter off, painfully, from her endearing father. He—small wonder—is "fresh out of songs" as they return home.

This story demonstrates that any daughter's first person self-representations will be conditioned and invaded by what she has watched her father do—what we all watch our fathers do as they construct the laws of genre. This daughter is blessed with a clowning father whose physical performance undermines those laws. Since the mother refuses to come out and play, the daughter must learn to clown from her father and to dance from the mock mother. The story itself and the "I" that is written is inside the paternal idea of craft, inside a world that is made. The power of the fiction, however, comes from what is excluded by that view of creation. We can begin to glimpse the implications of this for a woman's writing. Nora's writing—her signature, so to speak—is not read by us, but Nora (unlike the narrator and her mother) does have a name. The fact that it is not only her name, that it has been used by Ibsen and others, is a clue to Munro's method. The mock mothers that you meet when you run away from the "real mother" will direct you back to an acknowledgement of the other in mother and of the fact that the female subject, like the male subject, has to be constructed out of recycled fabric.

## "Images": Don't Tell Momma

"Images" is what we used to call a seminal story, rich in reflected and refracted images. The pattern of departure and return which was enacted in "Walker Brothers Cowboy" is here repeated with a difference, but this fact will not make us confident of possessing an archetypal pattern if we pay close attention. Catherine Sheldrick Ross uses this story as evidence for a claim that Munro "turns to myths and legends" for her patterns. The details add "texture" but they do not threaten that pattern. In Ross's view the "pattern is deepened with each reworking" but not challenged (Ross, 1983, 113–114). She notes that the structure of "Images" is "the familiar motif of the underground journey" (114). It is true that Munro works with "elements that have become central in the shared storehouse of story-telling conventions" (Ross, 1988, 122). What Ross fails to note, however, is that the details do challenge the pattern. Munro herself has observed (in conversation with Tim Struthers) that she admires a writer's focus on "the way the experience was looked at" and does not like a mythological "framework." She says explicitly, "I wanted to do without this. And that, I think, is my personal bias" (Struthers, 1983, 16).

I don't believe that Munro (or any other writer) can do without the myths or conventions, but I hope to demonstrate that she shows how the major myths do without the body of the mother. It is for this reason that she has to write against the grain of the conventions. The quest pattern in "Images" comes clear only if we turn a blind eye to the women left behind. In "Walker Brothers Cowboy" the mother was left behind and the substitute mother was the mock goal. In this case both mother and mock mother are left at home while the daughter goes adventuring with her father. As Lorna Irvine notes with relation to *Lives of Girls and Women*, "the women … pull against the straightforward development of the plot and will not allow clarification to occur" (Irvine, 1983, 107). The word "plot" here could be replaced with "myth" or "quest."

The most conspicuous presence in "Images" is that of a mock mother who parodies the role played by the "Intended" in Conrad's *Heart of Darkness*. Nowhere are women more firmly and ironically excluded from the quest formula than in *Heart of Darkness*. "'Did I mention a girl?'" asks Marlow.

> "Oh, she is out of it—completely. They—the women I mean—are out of it—should be out of it. We must help them to stay in that beautiful world of their own, lest ours gets worse. Oh, she had to be out of it. You should have heard the disinterred body of Mr. Kurtz saying, 'My Intended.' You would have perceived directly then how completely she was out of it." (Conrad, 1984, 84)

In *Heart of Darkness*, the "Intended" is in a kind of blind spot, alluded to briefly at crucial points in the narrative. At the end of the narrative she comes towards Marlow "all in black, with a pale head, floating towards [him] in the dusk" (117).

The Intended in "Images" is, by contrast, in the foreground. Mary McQuade is a conspicuous physical presence. The jokes lost on the mother swell her up "like a bullfrog" and make her "red in the face" (DHS, 34). The narrator pretends not to remember Mary's previous visit—the time of her grandfather's death. He lay in "near-darkness all day, with his white hair, new washed and tended and soft as a baby's, and his white nightshirt and pillows, making an island in the room" (DHS, 30). Mary McQuade, "the other island," is in her starched white uniform and sits "mostly not moving" waiting for the grandfather to die. This figure of power is dominant. The patriarch is infantilized by her and thus put on a level with the narrator who is "put to sleep in a crib." "Out in the daylight" Mary turns out (like Nora in "Walker Brothers Cowboy") to be "freckled all over, everywhere you could see, as if she was sprinkled with oatmeal" (DHS, 31).

She is waiting not only for birth and death but also for a lover. As Ben teases her about potential husbands, however, she does not fade into the shadows like Conrad's "Intended." On the contrary, we become increasingly conscious of her body: "Her laughter would come out first in little angry puffs and explosions through her shut lips, while her face grew redder than you would have thought possible and her body twitched and rumbled threateningly in its chair" (DHS, 34). Her ominous presence makes it impossible to give ourselves totally over to the quest pattern which dominates the story. It's astonishing how much power can be invested in one such person, simply a "practical nurse" given to playing practical jokes on members of her family. Her stay-at-home power is set up as a counter to the power of the ancient quest pattern—departure and return/descent and ascent. Munro takes the figure of the "Intended," costumes her in dazzling white, paints her face bright red, and sprinkles her body generously with freckles so that we can see her. This spectacle, in turn, changes the way we look at the body of the pregnant mother. The "large, fragile and mysterious object, difficult to move" (DHS, 33) is transformed, through Mary's mocking eyes, into a kind of circus balloon. The real pregnancy poses as a phantom pregnancy as the mother threatens to "'bob up to the ceiling, just like a big balloon'" (DHS, 33).

Mary's power is associated with the beginnings of life and with the end of life. The first time I read this story I assumed that the mother was dying and many of my students make the same assumption. There is an ambiguity in the story: the mother could as easily be dying as giving birth. Mary cannot control the time of either death or birth. The place where she sits is a place of waiting and what the young girl learns is the limits of power. The mother is reduced to being like an infant, whimpering "childishly" for Mary to rub her back (DHS, 33) and the mother's abdication makes a space for the activities of the mock mother. Although Mary's practical jokes are frightening, they are easier to cope with than is the "everlastingly wounded phantom" called "*Mother*." Her tricks serve to deflect and refract the power of the mother.

Swollen with jokes like a bullfrog, her body is a mocking reproduction of the body of the mother, swollen in pregnancy. At the same time, it mimics the male aggression suggested by the word *bull*. Her activities as trickster and clown make the text visible. They give the daughter something to interpret and encourage her to be wary while she reads.

The narrator's father is the victim of Mary McQuade's practical jokes and their pattern of interaction is consistent with what anthropologists know of the relation between permission to joke and kinship structures. A disturbing aggression is thriftily suggested by these jokes: "She gave him a fork with a prong missing, pretending it was by accident. He threw it at her, and missed, but startled me considerably" (DHS, 34). Like "Walker Brothers Cowboy," this story also puts the author herself in the position of a trickster and the quest pattern itself is part of her bag of tricks. The father claims to be the author of a joke on the Intended when he presents the story to Mary on his return: "We found the one for you today, Mary" (DHS, 43) but a double-take highlights the word "we." That "we" includes not only his daughter but also a larger collective—we who want these archetypal patterns and we who reinforce their rigidity. In actual fact (as the humble father knows perfectly well) it is by no means clear who is having the last laugh. Despite his "we found" it is clear that he did not go out hunting for the ideal husband for Mary; he went out to check his trapline for muskrats.

The trapline leads to the body of a muskrat: "the stiff, soaked body, a fact of death" (DHS, 36). The archetypal storyline, similarly, leads to a dead end. The mock mother is called Mary. The man who lives in the underground house is called Joe. The archetypal story, thus turned into a practical joke, leads to a repetition of the father's pattern of teasing. "His teasing of Mary was always about husbands. 'I thought up one for you this morning!' he would say" (DHS, 34). Mary enjoys "all these preposterous matings." This last one is a mating of Joseph and Mary that leads to a dead metaphor. Where is the baby? If we look too closely, the distortions multiply. The mother of the narrator, when she refers to herself "gloomily in the third person" as *Mother* is associated with "the name of Jesus" (DHS, 33). Efforts to fix the archetype, then, produce a mockery of the holy family.

Asked by Hancock if names are a "clue" to her characters, Munro answers (somewhat disingenuously) that she simply chooses names that "sound right" and does not think about why (Hancock, 1987, 213). The names Joe and Mary do "sound right" but not because they are clues leading to the end of a game. They are, however, clues to something that is intimated by the father's description of Joe to Mary: "'I thought up one for you this morning!'" (DHS, 34). The names, in short, are "thought up"—arbitrary fictions. Joe's talk of the Silases who burned his house may echo the biblical Silas but also, perhaps, a literary one. Silas Marner is a surrogate father in a novel by George Eliot alluded to in *Lives of Girls and Women* (LGW, 175). It is not possible to track down these echoes and nail them to the wall, because the narrator eats the nails. Joe Phippen feeds them to her in the form of a "tin of Christmas candies, which seemed to have melted then hardened then melted again, so the coloured stripes had run. They had a taste of nails" (DHS, 41). Eating this candy, the narrator consumes also the archetypal Christmas story about Mary and Joseph and, in so doing, makes it impossible for the holy family to be made up of this Mary and this Joe.

When the old symmetries are burned out, two houses are still left in this story. One is the building which houses the pregnant mother. The other is Joe Phippen's underground house. The trapline and the storyline make up a connecting journey between these two houses, when father invites daughter to "come with me and look at the traps" (DHS, 35). The storyline is riddled with traps for unwary readers and the dream-like atmosphere is itself a trap. The narrator corrects the people who ask "'What are you dreaming about?'" with an explicit "I was not dreaming. I was trying to understand the danger, to read the signs of invasion" (DHS, 35). She can read the signs of danger only if she watches "the shadows instead of the people." The journey leads to Joe Phippen's underground house, to a place of shadows that suggests primordial depths, Plato's cave, and "fairy stories" (DHS, 43). Ultimately, however, it is only a "hole in the ground" (DHS, 39) and we do well to pay heed to the advice that Joe gives to his visitors as they enter: "Mind your head here" (DHS, 39).

The severing of the head is an image already evoked by the stories that the narrator remembers her mother telling, about "a queen getting her head chopped off while a little dog was hiding under her dress" (DHS, 33). With the house destroyed, and the head of the symbolic order chopped off, does it come down to "the horror, the horror"? Our desire to believe in such essentials is what Munro, like Conrad, exposes. The quest pattern tantalizes, evoking our desire to reach a place of origin, perhaps identified with the "hidden place" in the Wawanash River (DHS, 37). This is a failed journey, however, for we do not arrive at a place where it all began. Joseph did not, after all, father Jesus. It's not that there is no quest; it's just that the quest is repeatedly displaced. What they find when they arrive is something made, not something born. The narrator recognizes it in retrospect as "the sort of place I would like to live in myself, like the houses I made under snow drifts" (DHS, 40). This recognition is anticipated by the reversal that takes place when Ben and his daughter encounter the man with the axe. The man threatening her father with an axe is

the sight that does not surprise you, the thing you have always known was there that comes so naturally, moving delicately and

contentedly and in no hurry, as if it was made, in the first place, from
a wish of yours, a hope of something final, terrifying. (DHS, 38)

"Made in the first place" is a crucial phrase in this passage because it under-
lines the story's focus on human reproduction and on beginnings.

Making and invention intersect with the world in which a grandfather
dies and a baby is born. It is possible to dismiss the danger in the story as a
fiction. Since Joe Phippen seems obviously paranoic, the narrator's fears of Joe
may be similarly imaginary. The axe remains there, however, lying on the table
in the underground house. The object of the child's fear may be constructed
from a wish of her own but that wish is shared and reproduced not only by
her but also by the machinery of popular culture. In her state of paralysis she
waits, "like a child in an old negative, electrified against the dark noon sky,
with blazing hair and burned-out Orphan Annie eyes" (DHS, 38). We wait
with her, hypnotized by the strong circle of the eyes. Like the child, we may
escape paralysis by becoming active readers but this will be impossible as long
as we project total meaning or essence into the places we cannot see. Our
eyes, in that case, will be "burned-out," like Joe's house: "they burned me out,
Ben" (DHS, 39). As she watches the surfaces in Joe's house (her father's good
manners, Joe's hospitality), the daughter begins to see the underground as a
repetition, not a rejection, of the house she left behind.

The return home after the visit is a return with a difference—a difference which draws attention to the act of storytelling and redefines those
secret "hidden places." The house left behind and the house to which they
journey are both, to adapt Ross's phrase, a "shared storehouse of story-telling
conventions" (Ross, 1983, 122). The "hidden places" are not where *the* story
hides but are simply what we do not understand. The recognition of this by
the narrator makes it possible for her to realize that she is no longer afraid of
Mary McQuade's power (DHS, 43). Power is not embodied in any one figure
or house, but dispersed. That does not mean there is no danger, that heads are
not chopped off queens or traps snapped on muskrats or cats victimized by
crazy men. The narrator learns to see all stories as partial. When her father,
for example, tells the story of Joe Phippen to Mary McQuade, the daughter
notes: "He left out the axe but not the whisky and the cat" (DHS, 43).

We are returned to the world of surfaces but, more important still, we
have discovered that what appeared to be underground is also made up of surfaces. There is no escape from the Conradian irony that civilization is built on
lies and manners. The "hole in the ground" where Joe, our mock father reigns,
is no more our place of origin than the belly of our mock mother. The quest
is a deliberate failure and we see this when we look at how the father, like
the one in "Walker Brothers Cowboy," tells a story to the mock mother. "She

served my father his supper and he told her the story of Joe Phippen" (DHS, 43). He makes a joke out of it. The joke is on Mary McQuade. She becomes the scapegoat of the story. The joke is also on Joe, however. Since we have witnessed the father's compassion towards Joe Phippen, it is troubling to see him so cavalierly reproducing Joe for the amusement of Mary. Who, in this version of storytelling, holds the power? We have learned that it is not Mary. It is not she who decides when life begins and ends. If the father in "Walker Brother Cowboy" teaches his daughter to clown, this one gives his daughter a lesson in "humility and good manners." When he was with Joe, he listened to Joe Phippen's story and went along with the idea of the Silases: "'I heard about that,' my father said" (DHS, 39). When he is with Mary, by contrast, he goes along with the fiction that the Silases are a fiction; here, at the supper table, he enters instead into the fiction of her search for an ideal lover.

This insistence on compassion as a motivating force in storytelling will come to fruition in the much later story, "The Progress of Love," where moments made up of compassionate lies are preferred in the end to the "old marriages, where love and grudges could be growing underground" (PL, 30–31). The underground in "Images" is not the place of the perfect story or of ultimate horror. It is the place where stubborn grudges are nurtured, a place of rigid convention and of obsessive and terrified behaviour. The father's world of good manners and playful clowning is a relief from those obsessions but it too is surface. The motive for telling the story—compassion—may be more important than the content of the story. The difference, however, between this compassionate lie and the lie that ends Conrad's *Heart of Darkness* is that this "Intended" is in on the joke and can hold her own with the father. The absence of the mother looms large in the two opening stories of this collection, but what is equally noteworthy is the comforting and solid presence of the father. His playful reproductions, his good manners, and his humility offer an alternative to grandiose quests. Instead of reaffirming the robust, individual male ego, his little acts of compassion and of failed understanding begin "the progress of love."

## "The Office": Writing on the Wall

This story demands attention, however briefly, since it is specifically about mothering and writing. The writer acquires a room of her own, but the walls of the room crumble for the simple reason that the narrator takes her mothering self with her and responds to Mr Malley, her landlord, as if he is a hungry child needing attention. She sees his portrait before she meets Mr Malley, and the "gilded frame" encloses a man in a business suit who looks "pre-eminently prosperous, rosy and agreeable." In person, however, Mr Malley moves "with a sigh, a cushiony settling of flesh, a ponderous matriarchal discomfort" (DHS, 63–64). As this mock matriarch fusses over the writer, bringing her assorted gifts, he begins to seem, however, more like a big fat baby who is "eatin' into" her time (DHS, 66). He seems to her "so wistful, so infantile" and she cannot turn away from his "obsequious hunger" (DHS, 67).

The repeated changes in the image of Mr Malley lead the narrator to see through the image of herself as a nurturer and to a confrontation with herself as a potential murderer. When he charges her with writing filthy things on the walls of the bathroom, she makes a confession: "I really wanted to murder him. I remember how soft and loathsome his face looked" (DHS, 73). Would this be matricide, patricide, or infanticide? The kaleidoscopic reversals expose the patterns of family behaviour as human constructs open to change. What holds the kaleidoscope still for the space of this story is the focus on the act of writing. His activity ("arranging in his mind the bizarre but somehow never quite satisfactory narrative of yet another betrayal of trust," DHS, 74) is seen as a mirror reflection of her activity ("While I arrange words, and think it is my right to be rid of him;" DHS, 74). The filthy writing on the wall in the washroom is yet another practical joke. Like the writing chalked on the sidewalk in "Walker Brothers Cowboy," this writing seems to be laughing at the narrator. The author of the writing on the wall is never identified and this throws the notion of authority into question, in contrast to the writing on the wall in the Bible. The narrator does get her vengeance, of course, by writing this story and thus nurturing him back with a vengeance. We cannot actually see him "in the flesh" so her reproduction is a conscious failure. Knowing this, the narrator cannot help but wonder why his arrangements and stories are obscene and hers are authorized and classified as literary.

We may say (anticipating the ending of "Material") that "this is not enough" and (anticipating the end of "Ottawa Valley") that she will never "be rid of him." This story, like so many of Munro's best stories, is about the failure of story. There is too much left over. The writer, the mother, the house, the office, the children, the husband, the landlord, the very trinkets in the office down to the last detail ("I forgot—a little plastic pencil sharpener") all appear separated, sharpened in their divisions, by this dramatic confrontation. At the beginning of the story the narrator claims to have discovered "the solution to my life." This is a failed solution and the details cannot be dissolved. After all the reproductions are done, the unincorporated flesh returns as a reproach. The self-representation in this little sketch questions any idea of art as final mastery. Nobody has the last laugh. Munro succeeds by a conscious failure and in this way her reproduction stands in sharp contrast to Mr Malley's self-portrait in the "gilded frame." This self-reproduction is that of somebody who watches—she watches herself in the act of watching the landlord watching her.

When the focus is on how we see, then nobody is the lord of the land. The naming of Malley reflects Munro's ironic view of power. The letters *mal* have been prefixed, since the sixteenth century, to many English words to convey the sense of something "ill," "wrong," "improper,"—as in the word *malevolent* (*OED*). Since the prefix *mal* also suggests the word *male* it may be tempting to fix blame and see the story as a stereotypical feminist rejection of the male figure of power. I hope my reading, however brief, has been enough to show that Munro does more than this. She shows the male figure to us as her reproduction and by this reversal we see, not his evil power, but her power. The story, after all, is about class as well as about gender. What we have is a diffusion of malevolence and power and a demonstration of the way in which we all live inside the "gilded frame" of the patriarchy.

## "The Peace of Utrecht": Breaking the Pink Bowl

"Walker Brothers Cowboy" and "Images" both sketch out ironic retellings of the quest pattern—departure from home and return to home. The mother is left behind as the daughter ventures forth with her father and this exclusion is the source of the irony. In "The Peace of Utrecht," the mother is not left behind. She is dead, and the result of this is that the "quest" is inverted: we begin with the daughter who is returning to the house. Alice Munro has spoken about this story and about her own mother:

> the incurable illness of a parent makes a relationship—its stresses become more evident that way. And so her illness and death and the whole tension between us—she had Parkinson's disease—was very important. The first real story I ever wrote was about her. The first story I think of as a real story was "Peace of Utrecht." It's about the death of a mother. (in Hancock, 1987, 215)

There is an ambiguity here. The narrator calls herself Helen but we know that Alice Munro is writing about herself; she admits candidly to Hancock that the story is "about" her own mother. The resulting confusion between fiction and reality disturbs our neat assumptions about the autonomy of art. The very awkwardness of the naming points to the transparency and inadequacy of our conspicuous fictions. Although this is probably one of the least funny stories Munro has ever written, it offers the strongest clues to the origins of her comic art. The details of Parkinson's Disease, like a "tasteless sideshow" (DHS, 195), will keep recurring as a signal that Munro refuses to dispense, entirely, with referentiality. This refusal will draw her repeatedly into a blurry area between life and art, an area where self-parody will be the only option.

Munro displaces and contains the situation by using the time of a visit as a framing device. Unlike a quest, a visit is acknowledged to be temporary, offering perhaps a flash of insight but never claiming to arrive at a fixed destination. A visit home, of course, is a contradiction in terms. In this story, Helen is both the girl who was once at home and the woman who is watching that girl. This eerie doubleness makes it possible to explore the issue of identity without collapsing inward into the claustrophobic centre of the story. Her sister Maddy is away when Helen arrives and she has left an absurd note on the door: "VISITORS WELCOME, CHILDREN FREE, RATES TO BE ARRANGED LATER (YOU'LL BE SORRY) WALK IN" (DHS, 197). The sign has the effect of playfully estranging the reality which ought to be home and of drawing attention to itself as a sign. It has meaning, of course, but the meaning is self-consciously detached from the gesture of signing and from the person doing the signing. "YOU'LL BE SORRY," for example, shows Maddy in the act of internalizing a pointing finger of blame that later becomes externalized for us. "WALK IN" has an ominous sound, as if the doorway marks the entrance to a family hell. The names of the sisters hint conspicuously at madness and hell.

The denial of the mother's body here precedes her actual death and the image of clothing makes this vivid. In the rare "periods of calm" that are part of the tricks of the disease, the mother employs her daughters in her efforts to be a lady. "She would demand that we rouge her cheeks and fix her hair; sometimes she might even hire a dressmaker to come in and make clothes for her, working in the dining room where she could watch" (DHS, 200). These are dresses that she will never wear "(for why did she need these clothes, where did she wear them?)" (DHS, 200). They are "unnecessary from any practical point of view" and they become like symbols without any symbolic significance, clothes that will never contain a body that can give them shape and meaning. Unlike the Emperor, whose clothes are the product of a shared collective self-deception, the mother's clothing is real but her body (indeed, her very identity) is an illusory construct. We can reproduce her clothes ("'I just got a new coat. I have several coats'" (DHS, 206)) but we cannot reproduce the mother.

In this story there is no mock mother like Nora or Mary McQuade. The daughters themselves mock the mother with their mimicry. They will not, however, be able to move ahead to construct themselves as active subjects until they have confronted the moral issues raised by their caricatures of the mother. When Helen enters the house upon arrival, she turns and waits, out of force of habit, for her "mother's ruined voice" to call: "Calling, *Who's there?*" (DHS, 198). It is a "cry for help . . . shamefully undisguised" (DHS, 198), but Helen disguises it, frames it. While remembering this cry, she looks into the hall mirror, which contains the reflection of a "habitually watchful woman" who is "recognizably a Young Mother" (DHS, 197–198). The watcher in the woman comes into conflict with the keeper because she opens herself up to this cry for help. "*Who's there?*" Who is really there? Who is in the mirror? Who is calling? Who is called? *Who Do You Think You Are?* These questions spell ruin for the daughter's notion of her own autonomous identity. The frame of the mirror is all we have to contain this ruin, and it contains a reproduction of the "Young Mother." The daughters responded to the call with the words "You go and deal with Mother" but they are never finished dealing with her because they cannot stop the reproduction of mothering. Years later, in the story "The Progress of Love," Munro writes a dramatic version of the other side of this estrangement: a young girl "was howling 'Mama!' she was howling 'Mama!'" (PL, 12). The mother calling "Who's there?" (in "The Peace of Utrecht") and the daughter calling "Mama" (in "The Progress of Love") are divided by the invisible walls of separate stories and cannot answer each other.

What is the cause of this agony and how can the daughter respond to it? Reproduction is at least a place to begin and it is here linked to having the courage to look at what is framed in the mirror. It may be because the phrase "your mother" is a reproduction that it is felt by Helen as a "cunning blow" to her pride: "at those words I felt my whole identity, that pretentious adolescent construction, come crumbling down" (DHS, 194). Now that the mother has died, the town has turned her into one of its "possessions and oddities, its brief legends." She too is a "construction" and the daughters' mimicry is based on that fact. Like many of the women in Munro's later stories, she is a joke. "Wild caricatures we did for each other (no, not caricatures, for she was one herself; imitations)" (DHS, 195). The trouble is that their imitations are internalizations of collective perceptions. Before the death, Maddy labels her: "'Our Gothic Mother' . . . 'I play it out now, I let her be. I don't keep trying to make her *human* any more'" (DHS, 195). But letting her be is precisely what the sisters cannot do and when they reproduce her they cannot ignore the town. The act of perception is invasive and invaded by convention. This particular label "Our Gothic Mother"—contains at least two conventions: Gothic fiction and the Lord's prayer.

The conventions are awkward and conspicuous failures. "In the ordinary world it was not possible to re-create her," writes Helen. The picture is never complete: "Our Gothic Mother, with the cold appalling mask of the Shaking Palsy laid across her features, shuffling, weeping, devouring attention wherever she can get it, eyes dead and burning, fixed inward on herself; this is not all" (DHS, 200). This is not all. It is never enough and the face remains hidden by a mask. Success of a kind can, however, be reached by an acknowledgement of failure. In many stories Munro invokes a mock mother to play out that failure. In this story she does it by showing how the past mocks us with its very deadness if we look for an accurate reproduction or copy. Maddy and Helen make Fred Powell a present of nostalgia, "a version of our childhood," says Helen, "which is safely preserved in anecdote, as in a kind of mental cellophane." The "child-selves" in these anecdotes are "beyond recognition incorrigible and gay." The sisters will have to break free of this paralyzing, false kind of safety and tear the cellophane to get to a deeper level of recognition.

Munro gestures the place of this tear when Helen opens the drawer of a washstand and finds pages from a loose-leaf notebook.

"I read: 'The Peace of Utrecht, 1713, brought an end to the War of the Spanish Succession.' It struck me that the handwriting was my own" (DHS, 201). The writing is distanced by time and by the fact that it is written from dictation. The words written and read become oddly irrelevant. They gesture in the direction of authorized historical reality, of wars fought by men and recorded by men. Reading these words, Helen feels her old life lying around her, "waiting to be picked up again" (DHS, 201). She sees the "rudimentary pattern" of the town as "meaningful" and "complete . . . under an immense pale wash of sky" (DHS, 202). This pattern, however, is an epiphany of false historicism as the repetition of the word "wash" suggests. What will stand and what will wash away with time? This question is condensed into the single word that locates this text: *washstand*. The historical "Peace" goes against the idea of a final peacemaking. It was not so much peace as a complicated narrative of temporary arrangements and realignments. The historical complexity points towards a meaning left blank in this story. There are two conflicting threads of referentiality in this story. One leads to Munro's mother, the other to military history. The very title, then, "The Peace of Utrecht," is like a blind spot, like a deliberately failed clue. Like "The Moons of Jupiter," which forms a kind of companion story to this one, the title is a careful mistitle. The "Peace" is an "understood" historical allusion which, by inversion, points to what we do not understand. It is in this sense that it is like the mother who also eludes possession and understanding. By this oddly oblique gesture, Munro claims a place in history for the maternal line.

Paradoxically, Helen reclaims the real mother that has become one of the town's possessions by confronting the fact that the mother *cannot* be claimed at all. Representations or re-creations of the "real mother" keep turning into mock mothers and the act of trying is so painful that it might be described as a recurring feeling of doing matricide. What is potent in this story is the courage to confront this guilt—the guilt of having murdered the real mother to make room for mock mothers. This guilt is brought into focus during the visit within the visit—Helen's visit to see Aunt Annie and Auntie Lou. Aunt Annie forces Helen to confront the absence of the mother's body in her empty clothes. As Helen watches helplessly, Aunt Annie holds up "for inspection" the items in this bodiless fashion show. This, in Aunt Annie's opinion, is the maternal heritage. It is what the daughter can possess. The daughter's revulsion at the very idea is a catalyst leading her in an opposite direction, to a fuller awareness of the mother's absence, her otherness. Guilt is realized in the finger of blame that Aunt Annie figuratively points at Maddy. The emotional climax of Aunt Annie's story is the mother's flight from the hospital. "*The snow, the dressing gown and slippers, the board across the bed . . .* all her life as long as I had known her led up to that flight" (DHS, 208). Helen has a "longing not to be told" about the failure of the flight: "Oh, Helen, when they came after her she tried to run. She tried to *run*" (DHS, 208). Literally, the mother is captured and returned to the hospital. In death, however, she does escape our clutches and this is oddly comforting. Although we may thus pay tribute by acknowledging the failure of our own representations, this does not alter or correct the exclusion of the mother from written history. Munro's choice of title here is an augury of her developing interest in history as it relates to the erasure of the maternal heritage.

With the realization of the silenced and marginalized mother comes also a heightened awareness of the otherness of other characters. Strike out the M in Mother and you see the other in Maddy. It is she, after all, who acted as surrogate mother to her own sick mother and it is she who is the object of the pointing finger of blame. Aunt Annie claims to have said to Maddy, after the funeral, "Maddy, may it never happen like that to you" (DHS, 208). In fact it is happening to Maddy like that. She too desires flight. It is in this sense that the flight "concerns everybody." The imprisonment of the real mother is an exaggeration of a brutality that lives at the heart of our society and Maddie too is a victim of it—a castout. Aunt Annie "was afraid of Maddy—through fear, had cast her out for good" (DHS, 209). As nurse and mock mother, Maddy has borne the full burden of the role of sustaining the idea of "mother" and she is most clearly imprisoned. Her reproduction of mothering is visible in her eager nurturing of Fred. With the mother dead, Helen transfers her guilt into an effort to help her sister escape. That sister, however, has her own ideas about the past and her own version of the mother.

The sisters look into "the desert that is between" them that is the product of trying to pin down a claim to the real mother. The dilemma is a product of attempts to make the mother fit into a pattern prescribed by the dressmakers of the symbolic order. Comfort comes, however, as a result of the fact that the sisters have a shared dilemma in the *now*. They have a job to do in this shared present. The ending of "The Peace of Utrecht" finds the sisters in the kitchen. Since Helen has just "got home" from her visit to the aunts, the prevailing emotion is one of relief. In contrast to her initial arrival, we now experience it as a genuine coming home. As the sisters share the chores of food preparation, we also feel the stress taken off any one female figure since both are involved in that act of mutual mothering which characterizes sisterhood at its most comforting. "I got some raspberries for dessert. . . . Do they look all right to you?" asks Maddy and Helen replies with an echo: "They look all right" (DHS, 210). They are in harmony in their actions, in what is understood between them, but their conversations are elliptical and ambiguous.

Since it is Maddy who has been bearing the full burden of the symbolic order, it is fitting that it should be Maddy who comes out of the dining room "carrying a pink cut-glass bowl, for the raspberries." The pink bowl stands in, mockingly, for the female vessel within the symbolic order. It is only when Maddy drops the bowl and it falls as if in dreamlike slow motion, that we notice it. It is "quite a heavy and elaborate old bowl" (DHS, 210). As Maddy picks up the "pieces of broken pink glass" we are dimly aware of the muffled violence in the word "cut-glass" and perhaps even in the colour pink, which could be watered down blood. Like a bowl in a painting by Mary Pratt, this one seems to be surrounded by a magical rim that lifts it out of ordinary reality even as it is in the act of shattering. We sense ourselves approaching, with Maddy, the madness of hysteria as she offers herself the hollow comfort: "It's no loss to me. I've got a whole shelf full of glass bowls. I've got enough glass bowls to do me the rest of my life" (DHS, 210). Arrayed on a shelf like items to be sold, Maddy's pink bowl turns out, after all, to have been a reproduction.

In his reading of this story, W.R. Martin fills the pink bowl up with raspberries. He claims that "Maddy drops and breaks the cut-glass bowl of raspberries" and concludes that "the symbolism is rather heavy and obvious" (Martin, 1987, 44). Perhaps Martin has in mind Henry James or Ecclesiastes and is forgetting that Munro asks us to colour this bowl pink, not gold. Martin's reproduction of Munro's story turns a blind eye to the implications of that shelf full of reproduced bowls. He is ignoring the challenge thus issued to our assumption that an original pink bowl might reproduce some essential metaphor of maternity. Although he does not spell out the symbolism, he seems to assume that it is too obvious to spell out. He assumes (I assume) that the bowl is an image of the mother's womb. Why then, is the bowl (in his mind's eye) full of raspberries?

If I seem to be mocking Professor Martin I do so to challenge my own assumptions and those of the reading masses. The ease with which an industrialized society can reproduce copies of the bowl is repeated in the ease with which both Professor Martin and I can reproduce the archetypal story of the Holy Grail. So obvious is this story, indeed, that he does not need to tell it. Like Ross (1983, 112–126), Martin fails to see that the archetypal level of Munro's stories does not exist in a place that is possible to separate from the reality of a technological society. Just as our reconstructions are shaped by the "understood" ideologies and stories that we live by, reinforced by the powerful apparatus of technology, so the mock bowls follow, down to the last detail of each angle, the pattern of the pink cut-glass bowl.

It is the bowl and not the symbolism that is "heavy and elaborate." The very elaboration is designed, moreover, to lead us to a confrontation with a sign that is emptied of symbolic significance. I do not deny that there is an awkwardness in the story. The clumsiness, however, is deliberate, like the stumbling of a sad clown. The clumsiness itself is a transparent disguise, like the naming of Helen and Maddy, and it is made real in the story when Maddy cannot hold on to the bowl which is itself a clumsily disguised grail. Leaving the raspberries out of the bowl for the moment (as Munro does) let us look at the pink bowl, then, as a metaphor. If we do this we see that the metaphor is as dead as the mother. The cup used to commemorate the death of Jesus Christ and the womb of our mother simply refuse to dissolve into an identity. Cirlot notes that the "loss of the Grail is tantamount to the loss of one's inner adhesions" (1962, 116). The breaking of this pink grail shatters the idea of the autonomous text and of the autonomous subject.

Munro's frequent allusions to Arthurian legend show her taking on the powerful story in order to juggle with it, rearranging, displacing and mocking. She uses old legends and conventions slyly, embodying them in order to question them. Cirlot notes that the "appearance of the Grail in the centre of the Round Table . . . closely parallels . . . the Chinese image of heaven (Pi), which is shaped like a circle with a hole (analogous with cup or chalice) in the middle" (1962, 116). This circle can be spotted in Munro stories but it is mockingly reproduced. I am thinking, for example, of the "Hole-in-One" doughnut shop in "Providence" (WDY, 136). The grail implies "above all, the quest for the mystic 'Centre'" (Cirlot, 1962, 116), but Munro is writing against the grain of this kind of symbolism. There are no knights at a Round Table here. Just two sisters working in a kitchen. The critic as treasure hunter, looking for a rich centre in the story, is doomed to failure. Such a reader could be compared to the character Arthur in "Something I've Been Meaning to Tell You." Arthur loves "schoolteacher's games" and when he wins a word game he is "immensely delighted. 'You'd think you'd found the Holy Grail,' Char said" (SIB, 3).

It is true that the pink bowl is described as "heavy and elaborate" but that very elaboration and heaviness is designed to lead us, not to symbolism but to a sign devoid of symbolic significance. Adapting the language of Naomi Schor, we might say that the pink bowl, so insistently demanding to be looked at, is a "disproportionately enlarged ornamental detail" which testifies "to the loss of all transcendental signifieds." Far from being full of

symbolic significance, heavily laden with raspberries, it is a "parody of the
traditional theological detail. It is the detail deserted by God" (Schor, 1987,
61). Like the chocolate cups in "Connection," the bowl waits for a ceremonial
use which never presents itself (MJ, 3). These are the kinds of cups you tend to
find in a woman's autobiography. Female autobiography is frequently like two
sisters playing house while the mother is gone. Unlike the "shattered dishes"
in the "children's house of make believe" in Frost's "Directive," however, this
shattered bowl does not lead us to a place where we can ever "Drink and be
whole again beyond confusion" (Frost, 1963, 253).

All is not lost, however. We do, after all, have the raspberries left over. If
we wish to have them for dessert, there's work to be done: "Oh, don't stand
there looking at me," says Maddy, "go and get me a broom!" (DHS, 210).
This is what happens when a symbol is shattered; it comes back to us as a
sign. Symbols are invested and filled up with meaning by the authorities that
control the symbolic order. Signs, by contrast, are fractured and defined by
context. This is not to say that we do not constantly try to see a symbol in a
sign but always we fail and the object is returned to us as an object, to be dealt
with as we go about our daily mental housekeeping chores.

### "Dance of the Happy Shades": Watching the Children Play
The title story of this collection is also the last one and in it Munro antici-
pates the directions she will take in later collections. She describes this as a
"fairly important story" but as one that "backs off quite a bit" from what she
calls the "real material" (in Struthers, 1983, 23). It also backs off from the
figure of the mother, but only in order to stage her powers on another level
where we can observe the interaction of those powers with artistic power.
The piano recital staged by Miss Marsalles (she calls it a party) dramatizes
the two activities I have isolated as central to the dilemma of the artist:
watching and keeping. The proud, bored mother, who watches her performing daughter play, appears as an ironic version of the maternal keeper.
The audience of mothers, in fact, exposes an almost total absence of the
compassion we associate with maternity. That compassion, instead, is grotesquely exaggerated and projected into the figure of the piano teacher, Miss
Marsalles. "The deceits which her spinster's sentimentality had practised on
her original good judgment" are viewed as "legendary and colossal" and she
speaks of "children's hearts as if they were something holy" (DHS, 213).

Our participation in the "embarrassment the mothers felt" (DHS, 216)
is gradually reversed until the unheard music of the "Dance of the Happy
Shades" becomes a place from which we ourselves are judged. The hospitality
of Miss Marsalles makes a space within which, however briefly, we may feel
liberated from ourselves. That liberation, however, is profoundly ironic. We

may feel a brief moment of moral superiority when we recognize the false and self-serving compassion of the neighbour who frets over Miss Marsalles. What we cannot escape, however, is our own misplaced pity for her. The narrator and her mother are dutifully kissed by Miss Marsalles, but the narrator comments: "It seemed to me that Miss Marsalles was looking beyond us as she kissed us; she was looking up the street for someone who had not yet arrived" (DHS, 217). The eyes of Miss Marsalles look on things that we do not see and it is this that teaches us the absurdity of our own self-importance.

When the special visitors do arrive, we experience a deepening shame as we have to admit, once again, to our own misplaced compassion. While the narrator plays her own "dogged and lumpy interpretation" of the "minuet from Berenice" (DHS, 220–221), the room is filled with the heavy bodies of the strange children. Their physical presence demands our attention and yet we are not able to join Miss Marsalles in her easy and innocent compassion. Situated between irony and compassion we experience the weight of the dilemma staged by Munro. We also see something of the view of art that will inform her subsequent stories. When Dolores Boyle plays, she "sits ungracefully" at the piano (DHS, 222), but her big body is the unwitting vehicle for a miracle. The fact that she is one of the "idiots," signals the importance that will be attached in Munro's fiction to the experience of the fool, to knowing the limits of our understanding. Like the name of the musical piece by Gluck, entitled "Dance of the Happy Shades," the story by Munro also entitled "Dance of the Happy Shades" will leave "nobody any the wiser" (DHS, 223) if we search for fixed meaning. There is an implicit story behind the music, namely Gluck's version of the story of Orpheus and Eurydice, but the descent and ascent pattern is now an allusion only, not something followed in the story as it was in "Images." Munro prefers to stay with the performance and with the surfaces of the world, aware of the flies that buzz over the food left too long in the kitchen.

These children, like the ones in Yeats's "Among School Children," remind us that both "nuns and mothers worship images" but that we must keep apart the bodies of real children from the images that "the candles light" for nuns (Yeats, 1963, 244). The awkward body of Dolores Boyle will not allow us to get to that place where we cannot "know the dancer from the dance" (Yeats, 1963, 245). Her "body is not bruised to pleasure soul" (244). Indeed, she seems untouched by her own music. Why, then, is it that her name makes one think not only of Mater Doloroso but also of dolour and of boils, of the kinds of protuberances denied by the mother in "Walker Brothers Cowboy"? There is only the slightest hint of comic effect in this story but that hint is a clue to the direction taken by Munro's subsequent fiction. Since the last lines of the story take away from us the inclination to say "*Poor Miss Marsalles*" (DHS,

224), we feel our own blindness. Miss Marsalles looks like "a character in a masquerade, like the feverish, fancied-up courtesan of an unpleasant Puritan imagination" (DHS, 217). The focus of the story is more on our misinterpretation of that masquerade than it is on exposing a truth that lies behind her disguise. If we look more closely we do notice that "the fever is only her rouge; her eyes, when we get close enough to see them, are the same as ever, red-rimmed and merry and without apprehension" (DHS, 217). With this clownish mock mother, Munro puts herself deliberately at an ironic distance from the real-life mothers. Doing so becomes a means of reappropriating, on another level, the compassion which is idealized in maternity.

KATHERINE J. MAYBERRY

# "Every Last Thing ... Everlasting": Alice Munro and the Limits of Narrative

Storytelling is the central activity of the characters of Alice Munro's fiction. It is of course the principal task of Munro's narrators—those characters who organize and focalize the events and reflections constituting the short stories (Blodgett 11–12); and it is also the frequent activity of a large group of secondary characters whose storytelling is narrated by the chief narrators and thus recessed within the main narrative. Whether seeking or evading truth, all of these characters enlist narrative as the central weapon in their dogged and usually inconclusive struggles with the disturbances born at the intersection of their pasts and their presents. All are impelled to manage their pain, ignorance, and occasional glimpses of knowledge by telling. Some are more successful than others in their struggles, but success, when it occasionally comes, seems more a matter of luck than desert, and is rarely a direct dividend of the narrative act.

Eventually, most of Munro's narrators, both primary and secondary, come to recognize, if only dimly, the imperfection and inadequacy of their medium. In most cases, this inadequacy is a function of the essential incongruence between experience itself and the narrative that would render it, an incongruence complicated by the necessary mediation of memory. The uneasy relationship between language and experience is a recurring concern of Munro's work—one that she neither solves nor despairs of solving. It is

From *Studies in Short Fiction* 29, no. 4 (Fall 1992): 531–41. © 1992 by Newberry College.

stated as early as *Lives of Girls and Women*, where a more experienced Del judges as "crazy, heartbreaking" her earlier project of fitting "every last thing ... radiant everlasting" within the narratives she would write (210). And with somewhat different implications, it dominates a late work like "Friend of My Youth," where the problem of narrative fidelity is confounded still further by the issue of proprietorship. As legatee of her mother's stories about her youth, the narrator insists on reshaping them into stories that will better suit her own version of the person she needs her mother to have been: "I saw through my mother's story and put in what she left out" (20).

The 1977 volume *Moons of Jupiter* is one of Munro's most intensely focused examinations of the capabilities and limitations of narrative. A collection of disturbing stories about middle-aged people—mostly women—facing often humiliating uncertainties, *Moons* has been called "a menopausal progression" (Rasporich xvii), a look at "the persistent psychological puzzle of women's masochistic complicity in their own humiliation" (Carrington 144), and (by Munro herself) an examination of "what men and women want of each other" (Munro, "Interview" 112). But *Moons* is also a work about what stories can do, about the relationship between truth and narrative, between knowing and telling. Confused and uncertain, the women of this volume are groping for knowledge of an unknowable male other: Lydia in "Dulse" telling a psychiatrist about her abusive relationship with Duncan; the narrator in "Bardon Bus" talking her way through a broken affair; Mrs. Cross in "Mrs. Cross and Mrs. Kidd" trying to devise a story about the speechless Jack. Repeatedly, it is through stories, through placing themselves and these others within narrative, that these women seek knowledge, a resolution of their confusion. To tell they hope, is to know. While some of these characters are temporarily relieved of the pressures of uncertainty, it is not, for the most part, the narrative process that affords this relief. Countless factors conspire against the composition of narrative truth—the failure of memory, the failure of nerve, the discontinuity between past and present, the alienation of language from experience. The stories these women tell must remain incomplete and finally barren of the truths they are seeking.

"Hard-Luck Stories," the tenth story in *Moons of Jupiter*, is the most direct treatment of the problem of narrative in the volume. Its principal characters storytellers and its principal dramatic action their storytelling, "Hard-Luck Stories" is a supremely meta-narrative work. The story-telling characters, Julie and the unnamed narrator, are not merely accessing the past through their narrative, not merely remembering, but creating, respectively, "entertaining" and "interesting" (192) stories for an audience of one—the silent and predatory Douglas. These characters are self-conscious storytellers, whose divergent management of the activity of telling affords a deep look into Munro's understanding of the narrative act. Through the stories of Julie and the narrator, Munro probes the impulses, varieties, capacities, and limitations of narrative, insisting once more on the uneasy, discontinuous relationship between narrative and experience, and identifying the various versions of lies and uncertainties that no narrative can escape.

Like all of Munro's work, "Hard-Luck Stories" virtually defies plot summary.[1] The story opens in the present tense, with the narrator meeting her friend Julie for lunch. Cryptically, they refer to a day two months earlier when they had been given a ride home from a conference by Douglas Reider, a previous acquaintance of the narrator. The narrative then moves back in time to the day referred to in the first section—the afternoon of the drive. While this afternoon, which includes the drive and a lunch shared by the three, is the principal setting of the story, we are taken back still further in time by three stories told by the two women as they eat lunch with Douglas. Their stories, two by Julie and one by the narrator, relate events occurring at different points in the women's pasts; their common subject is the deceits and stratagems that men practice on women. The telling of these hard-luck stories, which is rendered in direct, quoted speech, constitutes the main action of the work.

In their confessional rendering of sexual confusion and psychological disequilibrium, Julie's stories appear to be concerned with representing difficult personal truths. As a preface to the first story, she admits to having been bulimic at the time:

> I was one of those people who gorge, then purge. I used to make cream puffs and eat them all one after the other, or make fudge and eat a whole panful, then take mustard and water to vomit or else massive doses of epsom salts to wash it through. Terrible. The guilt. I was compelled. It must have had something to do with sex. They say now it does, don't they? (187)

And she refers to her condition at the time of the second story as "Miserable [and] mixed-up" (189). In each story, Julie represents herself as a credulous victim of the deceits of disturbed men—the first a mental patient pretending to be a graduate student, the second Julie's group therapist, pretending a passionate interest in Julie while sleeping with several other group members.

While the content of Julie's stories seems to be the stuff of wrenching confession, their manner is anything but pained. As the narrator recognizes, Julie's self-exposure is measured and self-conscious: she "set herself up to be preposterously frank. There was something willed and coquettish . . . about this" (186). Julie's words have little to do with the past that they would seem to represent; they mark instead a virtual severance of past and present, experience and language. Her narrative cuts her off from the experience it is ostensibly representing. We see evidence of this in the quality of her confession about bulimia quoted above, in the yawning gap between the bulimia itself—this powerful but speechless register of miserable protest—and the spare, businesslike language with which Julie renders it. Whatever pain expressed itself in that eloquent body language of bulimia is nowhere evident within Julie's recounting of the experience. And we see the gap between language and experience again in her reference to the condition of her inmate-almost-lover. When the narrator exclaims upon hearing from Julie that "He'd tried to cut his throat," Julie answers, "It wasn't that bad. He was recovering" (188).

Julie's language here and throughout her two stories is in a dialect common to a number of Munro characters—characters whose stories, with their controlled language and tone, operate at a considerable remove from the original events. The narrative of these characters exploits the inevitable discontinuity between language and experience; for them, narrative functions as a virtual false counter, standing for something, surely, but not for the lived experience their narratives pretend to render. Though variously motivated, the narrative modes of these characters are strikingly similar, marked by flat, sparse, spare language and linear chronology. For these characters, language behaves, protecting its users from the vitality and pain that might be uncaged by a less provident use of the medium. This is the narrative method used by Prue, the title character in another story in the *Moons* volume, whose "anecdotes" pry the told impossibly far apart from its lived antecedent.

> She presents her life in anecdotes, and though it is the point of most of her anecdotes that hopes are dashed, dreams ridiculed, things never turn out as expected, everything is altered in a bizarre way and there is no explanation ever, people always feel cheered up after listening to her; they say of her that it is a relief to meet somebody who doesn't take herself too seriously, who is so unintense, and civilized, and never makes any real demands or complaints. (129)

This is also the method of Wilfred, the younger brother in "Visitors," whose repertoire of stories is predictable and repetitious. As his wife recognizes,

> In Wilfred's stories you could always be sure that the gloomy parts would give way to something better, and if somebody behaved in a peculiar way there was an explanation for it. If Wilfred figured in his own stories, as he usually did, there was always a stroke of luck

for him somewhere, a good meal or a bottle of whiskey or some money. (215)

While the careful stories of characters like Prue and Wilfred may temporarily keep deep troubles at bay by depriving them of vivid language, these troubles insist on expression, ingeniously finding translation into a different discourse. Prue's mute rage at Gordon expresses itself in her petty theft of his belongings ("She just takes something, every now and then" [133]), and Wilfred's unutterable sadness surfaces in crying fits deep in the night.

Given their context of psychic disequilibrium ("I felt I wasn't too far from being loony myself" [188]), Julie's cool and breezy narratives must share some of the protective, distancing motivations impelling Prue and Wilfred. But another agenda also drives her: her stories, with their blithe and studied self-exposure, have the practical effect of attracting Douglas. Her confession to Douglas seeks neither expiation nor representation, but seduction. It is a trick of language and time that converts one thing into another (a painful experience into a "ridiculous" story [195]), just as Julie herself can exchange her earlier "hiking boots and ... denim jacket" (183) for a pink dress and flowered hat. Her preposterous frankness, her insistent insertion of sexuality into conversation with a man she has just met, is a not-so-thinly-disguised "come-hither" strategy that meets with complete success: Douglas is attracted to her, and, as we learn from the opening of the story, they become lovers. Julie's stories do, in a sense, authorize or empower her, in that their intentions are realized.

But we cannot be sanguine for her chances for happiness, for her hopes of finding "the one kind [of love] nobody wants to think they've missed out on" (182). For as we learn from the narrator's story, which recounts the ending of her earlier relationship with Douglas, like the inmate and the therapist, Douglas is another man who deceives and uses women. The practical effect of Julie's narrative calls into question Gayle Greene's claim that "all narrative is concerned with change ... [that] there is something in the impulse to narrative that is related to the impulse to liberation" (Greene 291). For Julie's story merely delivers her into another round of the same cycle, into an affair with a hard and voyeuristic man, about whom the best that can be said is, he "is better than crumbs" (182).

While Munro is not being harsh or moralistic about characters like Julie and Prue, their disinclination to revive their pasts through their narratives surely disqualifies them from the ranks of her heroines. As a writer of narratives whose recurring subject is the past and the use we make of it, who stubbornly insists on a thing called truth while repeatedly despairing of our ability to reach it, Munro appears not to endorse such an ultimately barren and repetitious narrative strategy, valorizing instead those narrative strategies (like the one practiced by the narrator of "Hard-Luck Stories") more dedicated to, if not more capable of, approximating truth. And while she doesn't always reward those characters who work this way, she does present the Julie's and Prue's as trapped in the ignorance constructed by their stories, condemned to reenact rather than to understand their past.[2]

Like Julie's stories, the narrator's single story in "Hard-Luck Stories" is about a man's manipulation of a vulnerable woman. But subject matter is the only common feature of the women's stories; the narrator's motives, methods, and intents are vastly different from Julie's. For the narrator, as for Del in *Lives*, words are consequential and vital, with physical properties of their own that, combined with the proliferation of associative logic set in motion by their use, are capable of sensuous, rich, sometimes uncontrollable signification. For Julie, the statement "He'd tried to cut his throat" is a cool, dry factual statement that can be easily contained and qualified by "It wasn't that bad. He was recovering." For the narrator, the statement associates itself with "suicide," a word with an almost unbearably physical reality: "Mention of suicide is like innards pushing through an incision; you have to push it back and clap some pads on, quickly" (188). The narrator's story demonstrates repeatedly the connection between language and physical experience, the ability of a word to call up, not shut down, a reality beyond the context of its present use. We see her acceptance of this connection in her account of an earlier conversation with Douglas:

> I asked him on the way up what Keith and Caroline were like, and he said they were rich. I said that wasn't much of a description. He said it was Caroline's money, her daddy owned a brewery. He told me which one. There was something about the way he said "her daddy" that made me see the money on her, the way he saw it, like long lashes or a bosom—like a luxuriant physical thing. (192)

This somaticizing of language is necessary to any narrator who seeks to resuscitate experience through language, through stories about the past. Unlike Julie, Prue, and Wilfred, the narrator's use of language invigorates rather than vitiates her narrative. Thus it continues the experiment initiated by Del in *Lives*—that insistence on the physical properties of both sides of the signifying transaction—the visual, oral properties of written and spoken language and the sensuality of its referents.[3]

We can't know, of course, how close the narrator's story comes to the events it narrates. This is a comparison quite impossible for Munro or any writer to make, as the original experience if indeed it existed at all—is unpresentable. But all the evidence suggests that the narrator's story is a far more faithful account than Julie's stories were. Whereas Julie's stories are compact summaries of her experiences, with little attempt made to recreate conversations or the effect the events had on her, the narrator remembers the language of the conversations she had that evening, recounts carefully her reaction to the evening's events—not, as far as we can tell, her reaction as mediated by the intervening time or the present, but her reaction at the time.

> Then she [the hostess] said in her wispy voice how much she loved the way it was in the winter with the snow deep outside and the white rugs and the white furniture. Keith seemed rather embarrassed by her and said it was like a squash court, no depth perception. I felt sympathetic because she seemed just on the verge of making some sort of fool of herself. . . . the man I was with got very brusque with her, and I thought that was mean. I thought, even if she's faking, it shows she wants to feel something, doesn't it, oughtn't decent people to help her? (193)

The most crucial difference between the stories of Julie and the narrator lies in what they are seeking. Julie's stories, though accounts of past events, are concerned with what they can effect in the present and the future; they demonstrate little concern with understanding the painful past that she rather cheerfully recounts. But the narrator does not tell her story as she would don a new dress—in order to achieve a certain effect. She is after something quite different, as she suggests when she distinguishes the effect of her story from Julie's: "It may not be very entertaining. . . . But it is interesting" (192). The different roots of the two words are revealing: tenir, to hold, in the first; esse, to be, in the second. The narrator's story will have something to do with being, with essence, with experience; Julie's holds that essence back.

Not until the narrator has finished her story do we realize that the "man I was in love with" (192) was Douglas himself, that a member of her audience is a principal character in the story she tells. It is this fact that helps us realize what she is after in giving this account: she is after no less than the actual experience itself as it was, a perfect retrieval of the past through narrative. Such a retrieval is only possible if the narrator can replace not just herself, but Douglas as well into the past. To gain Douglas's participation in the narrative would be to collapse present into past, to negate somehow the time that has elapsed between the original event and her story. If the recalcitrant present will cooperate, if Douglas will agree to be put back in the experience, the narrator stands a chance of understanding this troubling experience. And it is this desire for understanding that drives her narrative;

she tells so that she may know, so that she may understand the role of the other (Douglas).

The narrator's project is more coincident with Del's ambitions than with the reminiscences of later narrators in *The Progress of Love* or *Friend of My Youth*. Neither Del nor this narrator seeks to recover a past event by demonstrating its messy amalgamation with experience intervening between past and present; both would re-create experience by excising it, perfect and whole, from the matrix of the past. But in "Hard-Luck Stories," this tactic fails; time will not be collapsed, Douglas will not fill in the blanks, knowledge cannot be achieved. Douglas neither confirms nor denies the narrator's account; he remains the other that won't be contained, re-placed; understood.[4] His recalcitrance leads the narrator to recognize the futility of her story, its inability to freeze time by replicating the past and yielding the knowledge she seeks: "I could be always bent on knowing, and always in the dark, about what was important to him, and what was not" (197).

While the narrator's narrative project closely resembles Del's in *Lives*, the stakes to be won by its achievement have increased considerably. In perfectly retrieving the past, the narrator not only could gain understanding of that past, but also could realize the virtual identity between the concepts of inclusiveness ("every last thing") and timelessness ("everlasting" [210]). Her attempt to revive the past is also an attempt to stop time altogether, to fend off the changes overtaking her. She shares this ambition with a number of other characters in the volume—with Lydia, in "Dulse," and the narrator in "Bardon Bus," both desperately trying to understand failed relationships, and with Albert in "Visitors," stubbornly insisting on the truth of his narrative about Lloyd Sallows—"It's not a story. It's something that happened" (215). All middle-aged, these characters are concerned with change and death; in trying to suspend the past in narrative, they are trying to stop time, to ward off the death coming nearer to all of them. But as the abrupt insertion of the graveyard at the end of "Stories" reminds us, death will not be stopped by a trick of language or by any other contrivance. As the narrator realizes, language and story-telling are mocked by the obdurate fact of death: "I heard the silly sound of my own voice against the truth of the lives laid down here" (196).

However pessimistic "Hard-Luck Stories" may be about narrative—about its ability to retrieve the past, yield understanding, challenge the flux of time—it does not leave its struggling characters utterly hopeless. For the narrator, Julie, and Douglas (and indeed many of the characters in this and other volumes) do find solace, though not where they were seeking it, not in the stories they tell. As if to point up the inefficacy of narrative, Munro often offers its opposite as a source of comfort. Repeatedly, it is within the unmediated, unprocessed image and act that her characters find at least temporary peace. The three characters in "Hard-Luck Stories" are granted a moment of grace through the form of a trillium stitched on a footstool in a country church:

> I was pleased with this homely emblem ... I think I became rather boisterous, from then on. In fact all three of us did, as if we had each one, secretly, come upon an unacknowledged spring of hopefulness. (197)

The source of their pleasure in the trillium goes unidentified, the connection between the emblem and the comfort it casts remains uninterpreted, and hence, Munro seems to insist, the image is particularly powerful. A similar moment comes at the end of "Dulse," when Lydia, after desperately seeking shelter in the stories she tells her psychiatrist and her new telephone worker friends, finds relief in the seaweed left her by Vincent: "Yet look how this present slyly warmed her, from a distance" (59). Though Munro must present these moments within narrative, they remain the most immediate, unmediated, uninterpreted moments in the stories. It is as if she is saying that peace, truth, knowledge are unavailable through discourse, intellection; that they are accessible only within the unlocked, untranslated, silent image that, like Keats's "silent form dost tease us out of thought" (Keats 1186).

* * *

Munro's understanding of the function of narrative is mordantly paradoxical. Throughout her career, she has insisted on the existence of pre-linguistic experience, of a truth that originates outside of, independent of language. This truth is wholly experiential and wholly personal, never going beyond the bounds of individual perception.[5] Particular and circumscribed, it would seem a simple truth, though as Munro's vision matures, its constitution grows increasingly intricate, its excision from the surrounding web of falsehoods, uncertainties, silence, and alternative perceptions increasingly difficult. But simple or complex, this truth admits little access. The approaches attempted by most of Munro's characters are memory and narrative—virtually equivalent faculties in that they both order past experience, re-collect lived moments within a chronological frame. These characters attempt to understand their experience by going through it again, and only language allows this review. But as "Hard-Luck Stories" demonstrates, to go through it again is to change it utterly; there can be no coincidence between the experience itself and the language that would render it. Narrative is finally not the province of truth; to tell is at best to revise, but never to perfectly revive. The narrator's position at the end of "Hard-Luck Stories" is, for Munro, the predicament of all narrators who seek understanding through language—the predicament of being "always bent on knowing, and always in the dark."[6]

## NOTES

1. The difficulty of inclusively re-telling Munro's stories requires the re-teller to enact her repeated point about narrative—that it cannot exactly, inclusively, reproduce the original. And that Munro's own narrative is so unreplicable may indicate just how closely she has been able to approximate experience.

2. As early as *Lives of Girls and Women*, Munro had eschewed such dysfunctional narratives—stories that through mindless repetition or preoccupation with effect become unreal and meaningless to their tellers. Our first look at this vitiating process occurs in "The Flats Road," where Del observes the devolution, through narrative repetition, of fresh experience into unreflected, unreliable fiction.

> After a while we would all just laugh, remembering Madeleine going down the road in her red jacket, with her legs like scissors, flinging abuse over her shoulder at Uncle Benny trailing after, with her child. . . . Uncle Benny could have made up the beatings, my mother said at last, and took that for comfort; how was he to be trusted? Madeleine herself was like something he might have made up. We remembered her like a story. (23)

In "The Flats Road," this conversion process, this bleeding of life from experience through repeated tellings, is juxtaposed with another brand of narrative—that told by the first storyteller of the volume, Uncle Benny, whose rendering of his nightmarish visit to Toronto realizes his experience for Del:

> He remembered everything. A map of the journey was burnt into his mind. And as he talked a different landscape—cars, billboards, industrial buildings, roads and locked gates and high wire fences, railway tracks, steep cindery embankments, tin sheds, ditches with a little brown water in them, also tin cans, mashed carboard [sic] cartons, all kinds of dogged or barely floating waste—all this seemed to grow up around us created by his monotonous, meticulously remembering voice, and we could see it, we could see how it was to be lost there, how it was not possible to find anything or to go on looking. (22)

3. We see Del's sisterhood with the "Stories" narrator in passages like the following from *Lives*:

> I loved the sound of that word [tomb] when I first heard her [Aunt Elspeth] say it. I did not know exactly what it was, or bad got it mixed up with womb, and I saw us inside some sort of hollow marble egg, filled with blue light, that did not need to get in from outside. (45)

4. In this he is like the absent Duncan in "Dulse," who remains "an absolute holdout" (55) for the troubled Lydia.

5. Or as Munro herself has put it, "I write about myself because I am the only truth I know" (Wiseman 114).

6. "I work in the dark," says Munro of her own writing (Wiseman 114).

## Works Cited

Blodgett, E. D. *Alice Munro*. Boston: Twayne, 1988.

Carrington, Ildiko de Papp. *Controlling the Uncontrollable: The Fiction of Alice Munro*. Dekalb: Northern Illinois UP, 1989.

Greene, Gayle. "Feminist Fiction and the Uses of Memory." *Signs* 16 (1991): 290–321.

Keats, John. "Ode on a Grecian Urn." *English Romantic Writers*. Ed. David Perkins. New York: Harcourt, 1967. 1186.

Munro, Alice. "An Interview with Alice Munro." With Geoff Hancock. *Canadian Fiction Magazine*. 43 (1982): 75–114.

———. *Friend of My Youth*. New York: Knopf, 1990.

———. *Lives of Girls and Women*. 1971. New York: New American Library, 1983.

———. *The Moons of Jupiter*. 1982. New York: Penguin, 1984.

Rasporich, Beverly J. *Dance of the Sexes: Art and Gender in the Fiction of Alice Munro*. Edmonton: U of Alberta P, 1990.

Wiseman, Adele. *Chinada: Memoirs of the Gang of Seven*. Dunvegan: Quadrant, 1982.

GEORGEANN MURPHY

# The Art of Alice Munro: Memory, Identity, and the Aesthetics of Connection

Alice Munro's first collection of stories, *Dance of the Happy Shades*, published in 1968, won her the Canadian Governor General's Award but little fame. Her second book, however, *Lives of Girls and Women*, found in 1971 a wider audience, one ready to declare her "an important new talent"—even though she had been publishing fiction for nearly twenty years. Since then she has enjoyed, perhaps more than any of her contemporaries, a consistently high degree of both popular and critical success,[1] inspiring more book-length studies of her work than she has published books. Her most recent collection, *Friend of My Youth* (1990), was glowingly reviewed on both sides of the Atlantic: Peter Kemp in the London *Sunday Times* pronounced her "an unrivalled chronicler of human nature."[2] Such praise prompts readers to return to Munro's earlier stories, each so well crafted as to reward second and third readings, in order to search out new meaning in light of later developments. This critical approach is especially appropriate to a study of Alice Munro's writing, for returning to and re-evaluating what has gone before is both Munro's method and her great theme.

To an extraordinary extent, the raw material of Munro's work comes from her own life, a fact she readily admits.[3] Born in 1931 to Robert Eric Laidlaw, a farmer who raised silver foxes, and Ann Chamney Laidlaw, Munro grew up in relative poverty near Wingham, Ontario, not far from

From *Canadian Women: Writing Fiction*, edited by Mickey Pearlman, pp. 12–27, 155–56. © 1993 by the University Press of Mississippi.

Lake Huron. Married in 1951 to James Munro, she took her B.A. at the University of Western Ontario in 1952 and moved with her husband to British Columbia, where he opened a successful bookstore in Victoria. They had three daughters. Her mother, Ann Laidlaw, died after a long struggle with Parkinson's disease in 1959. Following her divorce in 1976, Munro remarried and moved back to Ontario, where she now lives.

The chronological and geographical settings of Munro's stories roughly reiterate this life pattern of departure and return. Many of the earliest, appearing in *Dance of the Happy Shades* and *Lives of Girls and Women* (a novel that is itself a progression of connected stories), are set in the "quasi-pioneer environment"[4] of southern Ontario, often depicting the brutality and squalor of life on the edge of a small rural community. Frequently, their point of view is that of a young girl scrutinizing the incomprehensible behavior of adults. Munro never abandons southern Ontario as a setting; many consider it the inspiration for her best work. But stories from her middle period, collected in *Something I've Been Meaning to Tell You* (1974), more frequently present young, troubled married life on the Canadian West Coast during an ironically rendered beat era, early feminist consciousness-raising, and the bewildering changes of the sixties. Munro acknowledges that she is "not at all sure" she acquired an authentic feel for British Columbia, even after twenty years of living there[5]: "I always felt when I lived in Vancouver and Victoria that I had to go home to die, because life on the west coast wasn't real in the same way."[6] Her collection *The Beggar Maid* (1978—published in Canada as *Who Do You Think You Are?*) begins and ends back in Ontario, following the progress of the protagonist Rose, whose life parallels Munro's in many ways. Munro's plots since 1978, often set near her childhood home, regularly concern strategies of coping and acceptance; in her own words, "I write about where I am in life."[7]

Because her work is so closely related to her life, and so thematically consistent (she has been criticized for her "continual elaboration of the similar"[8]), generalizations about setting and subject are possible and sometimes illuminating. They should not, however, obscure the variety in Munro's characterization. *Friend of My Youth*, for example, swells with a population of intensely realized characters—Calvinists, Polish and Croatian immigrants, ministers, gypsies, Scots, divorcees, teachers, laborers—each caught at different stages of life.[9] Some, while not exactly types, function symbolically: pilots stand for romantic, exciting, and irresponsible sex in "How I Met My Husband" (*SIBMTY*),[10] "White Dump" (*PL*), and "Hold Me Fast, Don't Let Me Pass" (*FMY*), and brassy, husband-hunting nurses in "Images" (*DHS*) and "Friend of My Youth" (*FMY*) embody coarse intrusions of the outside world on the sequestered, delicately balanced power structure of home. Fathers in

Munro's stories are often strong, courageous, traditionally masculine, and capable of transforming hardship with humor, like Ben Jordan in "Walker Brothers Cowboy" (*DHS*) or Fleming in "The Stone in the Field" (*MJ*). Typically, they are also intelligent and have a love of language, like Rose's father in "Royal Beatings" (*BM*, 5–6), or of astronomy, like the narrator's father in "The Moons of Jupiter," published two years after Munro's own father died during cardiac surgery.[11] Mothers, however, are more frequent and powerful figures in Munro's stories, a fact the narrator of "The Ottawa Valley" (*SIBMTY*), herself a writer, appears to acknowledge as she frets that she can never "*get rid*" of her mother. This plaint concludes both that story and the collection: "[My mother] has stuck to me as close as ever and refused to fall away, and I could go on, and on, applying what skills I have, using what tricks I know, and it would always be the same" (246). Munro's stories, taken collectively, provide a cohesive portrait of Munro's mother, most notably the exquisitely painful "Peace of Utrecht" (*DHS*), written the year Ann Laidlaw died. Mother figures in Munro, like Ada Johnson of *LGW*, are frequently martyrs to a disease either named as or similar to Parkinson's. They are dreadful housekeepers, visibly constrained by poverty and family obligations, independent, proud, and eager for their daughters to become even more so. Narrators speak of them with a mixture of exasperation, guilt, pride, and longing, like that of the narrator of "Friend of My Youth," who dreams of her dead mother "looking quite well" and saying she was always sure she would see her daughter again one day (3–4).

A character who appears with even more frequency than the mother who refuses "to fall away" from the narrator's memory and writing is the narrator herself. Munro's work is full of first-person retrospective narrators and third-person protagonists who are, themselves, writers or artists with "a need to picture things, to pursue absurdities" ("Royal Beatings," *BM*, 3). Often they are intelligent women[12] with lives animated by conflicts arising from a repressive Scotch-Irish Protestant upbringing; frequently they are torn by competing but equally compelling needs for freedom and domesticity. Rose in "Providence" (*BM*), kept from adventure and her lover Tom by her love and responsibility for her daughter Anna, is a good example. This double bind so common in women's lives since the sixties often reveals itself in Munro's protagonists' bifurcated attitude toward writing: they love language, but, like the narrator of "The Office" (*DHS*), they are tentative about writing as an activity: "I am a writer. That does not sound right. Too presumptuous; phoney, or at least unconvincing. Try again. I write. Is that better? I try to write. That makes it worse. Hypocritical humility" (59). Munro herself has always written in a room with a function other than simply providing her a place to write and has felt "less uneasy about writing because [she] was doing it in a room that wasn't a study." She wrote *Lives of Girls and Women*, for example, in her laundry room.[13]

Despite their attendant uneasiness about doing so, Munro's protagonists are driven to listen and watch, record, and reshape what they see around them. Mary in "The Shining Hours" (*DHS*) draws Mrs. Fullerton's story out of her by pretending to know less than she really does; Dorothy in "Marrakesh" is a retired schoolteacher driven to observe whatever is before her: "Beautiful or ugly had ceased to matter, because there was in everything something to be discovered" (*SIBMTY*, 163). Del Jordan, at the end of "Heirs of the Living Body" (*LGW*, 52), removes her dead Uncle Craig's historical manuscript from its fireproof and padlocked tin box and replaces it with her own writing, some poems and the beginning of a novel; she carries her uncle's perfectly typed thousand pages to the cellar, where they are ruined in a spring flood. Del's memory of the past and her connection to her family are linked to, but displaced by, her need to forge an identity in the present, and that identity, for Del—and for all of Munro's artist/protagonists—is connected to "the elegant channels of language" ("Age of Faith," *LGW*, 83). Munro's writers recognize that writing can be a strategy for dealing with life: Del carries with her the idea of her novel, her reshaping of a community tragedy, like "one of those magic boxes a favored character gets hold of in a fairy story: touch it and his troubles disappear" ("Epilogue: The Photographer," *LGW*, 204). Hugo in "Material" (*SIBMTY*) has reinvented his life, his ex-wife ruefully discovers, in his book-jacket biography, aggrandizing the enviable and eliminating the painful.

If writing can transform and re-create—"It is an act of magic ... of a special, unsparing, unsentimental love" ("Material," *SIBMTY*, 43)—it is also a challenging covenant between the writer and the world, one the narrator of "The Stone in the Field" despairs of getting right: "I no longer believe that people's secrets are defined and communicable, or their feelings full-blown and easy to recognize. I don't believe so" (*MJ*, 35). Furthermore, any failure of talent undercuts the artist's identity: Rose, an actress returning home to care for her senile stepmother Flo, is ashamed of a failure to accurately portray her characters in her acting, an especial embarrassment in a community where people might remember when her schoolgirl pride in performance resulted in her teacher's humiliating question, "Who do you think you are?" (*BM*, 200). Even in middle age, Rose is still unsure of the answer to that question. She struggles to reconcile her memories and her identity.

Writing can be that act of reconciliation for Munro's writers; writing is an act of magic and of love. But a love affair can impair a protagonist's ability to write, and thus imperil her identity. Lydia, the poet/editor of "Dulse" (*MJ*), is so devastated by the collapse of an affair that she believes she will probably write no more poems; she wonders how much money she could make as a cleaning lady (37). Writing, identity, and love are also problematically connected in "Bardon Bus" (*MJ*), when the writer/narrator recognizes in her friend Kay—as well as in herself—the tendency to reinvent her identity for a man (116): if the self can be forged by the act of writing, it can be lost in attraction to the opposite sex. Almeda Joynt Roth, Munro's turn-of-the-century "poetess" in the Canadian wilderness of "Meneseteung" (*FMY*), also recognizes a link between loving and loss of creative power, noticing that a married woman's creativity is focused on reinventing a man as a husband (60)—a task she herself does not want. At the end of her life, she channels the last of her creative juices not into the pursuit of Jarvis Poulter but into a poem.

The typical writer in Munro's fiction is, then, ambivalent about her work but driven to do it. She struggles for representative accuracy, which failures of love and/or talent undercut. Munro's writers labor to connect memory and identity, and the problems inherent in such connection provide the central conflicts of Munro's fiction. But always, connection itself is the subsuming theme. Three kinds of connection are especially important to the Munro *Weltanschauung*: travel, the connection of one place to another in a journey replete with metaphorical meaning; change, the connection between past and present; and sexual love, probably the most fundamental and highly problematic of human connections.

Eudora Welty has written that "writers and travelers are mesmerized alike by knowing of their destinations."[14] In this state of something like highway hypnosis, several of Alice Munro's characters experience significant realizations: the process of travel, involving as it does removal from quotidian obligations and attachments, focuses attention on the essential. A journey can thus be made toward a revelation as much as toward a destination, and not infrequently, Munro's characters make those journeys simultaneously. On a train to Vancouver, the narrator of "The Spanish Lady" (*SIBMTY*) reviews the disintegration of her marriage and meets a Rosicrucian who believes he knew her in a previous life; her unmet arrival in the station, coinciding with the sudden death of an old man who had been sitting on a bench there, is a "message" putting her life in sudden, graphic perspective (190–91). Rose Jordan has her first sexual pleasure from a man on board a train to Toronto in "Wild Swans" (*BM*). And Mary Jo of "Eskimo" (*PL*) encounters an unexpected—and unwelcome—reflection of her devotion to her lover/employer, Dr. Steeter, on board a winter flight to Tahiti. Munro herself finds train travel conducive to writing:

> One of the problems I used to have is getting really sort of seized
> up and not being able to write at all, not doing anything and

nothing happening. But if you are in the train you are going from place to place with no effort on your part. Something is being achieved, and so I don't think you get that really tight feeling about it. So I relax and write.[15]

What dislodges Munro's writer's block and what inspires her characters' epiphanies amount to the same thing: being in the process of making a physical connection between two places can lubricate intellectual and emotional connections as well.

Connection in Munro is both a hedge against and a barrier to change, that sometimes fearful and sometimes desirable fact of human life. While change is often remarked as a significant theme in Munro's work,[16] her focus is always on the connection between what went before and what comes after the change. Connection with the past is undeniably strong in Munro's writing, and characters who wish to sever their connections with the past discover they cannot. Maddy, the older sister in "The Peace of Utrecht" (DHS), finds that though her ten-year obligation of caring for her mother has ended, she can't retrieve her life from her guilt over putting her mother in the hospital where she died. Helena in "Executioners" (SIBMTY) longs for the time when everyone who remembers the terrible killing fire of her childhood will be dead so that it will finally and forever be over. Even Del, as she replaces that manuscript of Uncle Craig's with her own in "Heirs of the Living Body" (LGW), is not so much disposing of her past as she is confirming her familial destiny of becoming a writer herself—like the uncle whose work she tried to put behind her, work she will herself write about one day.

Familial connection is strong in Munro's stories, and it militates against change. Del Jordan believes that despite their apparent differences, her father, mother, and uncle are connected to each other and to their home: "This connection was plain as a fence . . . it would stay between us and anything" ("The Flat Roads," LGW, 22). Blood ties may sometimes be inscrutable, as they are to Mildred in "Visitors" (MJ), but they are undeniable. And in challenging situations when characters lack the protection of a present family, they form their own, no matter what their ages. Helen, the sixth-grader in "Day of the Butterfly" (DHS), betrays the only other outsider at school in her effort to be part of a group; "Mrs. Cross and Mrs. Kidd" (MJ) survive the indignities of old age through their connection to each other. In both cases, change, in the form of new friendships, threatens the old order, but the old order wins out. Teenagers threatened by the death of a classmate form an artificial and ceremonial connection in "Circle of Prayer" (PL): girls who don't know each other or the deceased at all well sing in unison and drop their jewelry into her open casket. Connection here is the only solace for the specter of the ultimate change, death.

Death as a violent, transforming upheaval is also at the center of "Accident" (*MJ*). When her lover Ted's son is killed, Frances's life changes forever: she ends up married with children of her own as a direct result of Ted's loss. Frances meditates, however, not on the changes made in her life but on how she has remained the same despite those changes (109). While Frances has change thrust upon her, other Munro characters try actively to impose changes, but with little success: they remain connected to what went before. "Jesse and Meribeth" (*PL*) attempt to re-create themselves by spelling their names in a new way; Jessie later marvels, like Frances, that she has stayed the same, even though she had thought she "could turn [herself] inside out, over and over again, and tumble through the world scot free" (188). Initiating change and trying to re-create themselves do not break characters' connection to the past and their identities shaped there: "People make momentous shifts, but not the changes they imagine" ("Differently," *FMY*, 242). Margot in "Wigtime" (*FMY*) breaks up the marriage of Reuel and Teresa while she is still a high-school student; later, Reuel's infidelity with another high-school student threatens to break up Margot's own marriage to him. She finds herself visiting Teresa, the woman she had earlier wronged, who is now a patient at the County Home and forever lost in the time when she was a war bride on the boat sailing to meet her husband in America. Margot recognizes that despite the momentous choices of her life—to seduce, marry, and then remain with Reuel—she is connected to a past pattern she cannot change: "'We're all on the boat,' says Margot" (274).

Margot's friend and confidant Anita mentally connects "war brides" with "war bonnets" when she hears this story. Her association suggests another sort of connection, one of key thematic importance in Munro's work: sexual love, as ever-present in Munro's writing as the image of flowing water, and just as dangerous.[17] Sex is a compelling but fearful mystery to the adolescent Del (*LGW*) and Rose (*BM*): Del's curiosity leads her to potential rape by Mr. Chamberlain, who masturbates in front of her ("Lives of Girls and Women"), while Rose's curiosity impels her to watch Shortie McGill raping his deformed sister Franny ("Privilege"). The dangers of sex for women especially impress the young in Munro's stories. Del scents coming from her Aunt Moira "a gynecological odor," marking her as "a likely sufferer from varicose veins, hemorrhoids, a dropped womb, cysted ovaries, inflammations, discharges, lumps and stones in various places, one of those heavy, cautiously moving, wrecked survivors of the female life, with stories to tell" ("Heirs of the Living Body," *LGW*, 34). Moira's daughter Mary Agnes, brain-damaged from being deprived of oxygen in the birth canal, has been assaulted by five boys who stripped her and left her lying naked in the cold mud of the fairgrounds (36). Ada Jordan's beloved teacher, Miss Rush, dies of childbirth in "Princess Ida" (*LGW*), as Callie's mother horrifically does in "The Moon in the Orange Street Skating Rink" (*PL*, 150); Ellie Grieves suffers constant pregnancies "full of vomiting fits that lasted for days, headaches, cramps, dizzy spells," terminating in miscarriages and stillbirths after "long, tearing labor[s]" ("Friend of My Youth," *FMY*, 11); Dotty in "Material" (*SIBMTY* 32) and Teresa in "Wigtime" (*FMY* 248) also report gory miscarriages. No wonder Jessie is "scared" when she sees Mrs. Cryderman's baby kick from inside her blotchy, swollen belly with its distended naval ("Jesse and Meribeth," *PL* 180).

As if rape and childbirth were not enough sexual danger, the female body itself is forever threatening Munro's characters with humiliation and exposure. The fear of tell-tale blood on the back of a skirt haunts the narrator of "Red Dress—1946" (*DHS* 150) just as it does Margot and Anita in "Wigtime," *FMY* 252; Rose fears the humiliation of dropping a Kotex pad in the high-school hall ("Half a Grapefruit," *BM*, 41). Dennis in "Bardon Bus" grotesquely reports that he envies women because "they are forced to live in the world of loss and death! Oh, I know, there's face-lifting, but how does that really help? The uterus dries up. The vagina dries up" (*MJ*, 122). Dawn Rose of "A Queer Streak" is so "affronted" by the onset of menstruation that she stops the flow for a year by sitting in the shallow, icy water of the creek; the neighbors believed the blocked, "bad blood" has affected her brain (*PL*, 215). The lonely Maria of "Five Points" endures the humiliation of paying boys to have sex with her in the shed behind her parents' store; her libido bankrupts her family and lands her in jail—while nothing is done about the boys who prostituted themselves (*FMY*, 40). Worse off yet are Marion Sherriff and Miss Farris (*LGW*), whose frustrated love lives lead them to drown themselves in the Wawanash River. Appropriately, it seems, Ada Jordan warns her daughter Del to use her brains and not be distracted by a man, lest she "get the burden, a woman always does" ("Lives of Girls and Women," *LGW*, 147).

The longing for sexual connection inflicts psychic as well as physical pain in Munro's fiction. Betrayal is common. From the high-school girl of "An Ounce of Cure" (*DHS*), so mortally depressed over being dropped by the boy who played Darcy in the Christmas production of *Pride and Prejudice* that she gets hugely drunk, to Prue, a woman in her forties who practices cynicism in a winningly lighthearted way and drowns her sorrow in a small revenge strategy of pilferage ("Prue," *MJ*), Munro's stories are filled with women—and sometimes men—who have "smelled love and hope" ("Providence," *BM*, 151) and suffer for it. Driven by a pursuit they may even view with disdain—Rose, for example, ruefully admits to herself that "nothing would do anymore but to lie under Simon, nothing would do but to give way to pangs and convulsions"

("Simon's Luck," *BM*, 170)—Munro's protagonists, like those in "Bardon Bus" (*MJ*), "Lichen" (*PL*), and "Circle of Prayer" (*PL*), often achieve only the loneliness and humiliation of being left. The spectacle of a woman waiting to hear from a man is a common occurrence: Edie lingers by the mailbox longing for a letter from her pilot ("How I Met My Husband," *SIBMTY*); at least one other woman besides the narrator writes desperate, unanswered letters to the same man in "Tell Me Yes or No" (*SIBMTY*); Rose's arranged tryst with Clifford in "Mischief" (*BM*) fizzles as she waits for him at an old logger's home; Matilda puts her life on hold for her English bigamist husband in "Oh, What Avails" (*FMY*). Once consummated, love brings an escalating sexual aphasia[18]: women under its influence can't study, like Del in *LGW*; can't read, like Rose in *BM*; can't work, like Roberta in "Labor Day Dinner" (*MJ*).[19] At its worst, sexual passion can leave behind an appalling residue of hatred: Rose's exhusband Patrick turns on her a "savagely warning face . . . a timed explosion of disgust and loathing" ("Beggar Maid," *BM* 100), and the sexually jealous Et in "Something I've Been Meaning to Tell You" (*SIBMTY*) may well have hastened her sister's suicide, poisoning her with invented stories of her ex-lover's exploits.

Despite its risks, though, connection is a subsuming theme of Munro's fiction. Her characters, particularly the writers among them, struggle to forge their identities in a crucible of connections: of one place to the next, of the past to the present, and of one sexual being to another. Her settings and plots rely heavily on Munro's memories of her own past, connected to and reassessed by her narrative personae. Munro's storytelling style, too, is a function of connection, its four coordinates a modernist narrative technique, a lapidary attention to point of view, a persistent undercutting of meaning, and a riveting attention to detail. Munro's narrative technique follows the modernist tradition of juxtaposing seemingly unconnected incidents to evoke a new meaning.[20] Contradictory narration, multiple storytellers, and leaps in time require the reader actively to connect and interpret divergent material. This is especially true of Munro's later stories, for her narrative strategies have grown more complex over time. "Labor Day Dinner" (*MJ*), for example, introduces multiple points of view. "The Progress of Love," title story of the 1986 collection, shifts the narrative action across three generations of contradictory stories, and "Fits" demonstrates virtuosic mastery of suspense, a technique put to good advantage throughout *FMY*.

Who tells the story is as important as how it is told, and Munro takes great care over point of view, frequently writing a story from both third- and first-person points of view before coming to a final decision about which is best.[21] Of special importance in her first-person narratives is the distance between the former (narrated) self and the present (narrating) self: for these retrospective narrators, realizations come only after the fact, if at all. Narrators, single or multiple, are likely to prove unreliable in Munro's fiction; she repeat-edly considers where meaning lies,[22] and frequently undercuts even the epiph-any-like closure of her earlier stories with speculation about the tricks memory plays. Rearranging details, confusing fact and fantasy, and simply mistrusting perception, Munro's characters stumble upon moments of "accidental clarity" ("Differently," *FMY*, 243) which lead nowhere and prove nothing.[23] Ada Jor-dan's stories of her mother, for example, differ from those of her brother Bill ("Princess Ida," *LGW*); her daughter Del does not know whom to believe.

A writing narrator in a Munro story, like the one in "Winter Wind," is likely to question the truth of her own tale:

> And how is anybody to know, I think as I put this down, how am I to know what I claim to know? I have used these people, not all of them, but some of them, before. I have tricked them out and altered them and shaped them any way at all, to suit my purposes. I am not doing that now, I am being as careful as I can, but I stop and wonder, I feel compunction. (*SIBMTY*, 201)

The narrator of "The Progress of Love" realizes she has made up a memory, a vivid image of her father's protecting her mother as she fed her inherited money into the kitchen wood stove. Though the narrator knows the scene could not have occurred—her father did not even hear about the incinera-tion until much later—"it seems so much the truth it is the truth" (*PL*, 30). Furthermore, this narrator allows her companion, Bob, to misapprehend her distress over his mentioning "sexual shenanigans" in her old home because, she says, "moments of kindness and reconciliation are worth having"—even when they're based on a lie (30). Needing to find the truth in a person or a situation, even when that "truth" contradicts the facts, Munro's characters, like most of us, "tell [themselves] stories in order to live."[24]

Balancing the uncertainty of meaning and truth in Alice Munro's fic-tion is her use of epitomizing detail, observation so meticulously acute that it gives the illusion of real life. The catalog is one of her techniques: the lists of what Ben Jordan, the "Walker Brothers Cowboy," sells (*DHS*, 3–4) and the detritus of Flo's life described in "Spelling" (*BM*, 180–81) clearly evoke one life in progress and one at its end. Catalogs can function as both vivid place descriptions and telling metaphors; Munro renders the emotional ste-rility of a bereaved couple's lives, for example, by revealing their collection of politically correct bibelots: "Eskimo prints and carvings, Indian wall hang-ings, ash trays, and bowls, and some gray porous-looking pots made by a former convict now being sponsored as a potter by the Unitarian Church" ("Memorial," *SIBMTY*, 211). Most memorable of all are Munro's arresting similes: "roots . . . like crocodiles" ("Walker Brothers Cowboy," *DHS*, 1); the grandmother who smells like "an old apple peel going soft" ("A Trip to the Coast," *DHS*, 183); a dead cow's open eye, like "an orange stuffed in a black silk stocking" ("Heirs of the Living Body," *LGW*, 37).

That the striking simile is the hallmark of Munro's style should come as no surprise: connection is her forte. Like the writer/narrator of "Meneseteung," Munro is curious, "driven to find things out, even trivial things. [Such people] will put things together. You see them going around with notebooks, scraping the dirt off gravestones, reading microfilm, just in the hope of seeing this trickle in time, making a connection, rescuing one thing from the rubbish" (*FMY*, 73). Munro's memories of her Ontario home, the Precambrian rock under her art, connect with her keen observation and descriptive skill to produce an uncannily accurate portrayal of how people conduct their lives. If she calls her identity as a writer into question with her series of ambivalent, self-conscious narrators, it is only because she would have us realize that none of us can be smug about labeling what we see "the truth." Like Millicent in Munro's recently published story, "A Real Life,"[25] we are bound to our past in ways we can't explain, ways which nevertheless shape our lives. And when it comes time to tell what has happened to us, as Munro herself has observed,[26] we edit the story as we go along.

## WRITINGS BY ALICE MUNRO

### STORIES

"The Dimensions of a Shadow." *Folio*, April 1950: 4–10.
"Story for Sunday." *Folio*, December 1950: 4–8.
"The Widower." *Folio*, April 1951: 7–11.
"A Basket of Strawberries." *Mayfair*, November 1953: 32–33, 78–80, 82.
"The Idyllic Summer." *Canadian Forum*, August 1954: 106–07, 109–10.
"At the Other Place." *Canadian Forum*, September 1955: 131–33.
"The Edge of Town." *Queen's Quarterly* 62 (1955): 368–80.
"How Could I Do That?" *Chatelaine*, March 1956: 16–17, 65–70.
"The Time of Death." *Canadian Forum*, June 1956: 63–66.
"Good-By, Myra." *Chatelaine*, July 1956: 16–17, 55–58.
"Thanks for the Ride." *Tamarack Review* 2 (1957): 25–37.
"The Dangerous One." *Chatelaine*, July 1957: 48–51.
"Sunday Afternoon." *Canadian Forum*, September 1957: 127–30.
"The Peace of Utrecht." *Tamarack Review* 15 (1960): 5–21.
"The Trip to the Coast." In *Ten for Wednesday Night*, ed. Robert Weaver, 74–92. Toronto: McClelland and Stewart, 1961.
"Dance of the Happy Shades." *Montrealer*, February 1961: 22–26.
"An Ounce of Cure." *Montrealer*, May 1961: 26–30.
"The Office." *Montrealer*, September 1962: 18–23.
"Boys and Girls." *Montrealer*, December 1964: 25–34.

"Red Dress—1946." *Montrealer*, May 1965: 28–34.

"Postcard." *Tamarack Review* 47 (1968): 22–31, 33–39.

*Dance of the Happy Shades*. New York: McGraw-Hill, 1968. Includes "Walker Brothers Cowboy," "The Shining Houses," "Images," "Thanks for the Ride," "The Office" (revised), "An Ounce of Cure," "The Time of Death" (revised), "Day of the Butterfly" (revision of "Good-By, Myra"), "Boys and Girls," "Postcard," "Red Dress—1946," "Sunday Afternoon," "A Trip to the Coast" (revised), "The Peace of Utrecht" (revised), and "Dance of the Happy Shades."

*Lives of Girls and Women*. Toronto: McGraw-Hill Ryerson, 1971. Includes "The Flats Road," "Heirs of the Living Body," "Princess Ida," "Age of Faith," "Changes and Ceremonies," "Lives of Girls and Women," "Baptizing," and "Epilogue: The Photographer."

"Material." *Tamarack Review* 61 (November 1973): 7–25.

"Home." In *New Canadian Stories: 74*, ed. David Helwig and Joan Harcourt, 133–53. Ottawa: Oberon, 1974.

"How I Met My Husband." *McCall's*, February 1974: 84–85, 123–27.

"Tell Me Yes or No." *Chatelaine*, March 1974: 34–35, 54, 56–60, 62.

"Forgiveness in Families." *McCall's*, April 1974: 92–93, 138, 140, 142, 144, 146.

*Something I've Been Meaning to Tell You*. Toronto: McGraw-Hill Ryerson, 1974. Includes "Something I've Been Meaning to Tell You," "Material," "How I Met My Husband" (revised), "Walking on Water," "Forgiveness in Families," "Tell Me Yes or No," "The Found Boat," "Executioners," "Marrakesh," "The Spanish Lady," "Winter Wind," "Memorial," and "The Ottawa Valley."

"Privilege." *Tamarack Review* 70 (1977): 14–28.

"Royal Beatings." *New Yorker*, 14 March 1977: 36–44.

"The Beggar Maid." *New Yorker*, 27 June 1977: 31, 35–41, 44–47.

"Providence." *Redbook*, August 1977: 98–99, 158–63.

"Accident." *Toronto Life*, November 1977: 61, 87–90, 92–95, 149–50, 153–55, 159–60, 162–65, 167, 169–73.

"Mischief." *Viva*, April 1978: 99–109.

"Wild Swans." *Toronto Life*, April 1978: 52–53, 124–25.

"Half a Grapefruit." *Redbook*, May 1978: 132–33, 176, 178, 180, 182, 183.

"The Moons of Jupiter." *New Yorker*, 22 May 1978: 32–39.

"Spelling" [excerpt]. *Weekend Magazine*, 17 June 1978: 24, 26–27.

"Characters." *Ploughshares* 4:3 (1978): 72–82.

"Emily." *Viva*, August 1978: 99–105.

"Honeyman's Granddaughter" [revision of "Privilege"]. *Ms*, October 1978: 56–57, 75–76, 79.

"Connection." *Chatelaine*, November 1978: 66–67, 97–98, 101, 104, 106.

*Who Do You Think You Are?* Toronto: Macmillan, 1978 [*The Beggar Maid: Stories of Flo and Rose* in the United States]. Includes "Royal Beatings" (revised), "Privilege" (revised), "Half a Grapefruit" (revised), "Wild Swans," "The Beggar Maid" (revised), "Mischief" (revised), "Providence" (revised), "Simon's Luck" (revision of "Emily"), "Spelling" (revised and expanded), and "Who Do You Think You Are?"

"A Better Place Than Home." In *The Newcomers: Inhabiting a New Land*, ed. Charles E. Israel, 113–24. Toronto: McClelland and Stewart, 1979.

"The Stone in the Field." *Saturday Night*, April 1979: 40–45.

"Dulse." *New Yorker*, 21 July 1980: 30–39.

"Wood." *New Yorker*, 24 November 1980: 46–54.

"The Turkey Season." *New Yorker*, 29 December 1980: 36–44.

"Prue." *New Yorker*, 30 March 1981: 34–35.

"Labor Day Dinner." *New Yorker*, 28 September 1981: 47–56, 59–60, 65–66, 70, 75–76.

"Mrs. Cross and Mrs. Kidd." *Tamarack Review* 83–84 (1982): 5–24.

"The Ferguson Girls Must Never Marry." *Grand Street* 1:3 (1982): 27–64.

"Visitors." *Atlantic Monthly*, April 1982: 90, 91–96.

*The Moons of Jupiter.* Toronto: Macmillan, 1982. Includes "Chaddeleys and Flemings, parts I ("Connection" [revised]) and II ("The Stone in the Field" [revised]), "Dulse" (revised), "The Turkey Season" (revised), "Accident," "Bardon Bus," "Prue," "Labor Day Dinner," "Mrs. Cross and Mrs. Kidd," "Hard-Luck Stories," "Visitors," and "The Moons of Jupiter" (revised).

"Miles City, Montana." *New Yorker*, 14 January 1985: 30–40.

"Monsieur les Deux Chapeaux." *Grand Street* 4:3 (1985): 7–33.

"Lichen." *New Yorker*, 15 July 1985: 26–36.

"The Progress of Love." *New Yorker*, 7 October 1985: 35–46, 49–50, 53–54, 57–58.

"Secrets Between Friends." *Mademoiselle*, November 1985: 116, 118, 120, 122, 124, 126, 128, 130, 228, 230.

"A Queer Streak. Part One: Anonymous Letters." *Granta* 17 (1985): 187–212.

"Eskimo." *Gentlemen's Quarterly*, December 1985: 262–66, 301–02, 304.

"Fits." *Grand Street* 5:2 (1986): 36–61.

"The Moon in the Orange Street Skating Rink." *New Yorker*, 31 March 1986: 26–36, 38–41, 44.

"A Queer Streak. Part Two: Possession." *Granta* 18 (1986): 201–19.

"White Dump." *New Yorker*, 28 July 1986: 25–39, 42–43.

"Circle of Prayer." *Paris Review* 100 (1986): 31–51.

*The Progress of Love.* Toronto: McClelland and Stewart, *1986*. Includes "The Progress of Love" (revised), "Lichen," "Monsieur les Deux Chapeaux," "Miles City, Montana" (revised), "Fits" (revised), "The Moon in the Orange Street Skating Rink" (revised), "Jesse and Meribeth" (revision of "Secrets Between Friends"), "Eskimo," "A Queer Streak" (revised), "Circle of Prayer," and "White Dump" (revised).

"Oh, What Avails." *New Yorker*, 16 November 1987: 42–52, 55–56, 58–59, 62, 64–65, 67.

"Meneseteung." *New Yorker*, 11 January 1988: 28–38.

"Five Points." *New Yorker*, 14 March 1988: 34–43.

"Oranges and Apples." *New Yorker*, 24 October 1988: 36–48, 52, 54.

"Hold Me Fast, Don't Let Me Pass." *Atlantic Monthly*, December 1988: 58–66, 68–70.

"Differently." *New Yorker*, 2 January 1989: 23–36.

"Goodness and Mercy." *New Yorker*, 20 March 1989: 38–48.

"Wigtime." *New Yorker*, 4 September 1989: 34–50.

"Pictures of the Ice." *Atlantic*, January 1990: 64–73.

"Friend of My Youth." *New Yorker*, 22 January 1990: 36–48.

*Friend of My Youth.* New York: Knopf, 1990. Includes "Friend of My Youth," "Five Points," "Meneseteung," "Hold Me Fast, Don't Let Me Pass," "Oranges and Apples," "Pictures of the Ice," "Goodness and Mercy," "Oh, What Avails," "Differently," and "Wigtime."

"Carried Away." *New Yorker*, 21 October 1991: 34–61.

"A Real Life." *New Yorker*, 10 February 1992: 30–40.

"A Wilderness Station." *New Yorker*, 27 April 1992: 35–51.

## ARTICLES AND LETTERS

"An Appreciation." *Room of One's Own: A Feminist Journal of Literature and Criticism.* 9:2 (June 1984): 32–33.

"Author's Commentary" In *Sixteen by Twelve: Short Stories by Canadian Writers*, ed. John Metcalf, 125–26. Toronto: Ryerson, 1970.

"The Colonel's Hash Resettled." In *The Narrative Voice: Short Stories and Reflections by Canadian Authors*, ed. John Metcalf, 181–83. Toronto: McGraw-Hill Ryerson, 1972.

"Everything Here is Touchable and Mysterious." *Weekend Magazine*, 11 May 1974: 33.

"On John Metcalf. Taking Writing Seriously." *The Malahat Review* 70 (March 1985): 6–7.

"On Writing 'The Office.'" In *Transitions II: Short Fiction. A Source Book of Canadian Literature*, ed. Edward Peck, 259–62. Vancouver: Commcept, 1978.

"An Open Letter." *Jubilee* 1 (1974): 5–7.

"What is Real?" *Canadian Forum*, September 1982: 5, 36. Reprinted in *Making It New: Contemporary Canadian Stories*, ed. John Metcalf, 223–26. Toronto: Methuen, 1982.

"Working for a Living." *Grand Street* 1:1 (1981): 9–37.

## Interviews

Frum, Barbara. "Great Dames." *Maclean's*, April 1973: 32, 38.

Gerson, Carole. "Who Do You Think You Are? Review-Interview with Alice Munro." *Room of One's Own* 4:4 (1979): 2–7.

Gibson, Graeme. "Alice Munro." In *Eleven Canadian Novelists*, 237–64. Toronto: House of Anansi, 1973.

Gzowski, Peter. "Interview with Alice Munro." *Morningside.* CBC Radio, 2 June 1987.

Hancock, Geoff. "An Interview with Alice Munro." *Canadian Fiction Magazine* 43 (1982): 74–114.

———. "Through the Jade Curtain." In *Chinada: Memoirs of the Gang of Seven*, 51–55. Dunvegan, Ont.: Quadrant Editions, 1982.

Horwood, Harold. "Interview with Alice Munro." In *The Art of Alice Munro: Saying the Unsayable*, ed. Judith Miller, 123–34. Waterloo, Ont.: Univ. of Waterloo Press, 1984.

Kroll, Jeri. "Interview with Alice Munro." *LiNQ: Literature in North Queenland* 8:1 (1980): 47–55.

Metcalf, John. "A Conversation with Alice Munro." *Journal of Canadian Fiction* 1:4 (Fall 1972): 54–62.

March, Ken. "Name: Alice Munro. Occupation: Writer." *Chatelaine*, August 1975: 42–43, 69–72.

Sandor, Suzanne. "An Intimate Appeal." *Maclean's* 99:46 (17 November 1986): 12j–121.

Scobie, Stephen. "A Visit with Alice Munro." *Monday Magazine* [Victoria], 19–25 November 1982: 12–13.

Slopen, Beverly. "Alice Munro." *Publishers Weekly*, 22 August 1986: 76–77.

Stainsby, Mari. "Alice Munro Talks with Mari Stainsby." *British Columbia Library Quarterly* 35:1 (July 1971): 27–30.

Struthers, J. R. (Tim). "The Real Material: An Interview with Alice Munro." In *Probable Fictions: Alice Munro's Narrative Acts*, ed. Louis K. MacKendrick, 5–36. Downsview, Ont.: ECW Press, 1983.

Twigg, Alan. "What Is: Alice Munro." In *For Openers: Conversations with 24 Canadian Writers*, 13–20. Madeira Park, B.C.: Harbour, 1981.

## Notes

1. David Stouck, "Alice Munro," in *Major Canadian Authors*, 2d ed. (Lincoln: University of Nebraska Press, 1988), 257–59.

2. 14 October 1990, 8:5.

3. E. D. Blodgett, *Alice Munro* (Boston: Twayne, 1988), 6.

4. Ildikó de Papp Carrington, *Controlling the Uncontrollable: The Fiction of Alice Munro* (DeKalb: Northern Illinois University Press, 1989), 16.

5. John Metcalf, "A Conversation with Alice Munro," *Journal of Canadian Fiction* 1:4 (1972): 56.

6. Harold Horwood, "Interview with Alice Munro," in *The Art of Alice Munro*, ed. Judith Miller (Waterloo: University of Waterloo Press, 1984), 135.

7. Interview by Peter Gzowski, *Morningside*, CBC Radio, 2 June 1987.

8. Blodgett, *Alice Munro*, 10.

9. Peter Kemp, *London Sunday Times*, 14 October 1990, 8:5.

10. References to Munro's collections are drawn from the following readily available paperback editions: *DHS* (*Dance of the Happy Shades*, Penguin, 1968); *LGW* (*Lives of Girls and Women*, Penguin, 1971); *SIBMTY* (*Something I've Been Meaning to Tell You*, Penguin, 1974); *BM* (*The Beggar Maid*, Penguin, 1978); *MJ* (*The Moons of Jupiter*, Knopf, 1983); *PL* (*The Progress of Love*, Penguin, 1987); and *FMY* (*Friend of My Youth*, Vintage, 1991).

11. Carrington, *Controlling*, 202.

12. Some narrator/protagonists who are *not* intelligent women include the appropriately named Dick in "Thanks for the Ride" (*DHS*); Helen, the obtuse jilted salesclerk in "Postcard" (*DHS*); Edie, the young and naive maid in "How I Met My Husband" (*SIBMTY*); Mr. Lougheed, a sensitive and lonely pensioner in "Walking on Water" (*SIBMTY*); Colin, the put-upon older brother in "Monsieur les Deux Chapeaux" (*PL*); and the wealthy widower Sam, still looking for past happiness in "The Moon in the Orange Street Skating Rink" (*PL*).

13. Horwood interview, 131.

14. Eudora Welty, *One Writer's Beginnings* (Cambridge: Harvard University Press, 1984), 44.

15. Horwood interview, 132.

16. Blodgett, *Alice Munro*, 33.

17. Munro frequently connects water and sex in her stories, often with an implied or overt threat of danger. Garnet French, to whom Del Jordan has lost her virginity, tries to baptize/drown her in "Baptizing" (*LGW*). Et likens her sister Char's "big and swollen" look to the sight of her drowned brother Sandy when she catches Char tangled with her lover, Blaikie Noble, in "Something I've Been Meaning to Tell You" (*SIBMTY*, 10–11). The seductive pilot of "How I Met My Husband" (*SIBMTY*) is named Chris Watters; in "The Found Boat" (*SIBMTY*), the spring-swollen Wawanash River is the site of a prepubescent sexual encounter between Clayton and Eva when, during their nude bathing, he spits a mouthful of river water at her and hits her breasts (136). Rose's crush on Cora in "Privilege" (*BM*), the beginning of sexual love, is compared to "the high tide; . . . the flash flood" (35). Rose later encounters on the train to Toronto the "minister" who masturbates her after telling her of a flock of wild swans he'd seen on a pond; his hand is able "to get the ferns to rustle and the streams to flow" ("Wild Swans," *BM*, 64). The menstruating "poetess" Almeda, ill and distracted both by the obscene racket on Pearl Street and her attraction to Jarvis Poulter, "channels" all her feelings into the composition of a poem about the river, "Meneseteung," which for her becomes the river—as a basin of grape juice for the jelly she's been making overflows its basin and runs across her kitchen floor, staining it a purple that will never come out (*FMY*,

70). In this stunning image, Munro links flowing water with creativity, both sexual and poetic.

18. Carrington, *Controlling*, 89.

19. Ibid., 156.

20. Stouck, "Alice Munro," 260.

21. J. R. (Tim) Struthers, "The Real Material: An Interview with Alice Munro," in *Probable Fictions: Alice Munro's Narrative Acts*, ed. Louis K. MacKendrick (Downsview, Ont.: ECW, 1983), 24.

22. Blodgett, *Alice Munro*, 85.

23. Robert Towers, "Short Satisfactions," *New York Times Book Review*, 17 May 1990, 38.

24. Joan Didion, *The White Album* (New York: Simon and Schuster, 1979), 11.

25. *The New Yorker*, 10 February 1992, 30–40.

26. Geoff Hancock, "An Interview with Alice Munro," *Canadian Fiction Magazine* 43 (1982): 94.

AJAY HEBLE

# "It's What I Believe": Patterns of Complicity in
# The Progress of Love

I am obliged to offer no more than this stubborn sentence: It happened
that way because that's how it happened.

Salman Rushdie, *Midnight's Children*

So that's life, then: things as they are?

Wallace Stevens, 'The Man with the Blue Guitar'

Τhe stories in *The Progress of Love* play out what perhaps is Alice Munro's
most cogent challenge to the tradition of realist fiction. Although the pieces
collected in this volume are not, for the most part, overtly metafictional,
although they do not engage in the kind of self-consciousness that one
finds, for example, in 'The Ottawa Valley,' 'Winter Wind,' and 'Home,'
they do nevertheless render problematic our ability to keep apart experience
and narration. Like so many of Munro's stories, these pieces promote and
undo reality at one and the same time; they tease us with expectations of
accuracy, objectivity, truth, and linguistic transparency, only to show us that
events which pose as accurate, objective, true, and transparent are fictions of
self-knowledge, narratives constructed by a narrating figure whose authorial
subjectivity can no longer go unquestioned.

From *The Tumble of Reason: Alice Munro's Discourse of Absence*, pp. 143–68, 198–99. © 1994 by
the University of Toronto Press.

In 'The Progress of Love,' Munro continues to probe the problems that have fascinated her from the start of her career. Of particular interest in this title piece is the way in which its narrator, Phemie, engages in an examination of the powers and the limits of storytelling. Abandoning the notion of truth as correspondence between story and event, the narrator instead presents her version of the past in a manner which suggests she is less interested in getting the facts straight than she is in coping with the world. The narrative that results is, like much of Munro's recent fiction, marked by a discontinuity, by an uneasiness which, in this case, reflects the narrator's own reluctance to get to the point of her story. As Blodgett points out, 'The story, simply by the way it is begun, suggests the narrator is hesitant to take the reader to the core of a matter whose truth she herself appears somehow unsure of' (*Alice Munro* 145).

The story begins with the narrator receiving a phone call from her father announcing her mother's death. While the subsequent sections seem to offer an account of her mother's life, what is worth noting is that many of the details presented by the narrator implicitly take up another issue: her mother's hatred of her own father, Phemie's grandfather. Thus the information we are given about such things as the colour of her mother's hair and the fact that Phemie's father had to wait to marry her mother turns on a hatred which will only be brought to the fore later in the story. The narration, in other words, is proleptic in its structure.

Prolepsis, of course, is a trope of deferral, of putting off, of holding in a kind of suspension. Phemie's reason for putting off discussing what seems to be at the core of her narrative involves not so much an aversion to confronting what she does not want to know as an unstated but implicit desire to challenge the importance of foundations and origins. What seems to be at issue here is the problem of truth, and Phemie's narration, rather than separating truth from falsehood, serves to conflate the two. When Phemie finally arrives at what appears to be the heart of the matter—her grandmother's suicide attempt—the prominence of the event is diminished by the fact that it is framed by another event: Aunt Beryl's visit. Although she 'said not to call her Aunt' (*PL* 14), Beryl, unlike Uncle Benny in *Lives of Girls and Women*, is a *real* relative, and this—perhaps—lends her a certain air of credibility. Beryl's visit occupies a central place in Phemie's narration because it functions, in effect, to put matters into perspective.

We first hear of the grandmother's near suicide from Phemie, but her narration is presented, as Mark Levene suggests, 'from her mother's point of view as though she [Phemie] were omniscient and the story a self-contained whole because of its dark impact on their lives' (8). In the extended passage describing the event (*PL* 9–13), the telling 'I,' the story's first-person narrator, suddenly disappears from the narrative. This shift from a first-person narration to the privileged position of omniscience fosters the illusion of—to adapt Emile Benveniste's distinction—historical utterance rather than discourse. Whereas discourse, for Benveniste, designates 'every utterance assuming a speaker and a hearer, and in the speaker the intention of influencing the other in some way' (209), historical narration is marked by the absence of the 'I' who tells the story: 'No one speaks here; the events seem to narrate themselves' (208). Historical narration, he writes, is a 'mode of utterance that excludes every "autobiographical" linguistic form "I"' (206). This exclusion, this absence, in Munro's story—or at least in the extended passage describing the near suicide of Phemie's grandmother—seems to constitute an attempt by Phemie to relive the original event, to experience what her mother, Marietta, went through—in short, to achieve a kind of hermeneutic empathy.[1]

Beryl's visit, however, illustrates the impossibility of such an empathy. Despite Phemie's attempt to recount, and by implication relive, what her mother went through upon discovering her own mother's near suicide, her version is called into question when Beryl—who, unlike Phemie, actually witnessed the event—turns up and insists that the whole incident was something of a joke designed 'to give Daddy a scare' (*PL* 21). Beryl further downplays the seriousness of the event by claiming that the rope her mother used to try to hang herself was not even tied to a beam: "My eyes followed that rope up and up and I saw it was just hanging over the beam, just flung there—it wasn't tied at all! Marietta hadn't noticed that, the German lady hadn't noticed it. But I just spoke up and said, Mama, how are you going to manage to hang yourself without that rope tied around the beam?" (*PL* 22). Beryl's version of the incident suggests that Phemie may not be remembering the past with complete accuracy. Although Phemie stands, for some time, by her mother's version of the episode, the opposing accounts of the story ask us to ponder the ultimate inaccessibility of a privileged founding moment of knowledge. The notion of truth is further undermined by means of another story which sheds light on this first. Because Phemie's mother hated her own father for the way he treated his wife, Phemie, in an effort to be rid of this inheritance of hatred, modifies an important part of a story concerning another kind of inheritance. Like Phemie's account of her grandmother's near hanging, this story too—which we are inclined to accept as accurate—will be challenged later in the narrative.[2] While visiting the farm where she used to live, Phemie, now an older woman, remarks to a friend that her mother once burned her paternal inheritance in the wood stove. The point of this story, for the narrator, is not so much the hatred which Marietta felt towards Phemie's grandfather, but rather the fact that Marietta's husband presided over the burning: "'My father letting her do it is the point. To me it is. My father stood and watched and he never protested. If anybody had tried to stop her, he would have protected her. I consider that love'" (*PL* 26).

The next section of the narrative, however, takes us back to the time of Beryl's visit, and here the narrator, still a child, listens to a conversation in which her mother and Beryl discuss the ways in which they have dealt with their respective inheritances. Phemie's mother talks about burning her share of the money, but we learn that Phemie's father was not present to witness, let alone approve of, the incident. Why, then, has Phemie presented us (and her friend) with the other version? As it turns out, the next segment of the narrative takes up precisely this question: 'My father did not stand in the kitchen watching my mother feed the money into the flames. It wouldn't appear so. He did not know about it—it seems fairly clear, if I remember everything, that he did not know about it until that Sunday afternoon in Mr. Florence's Chrysler, when my mother told them all together. Why, then, can I see the scene so clearly, just as I described it to Bob Marks (and to others—he was not the first)?' (*PL* 29). Here, the older Phemie admits that she has, in her narration, tampered with the past. Despite this admission, however, she has trouble believing that her account of the event is a fabrication. Of her version of the incident she says, 'how hard it is for me to believe that I made that up. It seems so much the truth it is the truth; it's what I believe' (*PL* 30). Here, Phemie appears to be appealing to the truth of created memory, to 'the truth of fiction.'[3] Ondaatje's phrase, I think, aptly gets at Phemie's desire to supplant conventional notions of truth as correspondence with a paradigmatic notion of truth as a need to be narratively or discursively faithful to the way things might have or ought to have been.

In the story Phemie twice supplies us with evidence to discredit the stories she has presented to us. In the second instance, however, despite open acknowledgment of her fictionalizing impulse, she clings to her initial version because, as Levene points out, 'even through distortion she wants to be assured of [her parents'] love' (8). As if to justify her practice of distortion, Phemie ends her narrative by explaining how she has told Bob Marks another lie in order to avoid disagreement: 'It was just as well to make up right away. Moments of kindness and reconciliation are worth having, even if parting has to come sooner or later. I wonder if these moments aren't more valued, and deliberately gone after, in the setups some people like myself have now, than they were in those old marriages, where love and grudges could be growing underground, so confused and stubborn, it must have seemed they had forever' (*PL* 30–1).

The story, then, in playing out what might be called a range of narrative attitudes, brings together two of Munro's central preoccupations: the problem of truth and the power of language. In telling her story, Phemie, to return to Benveniste's distinction, moves from a history—with its absent interlocutor—to a discourse in which the 'I' not only returns, but also explicitly declares its own involvement in constructing the narrative. In other words, Munro, rather than maintain a distinction between history and discourse, shows us that events cannot be narrated independently of a speaker. Having abandoned the notion of truth as correspondence to reality, Phemie comes to the realization that truth is largely a function of what she wants to believe. The 'progress' to which the story's title alludes thus becomes manifest, at least on a structural level, in Phemie's movement from an attempt at a kind of empathy—an attempt to enter into the experience and understanding of her mother—to her realization that any such attempt to experience what the 'original' mind went through is always subject to her own desires and motivations. By the time her narrative ends, Phemie's faith in the possibility of an objective ground for knowledge has diminished: rather than relive the past, she wants now to rewrite it to suit her own purposes.

Throughout the stories in this volume, Munro's protagonists frequently display a penchant for invention, for reshaping or fabricating events to accord with their own aspirations. In 'Jesse and Meribeth,' for instance—a story which, perhaps more than any other story in this volume, recalls Munro's earlier writing[4]—Jessie, the protagonist, lies to her friend MaryBeth by telling her that she is having an affair with her employer, Mr Cryderman. Jessie tells us, 'I had been planning to tease [MaryBeth] for a little longer, then to tell her that it was all a joke. I did not even have anybody's name in my head, in the beginning. I did now, but it was too outrageous. I couldn't believe that I would ever say it' (*PL* 177–8). After naming Mr Cryderman as her secret lover, Jessie feels 'wonderfully lightened, not burdened, by [her] lie' (*PL* 178). She then interrupts the narrative of her imaginary affair to offer, from what is presumably an older perspective, a kind of commentary on her behaviour:

> Once, I knew an old woman who said to me, when talking about her life, that she had spent three years having an affair with Robert Browning. She was not in the least senile; she was a very competent and straightforward old woman. She didn't say she loved Browning's writing, or spent all her time reading about him. She didn't say she had fantasies. 'Oh, yes,' she said, 'and then there was the three years' affair I had with Robert Browning.' I waited for her to laugh or add some little explanatory word, but she did not do so. I have to think, then, that the affair she conducted in her imagination was so serious and strenuous that she forbade herself to describe it as imaginary. (*PL* 178)

Like Phemie, in the title story, the old woman to whom Jessie refers clings to a notion of truth which is clearly divorced from the actual events of her life. Unlike Phemie, however, she seems unaware of the extent to which her story is a constructed one. In refusing to acknowledge the imaginary status of her affair with Browning, she presents her story as a kind of truth; but, as Jessie realizes, the story is based on an invented rather than an experienced relationship. Does the old woman actually believe that she has had this affair?[5]

It would appear that Jessie, at least during the time of her talk with the old lady, wants to maintain a distinction between truth and fiction, between narrative and experience: she expects the woman 'to laugh or add some little explanatory word.' What is interesting, however, is that Jessie—chronologically though not narratively speaking—has *already* confronted the impossibility of maintaining such a distinction. Even before her talk with the old woman, Jessie has been initiated into an awareness of the inseparability of truth and fiction. We, however, have yet to learn of Jessie's initiation; this information has been deliberately withheld from the narrative. Once again, progress, for Munro, is a matter of structure, a kind of language-game in which narrative must 'catch up' to chronology.

In 'Jesse and Meribeth,' the narrative does its 'catching up' when the protagonist of the story's time-frame—the young girl who invents stories about her affair with Mr Cryderman—reaches the level of awareness of a retrospective narrator who recognizes the seriousness and strenuousness of paradigmatic relationships.[6] Like Mr Chamberlain, about whom Del, in 'Lives of Girls and Women,' fantasizes, Mr Cryderman engages in behaviour which leads the young Jessie to understand that the real world and the world of her imagination cannot be kept apart.[7]

'Miles City, Montana' is another story in which the completeness of the opposition between these two worlds is called into question. The story begins with what appears to be an objective (or at least reliable) account of an event:

> My father came across the field carrying the body of the boy who had been drowned. There were several men together, returning from the search, but he was the one carrying the body. The men were muddy and exhausted, and walked with their heads down as if they were ashamed. Even the dogs were dispirited, dripping from the cold river. When they all set out, hours before, the dogs were nervy and yelping, the men tense and determined, and there was a constrained, unspeakable excitement about the whole scene. It was understood that they might find something horrible. (*PL* 84)

The narrator then proceeds to give us details about the drowned boy: 'The boy's name was Steve Gauley. He was eight years old. His hair and clothes were mud-colored now and carried some bits of dead leaves, twigs, and grass. He was like a heap of refuse that had been left out all winter. His face was turned in to my father's chest, but I could see a nostril, an ear, plugged up with greenish mud' (*PL* 84). What poses as an accurate representation, however, reveals itself to be a constructed memory. After describing 'the whole scene,' the narrator suddenly steps in and admits her own involvement in shaping what we have just been reading: 'I don't think so. I don't think I really saw all this. Perhaps I saw my father carrying him, and the other men following along, and the dogs, but I would not have been allowed to get close enough to see something like mud in his nostril. I must have heard someone talking about that and imagined that I saw it' (*PL* 84). Here, as elsewhere throughout the volume, we are asked to recognize the extent to which the subject—as the source of meaning—is always implicated in any attempt to tell about the past. In imagining mud in the drowned boy's nostril, the narrator shows us that her account of the incident belongs more to Benveniste's realm of discourse than to his realm of historical narration.

This insistence on reintroducing the subject into what appears to be an objective account is in keeping with Munro's movement away from a straightforward, unquestioned realistic discourse, one which posits a world of fixed, stable, and recuperable meanings. Richard Rorty has suggested that 'we do indeed need to give up the notion of "data and interpretation" with its suggestion that if we could get to the real data, unpolluted by our choice of language, we should be "grounding" rational choice' (325). Although Munro may not be entirely giving up what Rorty calls 'data and interpretation,' her fiction does illustrate the difficulty of articulating a founding moment of knowledge. Like Phemie, who, by the end of the title story, abandons the notion that the hermeneutic enterprise should be grounded on stable origins, the narrator of 'Miles City, Montana' shows us that any attempt to relive an experience from her past is always subject to her own motivated discourse.

In the second part of the story, Munro, in characteristic fashion, replays the first section, only now it is one of the narrator's own children who is in danger of drowning. The narrator, in the story's second section, is driving from British Columbia to Ontario with her husband, Andrew, and their children, Meg and Cynthia. 'We were driving back from Vancouver, where we lived, to Ontario, which we still called "home," in our new car,' she explains (*PL* 87). When the family stops at a pool in Miles City, Meg's near-fatal accident clearly recalls the Steve Gauley drowning with which the story begins. Worth noting here is that Meg's near drowning is presented as a memory which, like the narrator's recollection of the earlier drowning, is, to some extent, discred-

ited by her own admission that she has altered certain details. Hence, when
she remembers calling out to Cynthia to ask where Meg was, the scene she
comes up with contains the kinds of details which might lead us to accept it
as an accurate representation of what happened: 'It always seems to me, when
I recall this scene, that Cynthia turns very gracefully toward me, then turns all
around in the water—making me think of a ballerina on point—and spreads
her arms in a gesture of the stage. "Disappeared!"' (*PL* 100). After telling us
this, however, the narrator then corrects herself: 'She did say "Disappeared"
after looking all around the pool, but the strangely artificial style of speech
and gesture, the lack of urgency, is more likely my invention' (*PL* 100). Despite
her use of details to summon up this event, the narrator understands that her
memory of Meg's near drowning has been largely a product of her imagination. Once again the past—or at least the past as it is initially presented to
us, as readers—turns out to be subject to revision and reinterpretation. The
narrator's willingness to recognize her own position as subject in language
suggests the extent to which the past she wants to recover is intelligible only
through discourse. By demonstrating an awareness of the context in which
her account of the past is being constructed, she raises a problem that runs
throughout Munro's writing: the problem of whether one can be narratively
faithful to what happened in the past.

  The narrator thus situates both memories—the childhood recollection of Steve Gauley's drowning and the near drowning of Meg, which, in
fact, triggers the earlier memory—within a discursive context. The story's
structural preoccupation with patterns of complicity may, at some level, be
aligned with its thematic investigation of an analogous issue. As a child at
Steve Gauley's funeral, the narrator understands for the first time that her
parents have been complicitous in the boy's death: 'I was understanding
that they were implicated. Their big, stiff, dressed-up bodies did not stand
between me and sudden death, or any kind of death. They gave consent. So
it seemed. They gave consent to the death of children and to my death not
by anything they said or thought but by the very fact that they had made
children—they had made me. They had made me, and for that reason my
death—however grieved they were, however they carried on—would seem
to them anything but impossible or unnatural' (*PL* 103). After Meg's near
brush with disaster, however, the narrator, now herself an adult and a parent,
engages in a kind of speculative discourse which reveals her own complicitous behaviour. Although, on the surface, the narrator wants to promote a
sense of luck—'That was all we spoke about—luck' (*PL* 102)—what she is
compelled to picture is precisely the opposite. On an absent and potential
level of meaning, she plays out what *might have* happened had her daughter drowned: 'At this moment, we could have been filling out forms. Meg

removed from us, Meg's body being prepared for shipment. To Vancouver—where we had never noticed such a thing as a graveyard—or to Ontario? The scribbled drawings she had made this morning would still be in the back seat of the car. How could this be borne all at once, how did people bear it?' (*PL* 102–3). Realizing that 'there's something trashy about this kind of imagining' (*PL* 103), the narrator implicitly admits that she has been engaging in the very behaviour that she, as a child, resented in adults. Thus, at the end of the story, she holds out the hope that, in time, she will 'be forgiven . . . for everything that had first to be seen and condemned by those children: whatever was flippant, arbitrary, careless, callous—all our natural, and particular, mistakes' (*PL* 105).

What I have been suggesting is that 'Miles City, Montana' turns on the recognition of complicity on two discrete yet interconnected levels: the level of the subject represented in the fiction, and the level of the subject who narrates. The distinction here is between what, in Benveniste's terminology, we might call the subject of the *énoncé* (the protagonist caught up in the events of the story) and the subject of the enunciation (the retrospective narrator who calls attention to the fact that she has fabricated a past). Just as the protagonist comes to understand that she herself is, though perhaps inadvertently, giving consent to the death of her children, so, as a narrator, she undergoes a parallel process of discovery when, in the midst of her recollections, she intervenes and allows the story to define itself as discourse. Like those self-corrective moments in *The Moons of Jupiter*, moments I have discussed in the previous chapter, this intervention is also a kind of backing off from what cannot finally be known. Although the story begins in a manner which seems to suggest the possibility of an accurate representation of the narrator's past, it ends up, like so many of Munro's stories—in particular, the more recent ones—unable to offer a guarantee of its own truth.

Patterns of complicity emerge more indirectly in 'Fits,' yet another story which examines the implications of an altered detail in a reported event. At the centre of this story about a murder-suicide is Peg Kuiper's discovery of the dead bodies of her neighbours, the Weebles, and her unwillingness to talk about the incident. Although 'Peg was the one who found them' (*PL* 108), the story is told from the third-person point of view of her husband, Robert, who, as Ildikó de Papp Carrington notes, 'does not observe the violence' (52). In an attempt to reconstruct his wife's experience, Robert pieces together bits of information which he gathers from various sources.

Robert's attempt to reconcile the story as his wife finally tells it with the version presented to him earlier in the day by the constable leads us to an implicit recognition of a hidden level of unconscious motivation in Peg.

Although Peg appears essentially unshattered by her discoveries of the dead bodies, although she continues the day almost as if nothing extraordinary happened, her overt disinterestedness conceals a covert sense of morbid fascination. In thinking about 'one discrepancy, one detail—one lie—that would never have anything to do with him' (*PL* 130), Robert moves towards an awareness of the possibility that Peg's account of the incident has been motivated by a sense of self-interest.

Sensing that Robert would 'want to know' (*PL* 124) what happened, Peg tells him 'her part of the story' (*PL* 124). As with 'Miles City, Montana,' 'Jesse and Meribeth,' and the title story, here, once again, we are provided with an account which, chronologically, has already been rendered tenuous. Like the other stories, however, 'Fits' delays our discovery of the possibility that we have been presented with an impossible, because constructed, memory. Robert has already heard the constable's report of the Weebles' murder-suicide, but Munro puts off giving us Robert's memory of this report until the end of her narrative (see Carrington 54). By doing so, she generates surprise on the level of plot, but she also suggests that Robert, despite the evidence of two contradictory versions, does not himself recognize the implications of the discrepancy between these versions until he goes out for his long walk after dinner.

In telling her story to Robert, Peg says she 'knew there wasn't anybody but me alive in the [Weebles'] house. Then I saw his leg, I saw his leg stretched out into the hall, and I knew then, but I had to go on in and make sure' (*PL* 125). Later, during his after-dinner walk, Robert tries to understand why Peg has lied to him. The story ends with Robert's memory of the constable's account:

> At noon, when the constable in the diner was giving his account, he had described how the force of the shot threw Walter Weeble backward. 'It blasted him partways out of the room. His head was laying out in the hall. What was left of it was laying out in the hall.'
>
> Not a leg. Not the indicative leg, whole and decent in its trousers, the shod foot. That was not what anybody turning at the top of the stairs would see and would have to step over, step through, in order to go into the bedroom and look at the rest of what was there. (*PL* 131)

Only at the end of the story, then, do we realize that we have not, in fact, been given the whole story. In distorting this one detail, Peg seeks to appropriate the violent origins of the incident with her own metalanguage. Her distortion—her lie—forces us to recognize the extent to which Peg, despite appearances to the contrary, is riddled with a kind of curiosity that is not unlike that of her neighbours, who come 'poking around in a brutally curious way' (*PL* 126). Just as these neighbours drive by the scene of the incident in the hopes of 'getting a look' (*PL* 126), so Peg wants to get a good look at what Walter Weeble had done. So, as Carrington puts it, 'instead of screaming and running away, she stepped through whatever remained of Walter's exploded head and entered the bedroom to look at Nora's corpse' (55). Another critic, Charles Hanly, makes a similar point. He claims that the 'story hinges upon an implicit yet powerful motivation in Peg to witness such a scene' as the one she discovered in the Weebles' bedroom (171).

In leading us to recognize Peg's 'intense curiosity to see something for-bidden' (Hanly 171), these critics alert us to the possibility that her lie to Robert is itself an attempt to conceal her own self-interest. Peg, however, is unsuccessful in her attempts at concealment because we, like Robert, have access to alternative versions, to other histories.

The story, in fact, is rife with other histories, with loosely connected details from various pasts. Clayton, Peg's son from a previous marriage, reminds his mother about the fights she used to have with her ex-husband: "'When you used to have those fights, you know what I used to think? I used to think one of you was going to come and kill me with a knife'" (*PL* 126). Later, when he is out walking, Robert finds himself remembering violent scenes from his own previous relationship with Lee, and this memory from his past compels him to think about Peg and her ex-husband Dave, who suddenly left his fam-ily one day and headed off for the Arctic: 'A man doesn't just drive farther and farther away in his trucks until he disappears from his wife's view. Not even if he has always dreamed of the Arctic. Things happen before he goes. Marriage knots aren't going to slip apart painlessly, with the pull of distance. There's got to be some wrenching and slashing. But she didn't say, and he didn't ask, or even think much about that, till now' (*PL* 129). It is this sense of 'wrenching and slashing,' of eruptions of violence, which implicitly brings together not only Robert and Peg, but also Robert, Peg, and Walter Weeble. Unlike Peg, however, who wishes not to speak about either the violence from her past or the scene she discovered in the Weebles' bedroom—who, in fact, seeks to transform her own self-interest and fascination into a seemingly objective and distanced account—Robert, by the end of the story, gravitates towards an awareness of how much both he and Peg have been implicated in gestures of violence not entirely unlike those of Walter Weeble.

In the novella 'A Queer Streak,' Munro once again turns her attention to the ways in which the past can become the subject of stories.[8] Like 'The Progress of Love,' 'A Queer Streak' also concerns itself with the distance between generations and 'the possibility of bridging [that distance] through storytelling' (Gadpaille 74). Although the form of a novella may be new to Munro, the territory is familiar. A kind of variation on Peg's distortion of facts in a reported incident, the story dramatizes what happens when a family history is appropriated by a metalanguage.

That family history is an important issue is announced at the outset. The narrative begins with a description not simply of Violet's past, but of a past that she never experienced, a past to which she now has access only through the agency of other peoples' memories: 'Violet's mother—Aunt Ivie—had three little boys, three baby boys, and she lost them. Then she had the three girls' (*PL* 208). Just as Violet's knowledge of the brothers she never had is based on the stories that she is told—her meditations on the word 'lost' reinforce the fact that the term has been supplied by somebody else, undoubtedly her mother—her knowledge of her father's past is similarly based on the process of sharing and interpreting narratives. Consider, for instance, the following story about her father:

> He had gone to a dance, when he was a young man, up on the Snow Road, where he came from. Some other young fellows who were there had insulted him, and he had to take their insults because he did not know a thing about fighting. But after that he got some lessons from an old prizefighter, a real one, who was living on Sharbot Lake. Another night, another dance—the same thing as before. The same kind of insults. Except that this time King Billy lit into them and cleaned up on them, one by one.
> Lit into them and cleaned up on them, one by one.
> No more insults of that kind anywhere up in that country.
> No more. (*PL* 210)

The repetition of 'lit into them and cleaned up on them, one by one' and 'no more' suggests that Violet's knowledge of this incident from her father's past has come out of an oral reshaping of the past. As with Rose's knowledge, in 'Royal Beatings,' of her mother's death Munro here calls our attention to the fact that Violet's knowledge of her family history is based on the kinds of stories that have been handed down to her.[9]

Munro's work, as we have seen from other stories in this volume and in her earlier collections, is riddled with the problem of mediation. Her fiction is awash with constant reminders of gaps in time, of discontinuous histories, of distances from an origin. 'A Queer Streak,' as its opening scenes make clear, is no exception. The structure of the novella—with its two parts and its two perspectives from different generations—is itself indicative of the text's involvement with what philosopher Hans-Georg Gadamer has called *Zeitabstand*,

'temporal distance.' For Gadamer, temporal distance is the gap which separates the interpreter from the object of interpretation, a gap which he sees as
being a productive basis for the hermeneutic process. 'Time,' he writes, 'is no
longer primarily a gulf to be bridged because it separates, but it is actually the
supportive ground of process in which the present is rooted' (264).

In 'A Queer Streak,' this concept comes into play in various ways. The
second part of the novella is told primarily from the point of view of Dane,
Violet's nephew; hence we can speak about the temporal distance of generations. But it is also through the characters of Heather and Gillian, two young
women (one of whom claims to be a distant relative of Violet's) who show up
at Violet's door, that Munro explores the implications of the gap between an
interpreter and the object of interpretation. What Heather and Gillian want,
according to Violet, is information about her past: "'They are interested in our
family and what I can remember about what it was like,'" she tells Dane (*PL*
246). But, as we have seen elsewhere in Munro, the apprehension of facts is a
function of what one wants to believe. As if to highlight the point, Munro has
Heather and Gillian send Violet a card with the following message: '*Thank
you a million, million times for your help and openness. You have given us a wonderful story. It is a classic story of anti-patriarchal rage. Your gift to us, can we give
it to others? What is called Female Craziness is nothing but centuries of Frustration
and Oppression. The part about the creek is wonderful just by itself and how many
women can identify!*' (*PL* 248). By responding to Violet's story of her past in
these terms, Heather and Gillian seem to be promoting the productivity of
the concept of temporal distance. The past to which they are responding is the
past that formed the basis of the novella's first section. In this first section, we
learn about the 'queer streak' in Violet's family. As a young girl, Dawn Rose—
Violet's sister (later to become Dane's mother)—sends anonymous threatening letters to her father while Violet is away at school in Ottawa. 'Violet's
absence,' as Carrington notes, 'is crucial because she has been mothering her
two younger sisters ever since their mother, with whom the "queer streak"
begins, was unhinged by the deaths of her first three children' (177). When
Heather and Gillian receive this information about Dawn Rose, they seek
immediately to make it correspond with their own ideological perspective.
Thus, like Peg in 'Fits,' they too are implicated in gestures of appropriation.
In 'A Queer Streak,' these gestures serve to remind us that re-presentations of
the past inevitably involve a reconstruction of events not as they really were,
but rather as we have been led to see them from our own perspective in the
present. Like Gadamer, then, Heather and Gillian would probably subscribe
to the idea that 'every age has to understand a transmitted text *in its own way*'
(Gadamer 263; emphasis added). Unlike Phemie, who, in 'The Progress of
Love,' attempts to relive what her mother went through, Heather and Gil-

lian do not appear to be interested in attempting a complete and wholesale recovery of the past. For them, Violet's information about the family past is 'a wonderful story,' a transmitted text which interests them only insofar as they can interpret it in terms of the present. Thus Dawn Rose's threatening letters to her father are seen, by Heather and Gillian, as a classic example of 'anti-patriarchal rage.'[10]

Munro, however, while clearly recognizing the difficulty of separating history from narration, remains suspicious of all such unproblematized attempts to reclaim the past from a motivated perspective. For one thing, King Billy, as he is presented to us, could hardly be the object of anyone's 'anti-patriarchal rage' because he is not a father in the traditional sense (see Carrington 179). Given that 'it was Violet who ruled in the house' (*PL* 213), the interpretation offered by Heather and Gillian is clearly inadequate. In wanting to give Violet's gift to others, to dramatize Violet's memories for the women's theatre to which they belong, Heather and Gillian desire to re-enact what they see as a subversion of patriarchal authority. What I am suggesting is that their attempt to reinterpret Violet's painful past in terms of their own political agenda, to make the 'queer streak' from Violet's family history into a play about 'anti-patriarchal rage,' is itself a rehabilitation of structures of authority. Unlike Phemie at the end of the title story, these two characters lack a critique of their own metalanguage, an awareness that they too are implicated in a discourse of power and appropriation. As if to symbolize both their power and their insensitivity, Munro has Heather and Gillian precipitate Violet's death with their curiosity to see old documents from her past (see Carrington 182).

Heather and Gillian, then, are engaged in an attempt to reclaim the origin of the 'queer streak' in Violet's family. Their reshaping of Violet's memories nicely illustrates Gadamer's dictum: 'understanding is not merely a reproductive, but always a productive attitude as well' (264). The novella, however, with its constant reminders of mediation, asks us to recognize the extent to which the queer streak of the title refers not only to Dawn Rose's threatening letters, but also to an origin that is already beyond recovery. That Munro begins 'A Queer Streak' by emphasizing the mediated nature of Violet's knowledge about her past suggests that Heather and Gillian can only fail in their endeavours because the origin they seek is already distanced from itself.

While Munro's novella functions as a kind of implicit critique of systems of thought which, at the expense of trying to understand particular instances, seek to posit general principles, the closing piece in the collection, 'White Dump,' explicitly forces us to acknowledge the importance of individual points of view. Told from the perspective of three different women—Denise,

Sophie, and Isabel Vogelsang—who correspond roughly to the story's tripartite structure, 'White Dump' is without doubt one of Munro's most challenging stories, both structurally and thematically. With its emphasis on different points of view, the story recalls earlier pieces ('Accident,' 'Labor Day Dinner') in which Munro employs a somewhat similar method; in 'White Dump,' however, Munro's involvement with overlapping scenes and perspectives lends her fiction a new level of complexity. Her strategy in this piece seems to be an extension of the kind of circling round an event that takes place in 'The Progress of Love,' except that there—and this, to me, seems to be the point to the title piece—we are confined to the point of view of the first-person narrator, Phemie. Although her representations of the past may, at least initially, seem accurate, we are repeatedly urged to see Phemie's complicity, to recognize the extent to which she has constructed these representations according to her own needs and desires.

In 'White Dump,' the problem of complicity is addressed only peripherally, but then the story, insofar as it refuses to offer a unified centre of consciousness, is concerned with precisely that: the periphery. I say this not because the narrative takes up the plight of marginalized peoples, but rather because it is engaged in an investigation of a series of what might loosely be called colonizing (and decolonizing) moments. Part of the difficulty of the story stems from our inability to determine precisely *whose* story we are reading. By using overlapping points of view, Munro displaces the notion of a centre, thereby rendering unstable our reading of events in the narration. As Thomas Friedman points out in an unpublished paper, 'our perceptions, as readers, are being perpetually de-centered as the connections between the three generations of women are being broken and re-formed, deconstructed and reconstructed' (7).

In addition to posing the problem about *whose* story we are reading, 'White Dump' also renders problematic our attempt to fix any kind of determinate meaning, to say *what* the story is about. Although much of Munro's recent writing might accurately be discussed in terms of its refusal to offer a readily definable plot or story-line, the plot of 'White Dump,' by comparison, seems even more elusive.

Perhaps the best place to begin a discussion of the story is through an analysis of a number of its specific details. Although the narration begins in the present tense, with Denise as an older woman visiting her father, Laurence, and Magda (to whom he is now married), the story continually slips back into the past, in particular, into various recollections of Laurence's fortieth birthday, which, we discover, happened to fall on Bastille Day, 1969. The date, as anyone familiar with Munro's meticulousness would undoubtedly surmise, is far from incidental. Lest we forget, Laurence hastens to remind us that this was 'the year of the moon shot' (*PL* 278), an occasion which, although seemingly peripheral to the story's main sequence of events, acquires significance when read with other peripheral details in the text. Similarly, the fact that Laurence's birthday falls on Bastille Day is not as random as it may at first appear.

The moon shot and Bastille Day—what do these two historic occasions have in common? Or, given the story's rejection of a unified subject position, perhaps the more appropriate question would be, what sets the two apart? While the Apollo 11 space flight and moon landing will undoubtedly go down in the history books as 'a triumph for American science and technology,' as the fulfilment of an 'age-old dream of mankind' (von Braun 359), another way of looking at the July 1969 landing—in fact at the entire American space program—would be to see it as part of a larger colonial enterprise. One only need recall the rhetoric that surrounded the Apollo mission to see the program in these terms. In his comments to the astronauts on board the historic flight, President Nixon said, 'Because of what you have done, the heavens have become a part of man's world' (quoted in von Braun 360–1). His comment is telling because it reveals how the exploration of other worlds is itself a colonizing gesture. 'Man's' quest for knowledge—to know what is 'out there' not just in the world, but in the universe—is part of a larger desire to appropriate the unknown, to bring it into 'his' domain.[11]

Bastille Day, by contrast, is a national holiday in France commemorating the freeing of prisoners. According to popular thought, the storming of the fortress and state prison in the eastern district of Paris on 14 July 1789 was aimed at liberating the many prisoners who were being held captive within its walls. Traditionally seen as a symbol of the arbitrary power of the monarch to arrest and detain individuals without a trial, the Bastille, however, turned out to be housing only seven prisoners when it was captured. Furthermore, as David Thomson points out, the purpose of the attack was not so much to liberate prisoners as to capture more arms for revolutionary movements in Paris (696). The celebrated seizing of the state prison by a French mob, then, was partly motivated by a desire to replace the ancien régime with a new one.

Although peripheral to the story's main actions, these two experiences, the moon landing and the storming of the Bastille, serve implicitly to define the trajectory of the narrative in 'White Dump.' Moments of colonization and liberation (or at least what *seemed* to be liberation, thus making the Bastille reference doubly significant) punctuate the story. To put it another way, the story is marked by the interplay of these two discrete but interconnected experiences: freedom and colonization.

'White Dump,' as I noted earlier, begins with Denise's point of view. Although her narration offers hints about what transpired on Laurence's fortieth birthday, we do not really get a sense of what happened until the picture is somewhat filled in later by other perspectives. Denise, we are told in the first section, 'runs a Women's Centre in Toronto. She gets beaten women into shelters, finds doctors and lawyers for them, goes after private and public money, makes speeches, holds meetings, deals with varied and sometimes dangerous mix-ups of life' (*PL* 276). From this we gather that she is committed to liberating oppressed and victimized individuals. But she herself, we begin to realize, is trapped: she is 'too mired in a past that everyone else has abandoned' (*PL* 288). 'Unfair, unbidden thoughts' (*PL* 288) can strike her unexpectedly. What her section of the narrative suggests is that she cannot escape the guilt she feels for, in some sense, being responsible for the end of Laurence's marriage to her mother, Isabel. Thus when Magda asks Denise why her mother did not make the cake for Laurence on his birthday, Denise, in a 'voice gone cautionary and slightly regretful,' replies by saying that 'the oven wasn't working' (*PL* 279). The fact that Denise, unlike her mother, has regrets is significant because, although we have no way of realizing this until we complete the story, she is compelled to feel as though she set a whole series of unwanted events in motion by trying to surprise Laurence on his birthday.

Denise's present to her father is a trip in a small plane, flown by a local pilot who subsequently—we discover only near the story's end—has an affair with Isabel. While Denise may not tell us as much in her section of the narrative, we surmise that she is burdened with the guilt of having, as it were, introduced this pilot into the picture. Thus her comment about being an 'awful stage manager' (*PL* 279) takes on an additional meaning. While the immediate referent for her remark is the confusion that reigned during her attempts to surprise Laurence with the plane ride, when we return to it after a completed reading of the story we realize that the comment also carries a latent suggestion of Denise's own responsibility for initiating her mother's subsequent affair with the pilot. Denise, then, despite her commitment to liberation, reveals herself to be trapped by an inescapable link to her past. Or, to put it differently, she herself lacks the freedom which she seeks to bestow on the oppressed and the victimized. With this in mind, we can return to the passage about Denise's involvement with the Women's Centre in Toronto, and see that shades of a kind of (albeit ambiguous) colonizing impulse may already be evident in her attitudes and gestures. Although 'she gets beaten women into shelters, finds doctors and lawyers for them, goes after private and public money,' although she does, in other words, help other people, the description implies that she fails to help other people *help themselves*. Because the passage is worded in such a way as to emphasize Denise's actions (getting, finding, and going after), Munro calls our attention to the fact that attempts to liberate and help the oppressed can themselves hinge on colonizing impulses. As Linda Hutcheon has suggested in a recent article, 'the precise point at which interest and concern become imperializing appropriation is a hotly contested one' ('Circling' 153–4).

The second section of 'White Dump,' told from the perspective of Sophie, Denise's grandmother (and Laurence's mother), more explicitly examines this problematic interplay between colonizing and liberating gestures. Isabel, in the story's first part, has informed us that 'Sophie is such a pacifist and Socialist' (*PL* 281), and Sophie's own section of the narrative, at least ostensibly, appears to bear this out. In response to 'The Property Owners' Newsletter [which] had proposed a ban on long hair and "weird forms of dress"' (*PL* 291), Sophie had written in opposition: 'She stated in her letter that this entire side of the lake had once been Vogelsang property, and that Augustus Vogelsang had left the comparative comfort of Bismarck's Germany to seek the freedom of the New World, in which all individuals might choose how they dressed, spoke, worshipped, and so on' (*PL* 291). Sophie's tolerance for long hair and weird forms of dress, like her refusal to lie about not being married—about having conceived Laurence out of wedlock—suggests her own liberal perspective: she too wants to promote 'freedom' as a central fact of life. Yet after her 'bad experience . . . with the hippies' (*PL* 279)—whom she initially greeted 'in a cheerful, hailing tone' (*PL* 291)—Sophie is compelled 'to compose herself' (*PL* 292) with scenes from the past which undermine her liberal outlook. These scenes involve the Bryces, a family who owned the farm down the lake where Sophie, as a child, used to row to get milk. This is what Sophie recalls about the Bryce children: 'They were always pale children, in spite of the summer sun, and they bore many bites, scratches, scabs, mosquito bites, blackfly bites, fleabites, bloody and festering. That was because they were poor children. It was because they were poor that Rita's—or Annie's—eyes were crossed, and that one of the boys had such queerly uneven shoulders, and that they talked as they did, saying, "We-ez goen to towen," and "bowt," and other things that Sophie could hardly understand' (*PL* 293).

The young Sophie is attracted to the Bryce children because they belong to a world so completely alien from the world that she knows and inhabits. She likes to talk to them, to 'ask them questions and tell them things' (*PL* 293). But we quickly discover that Sophie's fascination with these neighbours from across the lake is tied to her desire to make them the recipients of her good will:

> She dreamed of giving them baths and clean clothes and putting ointment on their bites, and teaching them to talk properly. Sometimes she had a long, complicated daydream that was all

about Christmas for the Bryce family. It included a redecoration and painting of their house, as well as a wholesale cleanup of their yard. Magic glasses appeared, to straighten crossed eyes. There were picture books and electric trains and dolls in taffeta dresses and armies of toy soldiers and heaps of marzipan fruits and animals. (Marzipan was Sophie's favorite treat. A conversation with the Bryces about candy had revealed that they did not know what it was.) (*PL* 294)

In wanting to help the Bryce children, Sophie is engaged in an act of colonization: she wants to convert the Other into the Same. The fact that she dreams of bestowing upon them *her* favourite treat, marzipan, reinforces the notion that even the activity of giving is not innocent or value-free. Something is expected in return (thus even the Christmas setting for the daydream is not incidental). What Sophie expects in return for her good will is precisely that these children will become more like her. Her charity is problematic because it conceals a covert complicity.

When Sophie, 'in time,' does get her mother's permission to invite one of the Bryce children to her house, she has trouble understanding the girl's lack of preference: 'She wouldn't say what sort of sandwiches or cookies or drink she wanted, and wouldn't choose to go on the swing or the teeter-totter, or to play by the water or play with dolls. Her lack of preference seemed to have something superior about it, as if she was adhering to a code of manners Sophie couldn't know anything about. She accepted the treats she was given and allowed Sophie to push her in the swing, all with a steadfast lack of enthusiasm' (*PL* 294). What the young Sophie, here, perceives as the Bryce girl's lack of preference and enthusiasm, stems from her inability to conceive of a 'code of manners,' a system of signification, which is different from her own. The fact that she encodes and interprets the Bryce girl's hesitation in terms of superiority suggests that Sophie's own discourse is operating within this meta-level: to be in a position to give and offer is to maintain a position of superiority. By projecting her own sense of superiority onto the Bryce girl, Sophie sees her neighbour's lack of preference and enthusiasm as a rejection of the things that she has to offer.

If we examine this passage from the perspective which is not presented to us—the perspective of the Bryce girl—Sophie's position of authority becomes even clearer. By failing to indicate a preference, the Bryce girl wants to remain within a system of signification where all the choices presented to her by Sophie are available. To not choose between different types of sandwiches, cookies, and drinks is to remain within a system of infinite possibility, a system which the Bryce girl has never known at her own home. Unlike

Sophie, who, given her position of power, can always choose any one of these things, the Bryce girl is hesitant to make decisions because, for her, to choose would be to limit freedom and desire to a single object.

Not knowing what else to do with this neighbour whom she cannot assimilate into her own system of signification, Sophie takes the Bryce girl down to the water and initiates 'a program of catching frogs. Sophie wanted to move a whole colony of frogs from the reedy little bay on one side of the dock, around to a pleasant shelf and cave in the rocks on the other side.... By the end of the day, the colony had been moved' (*PL* 294). While the new space 'on the other side' may be 'pleasant,' what we do not know is whether it will contain the same requirements for living and spawning as 'the reedy little bay.' The fact that Munro uses the term 'colony' hints at the problem involved in Sophie's project. Even if the moving of the frogs is done with the frogs' best interest at heart (at least in the mind of the colonizer), Sophie's efforts replicate the project of the colonizers who, at their own whims, come in and move native inhabitants to reserves. As with Denise's efforts to liberate oppressed women, here too we see a potential problem with the project of good will. The passage, more precisely, asks us to recognize the extent to which colonies are inevitably victims—even of good will. In addition, it asks us to think about the ways in which space and location are perceived in terms of ownership and control. The 'reedy little bay' and the 'pleasant shelf and cave in the rocks' are—like the sandbox and the dollhouse—spaces that this little girl owns. The very fact that Sophie, in the first place, can think about moving the frogs implies that she considers this a space over which she has power and control.

These scenes from Sophie's childhood, scenes with which she *composes* herself, serve to undermine the liberal attitudes which she appears to espouse at various points in time in the story. Towards the end of her section of the narrative, Sophie, now a grandmother hovering in the air in a small plane, understands that the odd 'shrinking feeling' she is experiencing at the moment is a feeling she had known when she was young: 'This feeling—Sophie was realizing—wasn't new to her. She'd had it as a child. A genuine shrinking feeling, one of the repertoire of frightening, marvelous feelings, or states, that are available to you when you're very young. Like the sense of hanging upside down, walking on the ceiling, stepping over heightened doorsills. An awful pleasure then, so why not now?' (*PL* 296). The answer Sophie provides to her own question again poses a challenge to her liberal attitudes: 'Because it was not her choice, now. She had a sure sense of changes in the offing, that were not her choice' (*PL* 297). Although Sophie may indeed be sensing an intimation of her own mortality here, the fact that she wants to avoid change may also indicate her resistance to accepting the possibility of new and unexpected avenues of experience. Unlike Lydia in 'Dulse'—who understands that what she desires is not the world she knows but rather the world she cannot predict—Sophie, despite her apparent openness and free-mindedness, reveals herself in this passage to be opting for the safe and predictable world in which she is already comfortably ensconced. Sameness and routine, thus, are valorized at the expense of difference and possibility.

The third and final section of the narrative deals with Isabel's quest to liberate herself from the routine of her everyday life. When the section begins, Isabel is sitting 'in the shade of some scrawny poplar trees' thinking 'that this day, a pleasant family day, had been full of hurdles, which she had so far got over' (*PL* 297). The day, we realize, is Laurence's fortieth birthday, and while Laurence, Denise, and Sophie are flying above the Rideau Lake system in a small plane, Isabel takes the opportunity to evaluate the day's events. Already implicit in her description of the day as a series of hurdles to be got over is a sense that she is unhappy—or at least bored—with the way things are. A few pages into Isabel's section, we come across a passage which corroborates our suspicions about Isabel's problem: 'Not much to her credit to go through her life thinking, Well, good, now that's over, *that's* over. What was she looking forward to, what bonus was she hoping to get, when this, and this, and this, was over?' (*PL* 303). Later, we are told that Isabel sees her husband as someone who 'had to be propped up, kept going, by constant and clever exertions on her part, by reassurance and good management; he depended on her to make him a man' (*PL* 304). Isabel, we gather, feels trapped within her marriage; she wants to be free from Laurence. Thus, when the pilot remarks that perhaps Isabel could come out for her own flight the next day, Isabel sees this as an opportunity for liberation. She translates her own desire into the context of Sophie's episode with the hippies earlier that morning: 'It was the idea of herself, not Sophie, walking naked out of the water toward those capering boys. (In her mind, she had already eliminated the girl.) That made her long for, and imagine, some leaping, radical invitation. She was kindled for it' (*PL* 305). The 'leaping, radical invitation' which she longs for and imagines presents itself as a fantasy involving the pilot: 'She imagined that they turned at the same time, they looked at each other, just as in some romantic movie, operatic story, high-school fantasy. They turned at the same time, they looked at each other, they exchanged a promise that was no less real though they might never meet again. And the promise hit her like lightning, split her like lightning, though she moved on smoothly, intact' (*PL* 305).

Although 'in the years ahead' Isabel 'wouldn't be so astonished at the way the skin of the moment can break open' (*PL* 307–8), here she is astonished. The possibility which a relationship with the pilot offers her constitutes precisely what she feels has been missing in her relationship with Laurence.

Many years afterward, when discussing her affairs with 'her grownup daugh-ter Denise,' Isabel explains, "'I think the best part is always right at the begin-ning'" (*PL* 308). Then, in a manner reminiscent of many of the narrators in *The Moons of Jupiter*, she corrects herself: "'Perhaps even before the begin-ning," she said. "Perhaps just when it flashes on you what's possible. That may be the best'" (*PL* 308).

The comment recalls a memory of Isabel's which has been presented to us a few pages earlier, a memory from which the title of the story is taken. On the night of Laurence's fortieth birthday, after the plane ride and the tantaliz-ingly brief glimpse of a possible relationship with the pilot, Isabel remembers a childhood scene of promise, which now, as one critic has suggested, 'serves as a projection of her excitement at what may happen in the future, as an adult' (Friedman 13): "'You know we *used* to have the White Dump? At the school I went to—it was behind a biscuit factory, the playground backed on to the factory property. Every now and then, they'd sweep up these quantities of vanilla icing and nuts and hardened marshmallow globs and they'd bring it in barrels and dump it back there and it would shine. It would shine like a pure white mountain. Over at the school, somebody would see it and yell, 'White Dump!' and after school we'd all climb over the fence or run around it. We'd all be over there, scrabbling away at that enormous pile of white candy'" (*PL* 306). As a child, Isabel perceived this dump not as a dump, but rather as 'white and shiny. It was like a kid's dream—the most wonderful promising thing you could ever see' (*PL* 306). Even as an adult, looking back on this scene, she remembers her sense of intoxication; she is captured once again by the illusion of surfaces. The passage urges us to recognize the extent to which Isabel, from her childhood, has willingly suspended her disbelief. In looking for freedom and possibility, she has repeatedly been persuaded by surfaces. By interpreting the white dump within a kind of transcendental structure of imagery (candy as promise), Isabel diverts our attention from the fact that—as the word 'dump' suggests—this 'pure white mountain' is made up of somebody's garbage.

The force of Isabel's white dump recollection resides in the lesson which she fails to draw from it. When she comes to interpret other things in her life—the encounter with the pilot, for instance—she uses the same paradigm that she used as a child to interpret the white dump. Thus her initially roman-ticized view turns into a 'sordid' affair (*PL* 308), an affair which, furthermore, results in the end of her own marriage. What she fails to learn is explicitly introduced to us in the form of an omniscient commentary that comes prior to her recollection of the childhood memory. Immediately after Isabel, in her brief encounter with the pilot, experiences a sense of promise which 'split[s] her like lightning,' we are told that 'it isn't like lightning, it isn't a blow from outside. We only pretend that it is' (*PL* 305). This intrusive commentary from a first-person plural, omniscient 'we'—a 'we' which, in Gerald Prince's terminology, constitutes a 'sign of the "I" because it refers to a narrating self' (8–9)—undermines the sense of freedom and promise which Isabel thinks she is embracing.

The liberation Isabel thinks she attains by having an affair with the pilot, accordingly, turns out to be illusory. In fact, far from liberating herself, she ends up temporarily appropriating someone else's place and position. This, it seems to me, is where the scene with the catering woman—also the pilot's wife—crying in the dining room fits in. 'The spurts of sound' (*PL* 288) that Denise hears from this woman are a response to a kind of colonizing act, to a moving in and taking over which can occur only at someone else's expense.

Along with the allusion to the storming of the Bastille, therefore, various moments in the text alert us to the possibility that projects which appear to promote the goal of freedom can themselves be implicated in acts of appropriation and domination. Freedom, we may thus infer, is a kind of myth. But while the story thematically leads us to recognize the illusoriness of freedom, its structural configuration seems to take us in another direction. If, as I have suggested, Munro's de-centring strategy in 'White Dump'—her refusal to offer a unified centre of consciousness—is a kind of extension of her desire to examine the implications of complicity, then structurally the story seems to be getting at the fact that its writer too wants to break the shackles of an authoritarian discourse. While Munro clearly is not an overtly political (or post-colonial) writer, she remains engaged in an investigation of the relationship between form and ideology which leads us to suspect that 'White Dump' is, at least structurally, about the possibility of freedom.

Like many of the stories in Munro's earlier volumes, the stories in *The Progress of Love* render unstable what we think we know about Munro's fictional worlds. In explicitly declaring that we cannot take everything we read for granted, these stories—to return to the terminology I used in the previous chapter—clearly contribute to Munro's evolving poetics of surprise. What is new to these stories, however, is a more fully developed recognition of the impossibility of an unmediated access to reality. Thus, accounts which wear the mask of truth, which pose as direct representations of events, reveal themselves to be constructed memories or mediated narratives. Although much emphasis is placed on moments of revelation or awareness, the pieces collected in this volume ultimately leave us thinking not so much about the way 'the skin of the moment' appears to break open as about the way in which that breaking open shows the inseparability of language and discourse.

## Notes

1. The hermeneutic context for the notion of 'empathy' comes out of Wilhelm Dilthey's discussion of empathy as the 'state of mind involved in the task of understanding.' Empathy, he writes, gives rise to 'the highest form of understanding in which the totality of mental life is active—re-creating or re-living' (226).

2. It is worth noting that what challenges Phemie's story is an episode which, although coming *later* in the narrative, has *already* taken place chronologically. This disparity between narrative and chronological order might be seen as a part of the narrator's 'deconstructive' strategy. What initially masquerades as a true account of an incident—both in this instance and in the episode involving Phemie's description of her grandmother's near suicide—is subsequently revealed to be not just a possible version, but a version conditioned by her own desire to see the past in a certain way.

3. In a recent interview with Kay Bonetti for the American Audio Prose Library, Munro has said the following about created memory: 'what we use to make our lives possible . . . is the created memory or the created story or the interpretation poets and novelists make of life' (Bonetti).

4. The scenes with Mr Cryderman clearly recall Rose's encounter with the 'minister' in 'Wild Swans,' and Del's experiences with Mr Chamberlain in 'Lives of Girls and Women.' For a more detailed discussion of the way in which 'Jesse and Meribeth' echoes some of Munro's earlier stories, see Ildikó de Papp Carrington (128–31).

5. It is worth noting that there is an ambiguity here, an ambiguity which the narrator tries to close off, but which we as readers are not entirely willing to relinquish. What the old woman *does not say* (that 'she loved Browning's writing, or spent all her time reading about him') may, in fact, be what she *means* when she says she had an affair with the poet.

6. The shift into the present tense at the end of this passage tells us that we are, at this point, dealing with a retrospective narrator, with Jessie as an older woman, looking back on and revising her interpretation of the past.

7. As Carrington (129) notes, the names (Chamberlain and Cryderman) are strikingly similar.

8. We might here recall Munro's comment to Struthers about 'the whole business of how life is made into a story by the people who live it' (Struthers, 'Real Material' 33).

9. It perhaps comes as little surprise, then, that Violet, like Rose, should herself become something of a storyteller. After Violet tells her sisters 'that sometimes the butcher's man was not satisfied with the meat on the calves and went after juicy little children to make them into steaks and chops and sausages,' we are then informed that '[Violet] told this out of the blue and for her own amusement, as far as she could recall later on when she made things into stories' (*PL* 212).

10. For an excellent discussion of the way in which the card that Heather and Gillian send Violet functions as a kind of ironic version of the threatening letters Dawn Rose sends her father, see Carrington (177–8).

11. In these terms, the competition between the Americans and the Russians can be seen as a race to claim space.

MARK LEVENE

# "It Was about Vanishing":
# A Glimpse of Alice Munro's Stories

Some writers inspire in critics an awed silence (though rarely, of course, a gleeful contempt), others the most carefully honed and constrained of perspectives. Others still—for me, notably Joyce and Munro—trigger the instinct to reach, perhaps to overreach, to match their constant artistic surprises and their sheer humanity with a critical enterprise that is commensurately abundant and respectful, that spins its own sorts of 'tricks' (that signal word from Munro's 'Material,' *Something*, 43) to mirror the ones the writer has been performing with an ever-increasing sense of adventure and gracefulness. To use another of Munro's prime words, the compulsion is to find the broadest 'fit' between the interpretation and the fiction. Since a major emphasis of this essay is the extraordinary change in Munro's conception of the later stories, particularly 'Carried Away' and 'The Love of a Good Woman,' that is initiated by 'White Dump,' a change marked by the connection between 'vanishing' and the spatial character of the narrative, a reasonable course would have been a close reading of these few stories. But following Munro's own fascination with connectedness, it seemed essential in this exploration of her work to trace the continuities as well as the changes, to detail (within limits) how the shadings of one volume come to the edge or to the centre of another. At the same time, a brief theoretical approach to the short story also seemed desirable for the simple reason that

From *University of Toronto Quarterly* 68, no. 4 (Fall 1999): 841–860. © 1999 by the University of Toronto Press.

if Munro is indeed one of its pre-eminent writers, one reason might well be that her work cataylses, in D.H. Lawrence's terms, the pure 'carbon' of the genre (183). For these interwoven ends, particular words—transience, indeterminacy, absence, multiplicity, and space—recur throughout this inquiry, the last providing the immediate link between theory and practice.

Describing his preference for 'big books,' the American novelist Robert Stone provides an evocative perspective on the connection between the fictional construct and the reader's spatial and temporal zones of response. 'I use the white space. I'm interested in precise meaning and in reverberation, in associative levels. What you're trying to do when you write is to crowd the reader out of his own space and occupy it with yours, in a good cause. You're trying to take over his sensibility and deliver an experience that moves from mere information' (349). This process of habitation, with its suggestions of power, colonization, and education—an experience of absoluteness or totalization—is how novels, particularly panoramic ones rooted in some modification of the realist tradition, establish their presence, their claim on the reader's attention and expectation. But 'crowding the reader out,' occupying the reader's experiential and epistemological space with your narrative dominion, with what in 'Material' Munro calls 'the marvelous clear jelly' writers spend their lives 'learning how to make' (43), is also a process that sharply marks off the novel from the short story. The imminence of the ending, of closure, has increasingly seemed one of the most fruitful areas for theorists who are concerned to go beyond the modest definition that the short story is a story that is short. Following one element in Poe's analysis of the form, Norman Friedman observes: 'Because we can complete it at one sitting, the experience of closure in a story relates differently to our other life rhythms than reading a novel or a poem. It creates a rhythm of its own which is definite enough to displace our life rhythm until it is over. We can enter, move through, and leave story without interruption, and thus we build the story world as we read, apart for the other claims on our attention' (27).

Apart from the issue of interruption, Stone and Friedman are paradoxically fixing their attitudes toward both the novel and the short story on the nature of emotional and imaginative displacement. But it seems to me more reasonable to argue that the relative brevity of the story—and, I should add, even when a story strains a quantitative boundary, it often subverts a totalizing aesthetic—the heightened claim on the reader's attention of detail and the ubiquity of the ending produce something very different from complete displacement. If anything, there is a painful tension between the story's rhythm and our own 'life rhythms,' between presented, shaped narrative and our own jagged, graceless life stories. Short stories instil a profound ambivalence; they are complete, they are polished in an almost lapidary way, they create a compulsion, evoke a necessity around concentrated or distilled event and perspective, they cover a certain amount of moral space in a certain time, while pressing the limits of implication. The English short story writer William Sansom exults that the story 'should spread beyond its economy: short, it should be enormous' (9). Yet the relative brevity and imminent closure of short stories also announce a fragility that lacerates even as it confirms the reader's common, everyday sense of transience. One of the most striking qualities of Munro's later stories is how dramatically she redefines this process, establishing in spatial terms more of an experiential collusion than conflict between reader and narrative. But whatever the shape of the connection, whether collusion or conflict, our own narratives are never far from the foreground in reading a short story. We do not so much relinquish our stories as we keep them hovering around the margins of the very temporarily present twenty pages by Munro, Gallant, Calvino, or Lessing, less in a straightforward process of mimetic identification and comparison—yes, that's exactly how it felt, driving a stolen Mercedes across Montana (Ford, 'Rock Springs'), no, Mangan's sister did not make me see 'myself as a creature driven and derided by vanity' (Joyce, 'Araby,' 35)—than in a subtle balance of our own presences and absences with those of the written narrative.

Gallant, a master of absence, says in her essay 'What Is Style?' with a kind of triumphant resignation: 'What . . . fiction [and I'm reading this as short fiction] is about—is that something is taking place and that nothing lasts. Against the sustained tick of a watch, fiction takes the measure of a life, a season, a look exchanged, the turning point, desire as brief as a dream, the grief and terror that after childhood we cease to express. The life, the look, the grief are without permanence. The watch continues to tick where the story stops' (Geddes, 784). The *ars longa* cliché needs modification; in terms of the short story, particularly as shaped by Munro and Gallant in their concerns with absence, displacement, and the boundaries of language, art is short and so is life. In accounting for the appeal of the short story, its distinct appropriateness to modern life, Nadine Gordimer also concentrates metaphors of transience and fracture: 'The short story is a fragmented and restless form, a matter of hit or miss, and it is perhaps for this reason that it suits modern consciousness—which seems best expressed as flashes of fearful insight alternating with near-hypnotic states of indifference' (Geddes, 788). Short stories are inherently truer 'to the nature of whatever can be grasped of human reality' (787). Extended 'coherence of tone,' a quality the most thoroughly experimental novelist cannot expunge, contradicts the reader's fundamental experience:

> Each of us has a thousand lives and the novel gives a character only one. *For the sake of the form.* The novelist may juggle about

with chronology and throw narrative overboard; all the time his characters have the reader by the hand, there is a consistency of relationship throughout the experience that cannot and does not convey the quality of human life, where contact is more like the flash of fireflies, in and out, now here, now there, in darkness. Short-story writers see by the light of the flash; theirs is the art of the only thing one can be sure of—the present moment. (Geddes, 787; original emphasis)

Those thousand lives and the flash of the present moment are the intimate disjunctions and balances between the reader's 'life rhythms' and the narrative's.

These observations by Gallant and Gordimer point to the essential paradox which is one of the focuses of this inquiry: that the short story, the form that, in E. Annie Proulx's terms, demands the most 'control and balance' (xiii), is also the form that encapsulates impermanence, that militates against the sense of aesthetic wholeness and the substitution of one complete world— the narrative's for another—the reader's. Marjorie Garson's superb analysis of *Lives of Girls and Women* can readily be extrapolated to the genre itself: 'In Munro's writing the relationship of part to part and of part to the whole of which it is a part is not stable and natural but problematic and uneasy. *Lives of Girls and Women* continually subverts the organicist criteria of 'wholeness, harmony, and radiance' even as it seems to invoke them' (417). Indeterminacy, instability, formal and situational emblems of transience—these elements suggest anything but an absolutist aesthetic and evoke more general accounts of women's writing as 'resistance to tradition,' in Coral Ann Howells's words (5), as challenges to dominant generic as well as gender codes.[1] Munro's reconstruction of dominant modes is thus likened to the particular revisionism of writers such as Laurence, Atwood, Kogawa, and, one should now add, Urquhart and Michaels. The inevitable inference I am drawing is that the short story is especially hospitable to the more fluid 'rearrangements' which seem characteristic of women's writing, rearrangements that just as inevitably suggest a distinct though complex alliance of narrative and cognition (Howells, *Private and Fictional Words*, 4).

In her early interviews, Munro articulated a visceral aesthetic that arises from this alliance, an aesthetic that has been read more for its allegiance to literary realism than for its graceful but sharp lamentation for transience:

With me it has something to do with the fight against death, the feeling that we lose everything every day, and writing is a way of convincing yourself perhaps that you're doing something about this. You're not really, because the writing itself does not last much longer than you do; but I would say it's partly the feeling that I can't stand to have things go . . . I was talking about the external world, the sights and sounds and smells—I can't stand to let go without some effort at this, at capturing them in words. (Interview with Graeme Gibson, 243–44)

One of the first lectures I gave about Munro's work was attended by a former teacher of hers who gently and with Munro's own rhythms announced, 'That's how it was, that's how it felt.' It is a commonplace in Munro studies that her stories, spun from this dedication to the texture of experience, are also intensely imbued with an awareness of loss, of absence, and with the increasingly complex permutations—resonant of power and helplessness—of sounds into words and words into stories that hover between perception and vacancy.[2] Stories also become collections, and in her new *Selected Stories*, there is an overt, declamatory absence—the omission of 'The Peace of Utrecht,' her most explicit, early piece about her mother, which now stands in relation to the later 'Friend of My Youth' like the hidden and vanishing memories that punctuate her stories—in the words of 'Lichen' and likening, 'a pause, a lost heartbeat, a harsh little break in the flow of the days and nights as she keeps them going' (*Progress*, 70).

The first story of Munro's first volume, *Dance of the Happy Shades*, and the opening piece in the *Selected Stories* is 'Walker Brothers Cowboy.' It has a compounded prominence because of the ways in which it maps the physical and inner territory we have gratefully come to designate as 'Munro country.'[3] In strict, factual terms this is an area, Beverly Rasporich describes, in southwestern Ontario around Wingham where Munro grew up and which she 'mythologized as Huron or Wawanash County' (122), the Jubilee, Dalgleish, and Hanratty where her protagonists anchor their rich perceptions, where they weave their stories and complex roles, and where their creator can sometimes be found helping out with a book sale or even slinging beer. In the most obvious sense, Munro is a regional writer, but her regionalism, like her overt realism, is densely ambiguous not because she is really writing about covert biblical or Freudian realms, but because no world is intact, or can be assumed to be a whole or predictable, to be knowable.[4]

This provisionality emerges in 'Walker Brothers Cowboy' as the children accompany their father on his sales route and discover that they have left his accustomed territory and in visiting a woman known only to him have entered a separate realm in which the adults have names, drink, and suggest a privacy, a zone of memory and feeling that will always be separate from the narrator as both daughter and as teller. 'So my father drives and my brother watches the road for rabbits and I feel my father's life flowing back from our car in the last of the afternoon, darkening and turning strange, like a landscape that has an enchantment on it, making it kindly, ordinary and familiar while you are looking at it, but changing it, once your back is turned, into something you will never know, with all kinds of weathers, and distances you cannot imagine' (*Selected Stories*, 15). This new, unexpected, and uncertain territory is an essential feature of the Munro geography; it leads to the underground dwelling in 'Images,' to the adjacent world Uncle Benny inhabits in *Lives of Girls and Women*, 'a troubling distorted reflection' (28) of the surface, familiar world; it leads in 'Vandals' to the stark, almost Manichean border between Ladner's nature preserve and Liza's simple, unmysterious house; it leads most recently to the exquisite sensation Karin has in 'Rich as Stink' of her secret, 'immense' yet minuscule 'territory' (*The Love of a Good Woman*, 253). Munro's conflicting, distorting, even comforting territories lead perhaps most importantly to a revision of inner landscapes, the charting of what is one's 'real life.' The opening to such possibility which is at the heart of the later stories, 'Carried Away' and 'The Love of a Good Woman,' begins with the extraordinary perception in what is perhaps her masterwork to date, *The Progress of Love*, of intersecting or parallel lives. In 'The Moon in the Orange Street Skating Rink' the narrator asks: 'Do such moments really mean, as they seem to, that we have a life of happiness with which we only occasionally, knowingly, intersect? Do they shed such light before and after that all that has happened to us in our lives—or that we've made happen—can be dismissed?' (211). Ultimately, the unstable landscapes of *Dance of the Happy Shades* and *Lives of Girls and Women* lead in her most recent work to a spatial tapestry of figures within the shifts of story and perspective.

Throughout Munro's work the lack of stability in memory, in the relation of word to fact, and in place itself has an increasing reflection in her unsettled chronologies. In *Dance of the Happy Shades*, ambiguous temporality, while modest, is apparent in the uncertain retrospection Munro no doubt initially discerned in the first three stories in *Dubliners*. Like Joyce, she creates no firm border between childhood experience and 'the adult narrator's ability to shape these recollections for us' (Heble, 32). This indeterminacy extends to the very nature of her second book, *Lives of Girls and Women*. 'When I began to write *Lives*,' she said, 'I began to write it as . . . a much looser novel, with all these things going on at the same time, and it wasn't working. Then I began pulling the material and making it into what are almost self-contained segments' (interview with Gibson, 258). Like the Flats Road with which it begins, 'neither part of the town nor part of the country' (Heble, 43), the work hovers between novel and collection not in hesitation, but in an unmistakable declaration of fidelity to the intractability of experience and the exultant arrogance yet also the diffidence of the shaping imagination (Besner, 32ff; Ross, 68; Mayberry).

Critics who insist on the designation of *Lives of Girls and Women* as novel, besides implying a generic hierarchy, also diminish the book's compelling formal ambiguity, its scepticism towards a distorting and illusory completeness. Similarly, the need to repeat details from segment to segment is a withdrawal from structural wholeness, a positioning of the narrative between harmony and disjunction, a borderland measured too by Del's ambiguous retrospection and by the complexities in her compulsion to tell; these I need not recapitulate, except to emphasize the relation of words and power and the emerging sense of the multiplicity of truth, or put another way, of the distinction between truth and strict factuality.[5] The menace in Mr Chamberlain's sexual performance—'Quite a sight, eh?' he says—is entirely absorbed by Del's internal narration, her description of the landscape as 'post-coital, distant and meaningless' (187). In her relationship with Garnet French, initiated by hands reading one another, Del briefly submits to the seduction of wordlessness—they inhabit a 'world without names' (242)—but after they have sex, she must construct a story that melds metaphor and actual detail.[6] 'There's blood on the ground at the side of the house,' she tells her mother, 'I saw a cat there yesterday tearing a bird apart. It was a big striped Tom, I don't know where it came from' (249). At the end of the book, for all of the acknowledged discrepancy between Del's earlier, ironic, self-contained imagination and the Sherriff family, her recognition now that 'people's lives, in Jubilee as elsewhere, were dull, simple, amazing, and unfathomable—deep caves paved with kitchen linoleum' (277), her instinct as a writer is to deploy this multiplicity, to absorb it into that part of her mind to which no one else has access, to say rather than 'thank you' a private 'yes' to the 'stylized meaning,' the as yet unknown 'alphabet' Bobby Sherriff's spontaneous performance represents (278).

With *Something I've Been Meaning to Tell You* Munro shifts from the diffuse, provisional structure of Del's narrative, her ambiguous emergence as a writer, to an ostensibly even looser grouping of stories. But in so far as they intensify Munro's fascination with 'the limits of representation' (Heble, 74) and thus frequently resist closure, these stories are allied in tentativeness, in the power of absences, and in that paradox of control and transience I have been arguing is the essential condition of so much short fiction. Initially, 'Material' seems to focus a strictly ironic perspective on the power of male writers, a power often delegated to them by women 'with enormous transitory hope' (25). Hugo has written a story from material the narrator wants to reserve for life in all its awkward mystery, but the story 'is an act of magic . . . an act, you might say, of a special, unsparing unsentimental love' (43). Hugo's are 'lovely tricks, honest tricks,' and '[t]here is Dotty lifted out of life and held in light, suspended in the marvelous clear jelly Hugo has spent all his life learning how to make' (43). The narrator seems reconciled to the wholeness and therefore the primacy of imaginative transformation, but the letter she thinks to write him, '[a] few graceful, a few grateful, phrases' (43), gives way to 'short jabbing sentences' and her rage at both Hugo and her husband for their power, for not being '*at the mercy*' (44). The conclusion of the story seems to rest on the claims of experience, of human, unpolished material until we remind ourselves that the speaker, as W.H. New has observed (202), is herself prone to narratively shapely tricks, diffidently arranged as they are. The difficulty of harmonizing inventiveness and reality is compounded by the alliance between telling and power. The narrator is not so much a votary of unmediated experience as she is an artist who refuses the power and with it the deception that accompanies the deployment of story. The final piece in the volume, 'The Ottawa Valley,' concludes with the famous aesthetic hypothesis in Munro's work, 'If I had been making a proper story out of this, I would have ended it, I think, with my mother not answering and going ahead of me across the pasture' (246). But the purpose was not the kind of closure a submerged epiphanic ending can provide. The purpose of the entire narrative was to 'reach' her mother, '[t]o mark her off, to describe, to illumine, to celebrate, to *get rid* of her' (246). But the narrator's 'tricks' are inadequate, at least as exorcism; the mother and the narrator's bond with her are impervious to this sort of translation or completion. In fact, it is a 'proper' in the sense of 'paradigmatic' story ending, as Gallant puts it, as the 'watch continues to tick' (Geddes, 784).[7]

The five volumes, from *Lives of Girls and Women* to *The Progress of Love*, exhibit a striking fluctuation in mood. One collection, while displaying hesitations about the duplicities in narrative, nonetheless exults in the sheer livingness of language, the immense possibilities in invention. In the next the texture is darker, the edges sharper between the shaping imagination and the world from which it draws. The rich, writerly ambiguities in *Lives of Girls and Women* are followed by the narratological angst of *Something I've Been Meaning to Tell You*, which in turn leads to the verbal lavishness as well as the exhilaration in all sorts of journeys—sexual, geographical, and private—in *Who Do You Think You Are?* The difficulty, as Heble notes, of reconciling apparent opposites—public and private roles, invention and reality (99, 101)—persists here but without a sense of ontological crisis. Of course, Rose is an actor, not a writer; provisionality is inherent to the emphasis on performance throughout the volume. Even more than in *Lives of Girls and Women* there is a comic imprint on Rose's pictures and storytelling that tempers Munro's ongoing scepticism towards invention.

In contrast, the sombreness of *The Moons of Jupiter* is acute.[8] The dominant word in these stories is connection, the dominant perception that connections are at best unreliable and usually impossible to make. The imagination, Munro implies, flattens against the rock of simple mortality and inevitable loss, producing an elegiac note in recognition of the unknowable. At the end of the first sequence, 'The Stone in the Field,' the narrator starkly declares that whatever people's secrets are, about which an earlier version of herself would have tried to construct 'plausible connection[s],' however her mother's cousins actually 'behaved[,] they are all dead. I carry something of them around in me. But the boulder is gone, Mount Hebron is cut down for gravel, and the life buried here is one you have to think twice about regretting' (35). The only 'connecting tissues' (61) that are both accessible and comprehensible are in the bodies of turkeys one narrator guts for Christmas; the surrounding drama, its confusions of sexuality and violence, is impenetrable. In 'Accident,' the parts of Frances's life seem to connect, to construct a whole. But she thinks, '*What difference* . . . She's had her love, her scandal, her man, her children. But inside she's ticking away, all by herself, the same Frances who was there before any of it' (109). In the title story, the speaker concludes that hearing from her absent and solitary daughter or not hearing from her 'came to the same thing' (233). Like the moons of Jupiter, only some of which are visible, there are never clear, uncluttered views especially of those we love; there are no stable, consistent perceptions, only 'various knowns and unknowns and horrible immensities' (231). The loneliness in these stories is excruciating; it is the fibre, the essential connection between our sense of them as manifestations of imaginative order and as hostages to transience and the limits of understanding. Like the surface of Jupiter itself, however, Munro's world is perennially in flux, a revisiting of form and personal nuance out of what we as her grateful readers can only celebrate as a restless generosity. That grim phrase, '*What difference*,' is loosened of its pain in *Open Secrets* and *The Love of a Good Woman*, becomes refracted into the immensities of the possible through Munro's spatial reformulations of the real and the imagined, the interzones of choice and accident, a process Michael Ondaatje calls translation.

But *The Progress of Love* continues to explore the inescapability of epistemological gaps and the complexities of telling.[9] Indeed, the language of language permeates the volume to a far greater extent than in any of her previous work. In 'Lichen' Stella turns simile into a sudden, private transcendence, in 'Miles City, Montana' the parents invent characters for their children, and in 'Fits' Peg is 'hard to follow as a watermark in fine paper' (164). Although absence and loss are never far from the surface of these intricately narrated stories, the supple, expansive language, the moments of luminousness and mystery unfold a triumph *The Moons of Jupiter* pronounced impossible. It is

a triumph—or in the instance of 'Fits' simply an outcome—frequently registered through Munro's emerging deployment of particular spaces within
the narrative. The relation of the spatial and temporal in the title story is
astounding in its subtlety. Initially, the narration is restless, unsettled, moving
backwards and forwards in time, a process that marks the narrator's uncertain
entry into the past which is dominated by opposing versions of a family story.
Although the narrator's aunt says the grandmother's attempt to hang herself
was just 'to give Daddy a scare' (26), the narrator tells the story from her
mother's point of view as though she were omniscient and the story a self-
contained whole, a separate space within the framing narrative, because of its
dark impact on their lives. 'There was a cloud, a poison, that had touched my
mother's life. And when I grieved my mother, I became part of it' (15). She is
unable to break into the hardened shape of her mother's story and unable to
reconcile it with her aunt's account: 'It was my mother's version that held for
a time. It absorbed Beryl's story, closed over it. But Beryl's story didn't vanish;
it stayed sealed off for years, but it wasn't gone' (28). These closed spaces cannot, however, absorb her; because they allow no room for her emotions and
imagination, the narrator alters a crucial detail in another story as an antidote
to the poison and as a way of creating her own narrative space. She places
her father protectively beside her mother who burns her paternal inheritance.
His presence is demanded in the scene because even through distortion she
wants to be assured of her parents' love. She transfers the terms of hypothesis
to ostensible fact and the tones of certainty to imaginative construction. As
Heble suggests (146–47), truth and objective knowledge diverge in this tribute to 'moments of kindness and reconciliation' ('Progress,' 38).

    The story about the burned money—or rather, the factual and imagined
counterpoint of the event—is the first in a series of narrative deferrals that
punctuate the entire volume and that signal Munro's increasing fascination
with the spatial as the central element of her fiction. These are narrative units
displaced from the story's chronology only to re-emerge when the interior
condition of a figure is able to release it or when it is clear that it is a space
which in some way cannot become accessible. In 'Lichen' David is so terrified of aging that the visit to the nursing home drops out of the temporal
sequence; he fills the space instead with images of himself as a young man,
with misogynistic verbal constructions, with the picture of a new lover he
wants to have perceived as pornographic. But the description of visiting his
former father-in-law emerges in the narrative when even David cannot avoid
sensing the pathos of his desperate exertions, his various efforts to 'rewire'
his groin (50). The narrator of 'Miles City, Montana' can only reposition the
context for the 'furious and sickening disgust' (111) at adults she felt during
a friend's funeral when years later, her own daughter almost died and she

realizes that purposeful creation—of children or of stories—is not in conflict with mortality, but in collusion with it. In 'The Moon in the Orange Street Skating Rink' Sam defers the concluding part of the story about the 'escape' with Edgar and Calli to Toronto until half a century has passed and he returns to contemplate the layering of his ordinary life with moments of 'power' and 'possibility' and 'happiness' (206).

These are all instances of a narrative space being assimilated and made accessible within the story's concluding sequence. But 'Fits' presents an entirely different relation of language, cognition, and narrative deferral. In a complex interplay of hypothesis and direct report about a couple's death, the story follows Peg, their neighbour, to the point where she climbs the stairs, sees the open bedroom door, and discovers the Weebles' bodies. But the discovery exists by implication only; it is a white space within the narrative, one that is displaced at the end, yet remains absolute, utterly intact. In her refusal to describe the details or explain her feelings, Peg refuses mutual proprietorship through language in a community where telling, and thereby knowing, are a more profound need than love itself. Everyone except Peg assumes an innate correspondence between word and thing, designation and emotion. Peg told Karen the bare facts of the event, and Karen then started to shake. 'Telling Robert this, she shook again, to demonstrate' (151). Everyone wants Peg to do or say something that would confirm not only the expectation that she was 'shattered' by what she saw, but also the very meaning of the word 'shattered' (157). But she evades their linguistic rituals as audience as well as the reader's expectation of access to her covert responses, her subtle motives.[10] Peg's epistemological inaccessibility is suggested at the beginning of the story, in terms of Robert's description of her as 'self-contained.' 'Peg said she didn't know what he meant. He started to explain what a self-contained person was like … "I know what the words mean," Peg said smiling. "I just don't understand how you mean it about me"' (141). Words split off, do not fit. As Peg rubs lotion onto her hands while she tries to deflect her family's narrative compulsion, the reader makes the inevitable association with Lady Macbeth (163), but the analogy remains disconnected, inert, an unbridgeable gap in knowledge which is a perfect reflection of the spatial disjunctions that dominate the story. Like the murdered Nora Weeble, Peg took courses, but again the connection leads nowhere beyond itself, proving only that there are few things more appalling than symmetry without significance. Trusting nothing but 'transactional,' 'indicative' words (141, 171), Peg has usurped the story, sealed it into her own silent privacy, in the head that *somehow* fits with the shattered head in the hall. When Robert contemplates the one sundering 'discrepancy, one detail—one lie—that would never have anything to do with him' (169), he fills the earlier white space with his own perspective and the constable's words. We see the head; it supplants the leg Peg had inserted into the narrative. But like Robert, we remain cut off from Peg's actual vision. It is an adjacent or underlying blank, probably the most intimidating version of all those 'territories' in Munro's fiction, here a separate and separating space that means a diminished love.

Like 'The Progress of Love,' 'White Dump,' the concluding piece in the volume, is built up of embedded narratives, the layering of past and present experience, and the intricacies of the connections between the temporal and the spatial. Laurence and his daughter, Denise, tell a ritualized story about his fortieth birthday celebration which leaves out a great deal about a day when things 'split' open (406) in ways all the figures know (Isabel's affair, the collapse and eventual reconstruction of the family). But it is also a day when, beneath the evolving fractures, covert memories are sealed with others; connections, blessed and forgiving, are made, if only by the reader. Like the title story 'White Dump' also centres on three generations of women, but instead of blending their narratives, it sets out their stories in distinct though non-chronological units. Indeed, this multi-focal, sectioned anatomy of love, memory, and language is the primal narrative behind those elongated social histories and dramas about knowing and possibility, those epistemological mysteries ('Carried Away,' 'The Love of a Good Woman'), that for many readers have opened up an entirely new place in the world in fiction. Two passages from the later volumes clarify the directions Munro is taking in 'White Dump.'

> It was about vanishing. I knew that Charlotte and Gjurdhi had not actually vanished—they were somewhere, living or dead. But for me they had vanished. And because of this fact—not really because of any loss of them—I was tipped into dismay more menacing than any of the little eddies of regret that had caught me in the past year. I had lost my bearings. I had to get back to the store . . . but I felt as if I could as easily walk another way, just any way at all. My connection was in danger—that was all. Sometimes our connection is frayed, it is in danger, it seems almost lost. ('The Albanian Virgin,' *Open Secrets*, 126–27)

> To me it seems that it was only then that I became female. I know that the matter was decided long before I was born and was plain to everybody else since the beginning of my life, but I believe that it was only at the moment when I decided to come back, when I gave up the fight against my mother (which must have been a fight for something like her total surrender) and when in fact I chose

survival over victory (death would have been victory), that I took
on my female nature. ('My Mother's Dream,' *The Love of a Good
Woman*, 337)

Vanishing and survival—these are the prisms through which one can
read the sort of story 'White Dump' initiates. A year after the birthday,
Denise says of her grandmother: 'Sophie had not been at the Log House
since the beginning of summer. She was in Wellesley Hospital, in Toronto,
having some tests done' (378). In terms of the story's emerging, inferred chronology, this is where Sophie vanishes, but she is far from absent in the actual,
spatial arrangement of the narrative. Not only does she have her own discrete
section between her granddaughter's and her daughter-in-law's, she 'survives'
in Denise's behaviour as well as in her appearance and even more strikingly
in Isabel's memories of her own childhood. 'A rich man's daughter, now poor'
(370) is applicable to Sophie (described as having 'a crown of yellowish-white
braids' [372]) and to Denise, who in the last sentences of her section sees herself '[i]n the darkening glass . . . a tall, careful woman with a long braid' (382).
Apparently unaware of the repetitions, Denise curtails Sophie's vanishing, if
only in an overt, public way.

The privacy of Sophie's narration leads to connections both lost and
rewoven. At its centre is her recollection of trying to play with and be generous to the poor Bryce children, in one of whom she detects 'something superior . . . a code of manners Sophie couldn't know anything about' (390). Like
her 'marvellous' sensation during the plane ride for Laurence's birthday of
'[s]till shrinking, curled up into that sickening dot, but not vanishing' (394)—
though she tells her family only that '[i]t was most enjoyable' (405)—the
memory of the frog march she organized with the Bryce child cannot apparently survive her. Inaccessible to others, memories like this one will shrink
and vanish. Yet, inaccessible to Sophie are comparable and comparably secret
nuances experienced by Isabel, who sees in the pilot 'something vigilant . . .
and careless or even contemptuous of them, sharply self-possessed' (402). We
make the connection between the Bryce child and the pilot and therefore the
connection between two women whose overt link has been mutual distaste
and dismissiveness. Even more resonant than this evocation is Isabel's sealed
association between her tumultuous sexuality and an almost 'perverse' longing
for her own childhood (404), a longing prefaced by Sophie's extended, loving account of her own childhood. There is nothing declamatory about these
ties between Denise and Sophie, Sophie and Isabel. Munro is not making
a 'statement' about legacies and continuities such as we find in Laurence's
*The Diviners*. The gaps of understanding, the absence of mutually recognized
memories, the tremendous loss, are still paramount, still create the elision

between the ephemerality of life and of story. But as she has done throughout the volume, Munro layers the temporal and the spatial. Here too there is a displaced sequence. What happens between Sophie's morning swim and the afternoon plane ride is a blank space in her narration. But in her section Isabel completes the sequence, recalls the naked Sophie returning to the cabin. The 'perverse old fraud' (399), for reasons to which we have no access, has lost this transition. It remains a permanent deferral, a vacancy set in equilibrium with the layering of Sophie's presence and memories in the narrative spaces inhabited by the other women. We gratefully infer from *The Progress of Love* that vanishings are not complete, that there are flickering survivals.

After the largely elliptical collection *Friend of My Youth*, with its emphasis on absence and the unknowable, we encounter the lengthy, multi-layered stories in *Open Secrets* and *The Love of a Good Woman*.[11] Here the sense of possibility in form as much as in the experience literary form registers expands in remarkable ways. In the first, as Munro told Peter Gzowski, she tried 'riskier' things than ever before.[12] In 'The Albanian Virgin,' she creates an extraordinary imitation of early twentieth-century travel writing in a romance that envelops a more strictly realistic romance in the present. In 'A Wilderness Station' letters (which figure prominently throughout the volume, some of them 'sent,' some 'unsent,' many of them misunderstood) chronicle local history and present differing versions of a murder.[13] But for all of the details of settlement and individual perspectives on events, the story ends with what is unseen and unheard; it too is about coming back, not vanishing, about survival. As Munro has said, in the opening narrative, 'Carried Away,' there is 'a ghost that is not exactly a ghost, there is the social history of a piano factory in a small town,' there is the intersection of letters and again of unshared memory (interview with Gzowski). That readers do not quite *know* what happens in the story should, she feels, be catalytic in that its shifting dimensions, its fluid discourses, suggest that sense of alternate lives which has lapped at the edges of Munro's fiction from the start—that we inhabit fantasy as much as fact, that our familiar lives are accompanied by phantom existences that *must* be allowed. As Nathalie Foy so adroitly remarks about *Open Secrets*, 'There is no interrogation of fiction and language in this collection, of the clash between realist narrative and epistemological uncertainty. There is a move away from concern about the limits of representation and toward respect for inspiration' (148). The sort of dense, complex, elongated structure Munro seems fascinated by now is one that resists, even denies, closure; it therefore reinvents the existential tension typical of the short story that she used to write. What her new fictions present are not so much conflicts between completeness and transience, but endless, parallel narratives to our own, in which not knowing is a shared 'pause, a lost heartbeat' ('Lichen,' *Progress of Love*, 70) rather than a source of anguish. These recent narratives are far more spatial than they are temporal; particular sections and their layered stories provide a territory, a space, in which figures appear, disappear, and re-form in different shapes, what Louisa in 'Carried Away' senses as 'sudden holes and impromptu tricks and radiant vanishing consolations' (*Open Secrets*, 50). And to these spaces, these rooms Munro sets out with dazzlingly familiar objects and open secrets, we bring our local habitations, our jagged but multiple 'life rhythms' which are the pulse of reading short fiction.

But if this celebratory language suggests a whiff of incense or the gleam of a polished solar panel, a new-age narrative Ontario chapter, we should remember that in *Open Secrets* and *The Love of a Good Woman* Munro allies multiplicity, the seemingly limitless possibility of intersecting or parallel stories, with terrible acts of willed or accidental violence. From 'Fits' on, there is a striking incidence of decapitation in her work, and although we should be wary of demeaning its complexity with schematic Viennese imports—severed heads as mutant cigars—there is in her spinning of possibility a discernible sense of the eradication of a modernist epistemological tyranny. For Louise in 'Carried Away,' gaps in perception are initially troubling: 'She could not remember shaking out her hair, as he said she had done, or smiling at any young man when the raindrops fell on the radiator' (10), and on the night he left her a note about his engagement, '[h]e had been in the same room with her, watched her, and taken his chance. But never made himself known' (18). After the accident to her letter-lover, these gaps, these 'sudden holes,' become a source of implied, lacerating anguish, an absence compounded by Jack Agnew's space in the library and in her memory, never being open to any sort of definition. 'I never saw him. I never saw him, to know who he was' (37). Arthur cannot help Louisa to 'picture' (29) the accident or the head itself. Her wanting to know amounts to a chain of 'nevers,' a generation of mysteries which lead to a connection between Louisa and Arthur, to years of marriage (abbreviated in the last section by Munro's persistently parenthetical manner about mortality), to 'a normal life' (48). For Louisa, Jack Agnew 'was about vanishing' ('Albanian Virgin,' *Open Secrets*, 126), but a visible and vocal Arthur begins filling that empty space in the library on Saturday nights, reversing the source of mystery from Agnew to Louisa herself. After the accident, Arthur could only imperfectly 'fit' the head to the body; the phrase 'just more or less in place' (34) applies as much to the perpetuating, surviving Arthur, in the library, in Louisa's life. In the concluding section, Louisa explains to a fully bodied Jack Agnew, complete with a pattern of experience which would seem to contradict the past, that she 'used to look' at Arthur sitting in the library, 'at the back of his neck and think, Ha, what if something should hit you there! None of that would make sense to you' (48). Munro has no interest here in reconciling the gaps, the secrets, the parallels, the possibilities. Like Louisa, they go 'under a wave' (50); denying the ordering, roiling mind, they inhabit altered spaces within the narrative to which we accord our own sense of alternatives, of the survival of fantasy as much as fact.

The apparent alternation between fantasy and fact is among the many brilliant elements of 'The Albanian Virgin.' Within this movement is the counterpoint between the insistent clues that connect the two romances—the priest's moustache and crucifix, the same details connected with Gjurdhi, Charlotte, and Claire in the present—and the narrative's unresolved, open-ended multiplicity. Whether the couples are actually the same is inconsequential, since, despite another severed head, the danger again is in our 'frayed . . . almost lost' connections, where 'views and streets deny knowledge of us, the air grows thin' (127). In story, in fact, or in both connections can be made and can be made to seem endless. When Claire, providing a parallel story to that of Lottar, the Albanian virgin, invokes Munro's version of entropy, that '[i]t was about vanishing' (126), she immediately imagines 'a destiny,' a brief narrative of life with Nelson, her former lover, only, it seems, to discover him at her bookstore. 'For this really was Nelson, come to claim me. Or at least to accost me, and see what would happen' (127). What happens is recorded as a sort of experiential haiku, notes towards parallel lives—'*We have been very happy. I have often felt completely alone*' (128)—which serve as ellipses to the lush, cinematographic details of Lottar's rescue by the Franciscan and the limitless extension of their story: 'She called him and called him, and when the boat came into the harbor at Trieste he was waiting on the dock' (128).

In contrast, the spatial relation of stories in the infinitely darker 'Vandals,' which Foy persuasively argues is a coda to the volume, is more restricted, pointing to a stark dualism rather than an unfolding multiplicity. Here Munro seems to revisit and counter the exhilaration of sexual play in *Lives of Girls and Women* and *Who Do You Think You Are?* A grimmer version of many of Munro's weavers of the real and the artificial (Stella in 'Lichen,' Laurence in 'White Dump'), Ladner is a taxidermist and the creator of a complex, 'bruised' Eden of labyrinthine forest and walkway and water.[14] On the side of the road where, as children, Liza and Kenny live out one current of their lives, there are no trees, 'no secret places—everything is bare and simple' (291). Across the road, however, Ladner's is 'a world of different and distinct countries':

> There is the marsh country, which is deep and jungly . . . A sense
> there of tropical threats and complications . . . And the dark rooms
> under the downswept branches of the cedars—entirely shaded and
> secret rooms with a bare earth floor . . . Smells are harsh or enticing
> . . . Here are the scenes of serious instruction where Ladner taught

them how to tell a hickory tree from a butternut and a star from a planet; and places also where they have run and hollered and hung from branches and performed all sorts of rash stunts. And places where Liza thinks there is a bruise on the ground, a tickling and shame in the grass. (291)

This passage concentrates the implied connection in Munro's earlier work between adjacent, alien territories (Uncle Benny's world in *Lives of Girls and Women*, the father's private geography in 'Walker Brothers Cowboy') and the emerging prominence of parallel or multiple lives. But in 'Vandals' Munro limits mystery and continuation to a repetitive, disorienting fluctuation. Ladner is both teacher and violator; the expression on his face and the movement of his hand do not 'fit.' 'He could switch from one person to another and make it your fault if you remembered' (289). Beneath the details of natural life Liza has taken on from Ladner, there is 'the secret life she had with him [where] what was terrible was always funny, badness was mixed up with silliness' (289–90), a secrecy she vainly hopes Bea can redeem. But as Foy notes, 'Bea and Liza ... occupy entirely different spaces on Ladner's property and in his narrative life' (155). The dualism persists and 'splits open' years later when, virtually simultaneous with Ladner's death, Liza, now a born-again Christian, and her husband come as helpers to the curiously protean yet 'solid' (277) territory and become its vandals. Whether by collapsing the artificial and the real in Ladner's constructions, by destroying his open and covert space, Liza is liberating or sealing her own 'shaded and secret rooms' (291) is unclear. What Munro quietly, even graciously, suggests is that Liza is not only Ladner's scourge, she is also his inheritor, his survival.[15] He persists in the knowledge about trees that Liza extends to Warren, and he persists in the lack of 'fit' between that knowledge and the fluid, convulsive melding of faith and rage which is, in Foy's terms, her 'dark space' (159).

Like 'Meneseteung' and 'Carried Away,' 'The Love of a Good Woman' possesses a sort of burnished localization, with its opening display of 'optometrist's instruments' that 'belonged to Mr. D.M. Willens, who drowned in the Peregrine River, 1951' (3), with the account of the day three boys discover the body, and with the care given the dying, venomous Mrs Quinn by Enid, 'a good woman' who creates divergent narrative possibilities for herself and Rupert, the surviving husband. Over a third of this lengthy story is taken up with the quotidian details of the boys' lives, with relatively little attention paid to the drama of the discovery itself. Their respective characters, their contrasting families, the very nature of their meals are accorded a meticulous importance, an essential texture that from the start of her career Munro has identified as the writer's weapon against death, against vanishing.

Yet, with the shift from the first to the second sections of the story, Cece Ferns, Bud Salter, and Jimmy Box seemingly disappear from the narrative; their connection with the following sequences seems at best accidental. But at one point Enid thinks of the adult Rupert and the boy she knew in school: 'And whatever troubled him and showed in his face might have been just the same old trouble—the problem of occupying space in the world and having a name that people could call you by, being somebody they thought they could know' (47–48). This 'problem' is perhaps the submerged mystery in so much of Munro's recent work—that of 'occupying space' in the narrative, having a particular name and character. This is the perspective that shades the transition from Sophie to Denise and Isabel in 'White Dump,' the mirroring of Louisa's men in 'Carried Away,' the secret connection between Ladner and Liza in 'Vandals.' The sense of 'occupying space' is Munro's reworking of that phrase, *What difference*, once cynical, now celebratory. In the section devoted to the boys' outing, the narrative acknowledges that out there, they are nameless, they are free, that others could be ready substitutes for them. The 'difference' is in story itself. The boys do not so much vanish as give way to the habitation of narrative space by the story of Enid and Mrs Quinn's story of the optometrist's sexual assault and Rupert's reciprocal violence. That narrative space itself is never settled, always open to transitions and alternatives, is again revealed in the humane luxury of the opposing directions Enid imagines for herself and the story that encompasses the boys and the box of optometrical instruments. As long as she does not ask Rupert about the death, '[t]he different possibility was coming closer to her, and all she needed to do was to keep quiet and let it come' (76). Instead of a nurse, a refracted missionary, a devoted visitor to a chastened Rupert in prison, she will have a house and make it 'into a place that had no secrets from her and where all order was as she had decreed' (77).

In 'The Love of a Good Woman,' Munro elongates the narrative with a loving devotion to the various textures of the spaces the figures inhabit. In 'Rich as Stink' 'the problem of occupying space' in the story 'and having a name that people could call you by' ('Love,' 48) is concentrated on the gloriously innocent ten-year-old Karin (whose name might also be Maisie Farange), who extends her emotions in terms of the spaces around and inside her. Her missing of Derek, her mother's 'friend,' she thinks of as 'the sense that there was space to fill, and a thinning out of possibility' (220). After the accident in which she is burned wearing a wedding gown, Karin evades her mother's encroachment, her 'absurd' sorrow, by becoming both 'a continent' and its minute contraction: 'something immense and shimmering and sufficient . . . stretched out like this and at the same time shrunk into the middle of her territory, as tidy as a bead or a ladybug' (253).

But the most audacious and magical of Munro's creations of narrative space is the concluding 'My Mother's Dream,' a story destined to have
a supra-artistic, even therapeutic, prominence in the literature of mothers
and daughters. Here Munro counterpoints the eerie, layered dream which
suggests the death of the child with the raucous comedy of the daily life
surrounding the very much alive infant. In the dream the mother's sorrow
inhabits her completely: 'There would never be any room in her for anything
else. No room for anything but the realization of what she had done' (295).
But it is the child's storms of fury, 'a birthright rage free of love and pity, ready
to crush your brains inside your skull' (322), that occupy the house and the
lives of everyone in it. Munro's astounding decision for arranging this story of
love, femaleness, and survival was to create an absolute equation between retrospective and immediate or simultaneous narration. The wrathful infant and
the nuanced adult are entirely the same, occupy the identical space within the
narrative; neither vanishes for an instant, a virtually miraculous version of that
signal phrase, 'What difference.' Indeed, time collapses utterly as 'she/they'
record the upheavals and the gorgeously quiet resolution—'I stayed still—not
yet being quite able to turn over—and I stayed quiet' (336)—of the preference for the mother, for 'coming back.' 'I don't believe that I was dead, or that
I came back from the dead, but I do think that I was at a distance, from which
I might or might not have come back' (337). Relinquishing the battle against
her mother, she—in both the nursery and the study—'chose survival over victory' and 'took on [her] female nature' (337).

Survival and vanishing, possibility and the habitation of space—these
are the terms that help us describe the new rooms in Munro's edifice of fiction, those houses she so accurately speaks of as emblematic of her imagination (Geddes, 825). Beneficent as her new stories generally are, they are hardly
denials of transience. They change the angle, seeing, revealing, plenitude which
is the other side of (an adjacent room to) the 'rag-and-bone shop.'[16] And we
visit these extraordinary rooms, fully conscious of our connections with them
as both enormous and minuscule, 'frayed' and rewoven, fully conscious, too,
that we have no choice but to bring with us in that 'fit' between story and self
our habitual, splintering carapaces.

## NOTES

1. I am deeply indebted to Coral Ann Howells for her arguments about multiplicity and indeterminacy in *Private and Fictional Words*. Also Rasporich, 165.

2. See in particular Heble. Also Carrington, *Controlling*.

3. Howells's recent book on Munro arrived when the majority of this study
was already written, but in time to note some similarities in perspective, here about
mapping, psychological geography. See *Alice Munro*, 16–19.

4. See Carscallen's dense and fascinating readings. Also Redekop, 42.

5. Heble effectively details Munro's 'double-time scheme' (49) and is particularly astute about truth and invention in the chapter on *The Progress of Love*, 143–68. Also Thacker.

6. Cf Kamboureli, 37.

7. 'Paradigmatic' is one of Heble's central terms (34). Redekop reports that composing the story was almost the end of Munro's life as a writer (104).

8. See Redekop's discussion of loss here (149ff).

9. This section is a version of my 1987 review of the book in the *University of Toronto Quarterly*.

10. I cannot see the justification for the notion (Carrington, *Controlling*, 55; Heble, 153, and elsewhere) of Peg's morbid 'curiosity' and 'self-interest.' We simply cannot know.

11. See Redekop on *Friend* (209ff).

12. Interview with Peter Gzowski. Also Carrington, 'Title.'

13. See Howells, *Alice Munro*, 125.

14. Foy connects Munro's 'fairy-tale style' (156) here with the relation Lamont-Stewart describes of the ordinary and the grotesque.

15. Cf Foy, 159.

16. Yeats, 'The Circus Animals' Desertion,' *Collected Poems*, 392.

## Works Cited

Besner, Neil. *Introducing Alice Munro's Lives of Girls and Women: A Reader's Guide*. Toronto: ECW 1990

Carrington, Ildikó de Papp. *Controlling the Uncontrollable: The Fiction of Alice Munro*. Dekalb: Northern Illinois University Press 1989

———. 'What's in a Title? Alice Munro's "Carried Away."' *Studies in Short Fiction* 30 (1993), 555–64

Carscallen, James. *The Other Country: Patterns in the Writing of Alice Munro*. Toronto: ECW 1993

Ford, Richard. *Rock Springs*. New York: Vintage 1988

Foy, Nathalie. '"Darkness Collecting": Reading "Vandals" as a Coda to *Open Secrets*.' Forthcoming. ECW, 147–68

Friedman, Norman. 'Recent Short Story Theories: Problems in Definition.' *Short Story Theory at a Crossroads*. Ed Susan Lohafer and Jo Ellyn Clarey. Baton Rouge: Louisiana State University Press 1989, 13–31

Garson, Marjorie. 'Synecdoche and the Munrovian Sublime: Parts and Wholes in *Lives of Girls and Women*.' *English Studies in Canada* 20:4 (1994), 413–29

Geddes, Gary, ed. *The Art of Short Fiction: An International Anthology*. Toronto: HarperCollins 1993

Heble, Ajay. *The Tumble of Reason: Alice Munro's Discourse of Absence*. Toronto: University of Toronto Press 1994

Howells, Coral Ann. *Private and Fictional Words: Canadian Women Novelists of the 1970s and 1980s*. London: Methuen 1987

———. *Alice Munro*. Manchester: Manchester University Press 1998

Joyce, James. *Dubliners*. 1914; Harmondsworth: Penguin 1976

Kamboureli, Smaro. 'The Body as Audience and Performance in the Writing of Alice Munro.' *A Mazing Space: Writing Canadian Women Writing*. Ed S. Neuman and S. Kamboureli. Edmonton: Longspoon/NeWest 1986, 31–38

Lamont-Stewart, Linda. 'Order from Chaos: Writing as Self-Defense in the Fiction of Alice Munro and Clark Blaise.' *The Art of Alice Munro*. Ed Judith Miller. Waterloo: University of Waterloo Press 1984, 113–21

Lawrence, D.H. *Letters of D.H. Lawrence* Vol. 2: June 1913–October 1916. Ed George J. Zytaruk and James T. Bolton. Cambridge: Cambridge University Press 1981

Levene, Mark. Review of *The Progress of Love*. University of Toronto Quarterly 57:1 (1987), 7–9

Mayberry, Katherine J. '"Every Last Thing . . . Everlasting": Alice Munro and the Limits of Narrative.' *Studies in Short Fiction* 29 (1992): 531–41

McPherson, Hugo. 'Fiction (1940–1960).' *Literary History of Canada: Canadian Literature in English*. Gen ed Carl F. Klinck. Toronto: University of Toronto Press 1965, 694–720

Munro, Alice. *Dance of the Happy Shades*. 1968; Toronto: McGraw-Hill 1988

———. *Lives of Girls and Women*. 1971; Harmondsworth: Penguin 1997

———. Interview with Graeme Gibson. *Eleven Canadian Novelists*. Toronto: Anansi 1973

———. *Something I've Been Meaning to Tell You*. 1974; Harmondsworth: Penguin 1990

———. *Who Do You Think You Are?* 1978; Harmondsworth: Penguin 1991

———. *The Moons of Jupiter*. 1982; Harmondsworth: Penguin 1986

———. *The Progress of Love*. 1986; Harmondsworth: Penguin 1995

———. *Friend of My Youth*. 1990; Harmondsworth: Penguin 1991

———. 'What is Real?' In Geddes, 824–27

———. *Open Secrets*. Toronto: McClelland and Stewart 1994

———. Interview with Peter Gzowski. 'Morningside.' CBC Radio, 30 Sept 1994

———. *Selected Stories*. Toronto: McClelland and Stewart 1996

———. *The Love of a Good Woman*. Toronto: McClelland and Stewart 1998

New, W.H. *Dreams of Speech and Violence: The Art of the Short Story in Canada and New Zealand*. Toronto: University of Toronto Press 1987

Proulx, E. Annie, ed. *The Best American Short Stories 1997*. Boston: Houghton Mifflin 1997

Rasporich, Beverly J. *Dance of the Sexes: Art and Gender in the Fiction of Alice Munro*. Edmonton: University of Alberta Press 1990

Redekop, Magdalene. *Mothers and Other Clowns: The Stories of Alice Munro*. London: Routledge 1992

Ross, Catherine Sheldrick. *Alice Munro: A Double Life*. Toronto: ECW 1992

Sansom, William. 'The Short Story.' *London Magazine* 6 (1966), 9

Stone, Robert. *Writers at Work: The Paris Review Interviews*. 8th series, ed George Plimpton. Harmondsworth: Penguin 1988

Thacker, Robert. '"Clear Jelly": Alice Munro's Narrative Dialects.' *Probable Fictions: Alice Munro's Narrative Acts*. Ed Louis K. MacKendrick. Toronto: ECW 1983, 37–60

Yeats, W.B. *Collected Poems*. London: Macmillan 1958

DEBORAH HELLER

# Getting Loose: Women and Narration in *Alice Munro's* Friend of My Youth

About midway through Alice Munro's *Friend of My Youth*, the protagonist of "Oranges and Apples," recalling his mother's disparagement of his
wife, reflects on the phrase "loose woman":

> When he heard people say that, he'd always thought of an
> unbuttoned blouse, clothes slipping off the body, to indicate its
> appetite and availability. Now he thought that it could also mean
> just that—loose. A woman who could get loose, who wasn't
> fastened down, who was not reliable, who could roll away. (132)

Most of the stories in *Friend of My Youth* are about characters—principally,
but not exclusively, women—who in one way or another "get loose," are not
"fastened down." They get loose from the roles expected of them by other
characters in their fictional lives and from the roles that readers may expect
them to play in predictable plots. In crucial instances, characters also seem
to get loose from the narrator's knowledge and control. The image of the
"woman who could get loose" is thus suggestive for the collection as a whole,
hovering as it does at the intersection of substance and technique, subject
matter and the manner of its narration.

From *The Rest of the Story: Critical Essays on Alice Munro*, edited by Robert Thacker, pp.
60–80. © 1999 by ECW Press.

The openness of Munro's characters to metamorphosis, as well as her refusal of closure in favour of open-ended narrative structures, have received considerable critical attention.[1] This essay is concerned more specifically with Munro's new departures in her seventh collection of stories and with how, even as Munro revisits familiar situations, structures, and concerns there, she develops them in fresh ways. The opening story, "Friend of My Youth," immediately points in several directions at once, introducing strategies and motifs—including that of getting loose—that are picked up throughout the eponymous collection while also returning to material familiar from earlier "autobiographical" stories, notably "The Peace of Utrecht" in *Dance of the Happy Shades* and "Winter Wind," "Memorial," and "The Ottawa Valley" in *Something I've Been Meaning to Tell You*: the mother's debilitating illness and the young daughter's inability to respond adequately to the challenge of her mother's needs, her youthful shame, and her adult guilt, experienced as especially powerful and tenacious in retrospect.

Although critics have commented on the broad similarity between the mother–daughter situation in "Friend of My Youth" and earlier versions of Munro's treatment of what appears to be the same material, none has noted how the crucial framing dream in "Friend of My Youth" echoes and reworks an earlier account of a dream in "The Peace of Utrecht," the story in which Munro "first tackled personal material" (Munro, "Real Material" 21).[2] In both stories, these are presented as recurrent wish-fulfilment dreams, revealing a narrator-daughter's fantasy that if only the mother had not been so ill, had not made so many demands, how simple it would have been to be a better daughter and not to have had to be guilty. In the early story, the account of the dream is brief, momentarily emerging out of the adult narrator's reflections about her mother on her first visit home after her mother's death. Moving from painful memories of her long suffering mother and her own failures to meet her mother's demands, the narrator recalls how

> the disease is erratic and leisurely in its progress; some mornings . . . she wakes up better . . . [and] tries to make up for lost time, tidying the house, forcing her stiff trembling hands to work a little while at the sewing machine. She makes us one of her specialities, a banana cake or a lemon meringue pie. Occasionally since she died I have dreams of her . . . in which she is doing something like this, and I think, why did I exaggerate so to myself, see, she is all right, only that her hands are trembling—(*Dance* 200)

The dream breaks off, and, even though the story is concerned with the two sisters' different ways of coping with the aftermath of their mother's illness and death, we do not hear of it again.

Until, that is, it resurfaces in the framing dream of "Friend of My Youth":

> I used to dream about my mother, and though the details in the dream varied, the surprise was always the same. The dream stopped, I suppose because it was too transparent in its hopefulness, too easy in its forgiveness.
>
> ... Sometimes I would find myself in our old kitchen, where my mother would be rolling out piecrust ... or washing the dishes. ... But other times I would run into her on the street, in places where I would never have expected to see her. ... She would be looking quite well—not exactly youthful, not entirely untouched by the paralyzing disease that held her in its grip for a decade or more before her death, but so much better than I remembered that I would be astonished. (*Friend* 3)

But when Munro returns after more than twenty years to the recurrent dream of the daughter's wish to find her mother alive again and almost well, in the very early stages of her illness, she uses it in a much more purposeful and deliberate fashion. Prominently placed at the opening of the story, the dream is virtually deconstructed before it is recounted, by the narrator's unsparing explanation of why it stopped. But the narrator is then free to develop the dream fantasy more amply and leisurely, revealing its comfort value directly after she has denied its legitimacy. "I recovered then what in waking life I had lost—my mother's liveliness of face and voice before her throat muscles stiffened and a woeful, impersonal mask fastened itself over her features ...," her "casual humor," and her "lightness and impatience and confidence" (3–4). The "recovered" dream-mother does more than forgive her daughter; she renders superfluous any apology or guilt:

> I was sorry I had kept a bugbear in my mind, instead of this reality—and the strangest, kindest thing of all to me was her matter-of-fact reply.
>
> Oh, well, she said, better later than never. I was sure I'd see you someday. (4)

Although offering an already discredited comfort, the recounted dream, by helping her to recapture the youthful mother, then serves as a springboard from which the narrator launches into a story told to her by her mother, stemming from her mother's single days teaching in a one-room country schoolhouse and boarding with the Grieves family, whose tangled lives form the substance of her tale. In the narrator's recounting of her mother's story, we successively witness the apparent self-effacement of two storytellers, for the narrator seems to disappear in giving voice to her mother's tale, and then the mother is lost to view within *her* story, which constitutes the bulk of "Friend of My Youth." Just when we have all but lost sight of any storytelling presence, however, the apparent self-sufficiency of the tale is abruptly undercut by a series of codas that jolt us into an awareness of the mediating role of the narrative voice. The codas provide glimpses of successively shifting stages in the narrator's own development and in her relation to her mother, each constituting a different attempt to understand the recalcitrant mother material. The last coda returns to the dream, which now upstages the story that it frames. The closing dream provides a new take on the mother–daughter drama at the same time that it offers suggestive avenues of approach to the stories that follow; for these stories ring their own variations both on Munro's familiar albatross story and on the wider issues raised in the codas to "Friend of My Youth"—issues of women's relations to one another and of "relation" itself, in the sense of narration.

The central story in "Friend of My Youth," which concerns the strict Cameronian Flora, twice betrayed by her one-time fiance Robert, has been pieced together by the narrator's mother from firsthand experience and from gossip and letters telling of events before and after her stay in the community. The account ends with an exchange of letters between the mother and Flora in which the mother writes from afar to express sympathy and profess outrage and in which Flora replies to reject the sympathy and outrage and, essentially, to tell her former friend to mind her own business. At this point, the apparent neutrality of the account comes to a sudden end. The original narrator, temporarily lost to view, reemerges, offering successive codas, or exegeses, to the interpolated story that we have just read. First, reminding us of the source of the story, the narrator resentfully recounts her mother's attempt to package it as a moral tale:

> In later years, when she sometimes talked about the things she might have been, or done, she would say, "If I could have been a writer—I do think I could have been; I could have been a writer—then I would have written the story of Flora's life. And do you know what I would have called it? 'The Maiden Lady.'" (19)

*If I could have been a writer....* The mother's wistful evocation of her unfulfilled potential highlights the fact that the lively, often comic, rendition of the sad tale that we have been reading is the achievement of the narrator-daughter, the real writer after all. The story of Flora's life emerges as a site of contestation between the narrator and her mother, implicitly posing the questions of who will give it definitive voice and to what end. Next, the narrator recalls her teenage rejection of her mother's reverential account of Flora as "a noble figure, one who accepts defection, treachery, who forgives and stands aside, not once but twice" (19). More than Flora is at stake in the narrator's dismissive youthful response to her mother's moralizing:

> In her own plight her [the mother's] ideas had turned mystical, and there was sometimes a hush, a solemn thrill in her voice that grated on me, alerted me to what seemed a personal danger. I felt a great fog of platitudes and pieties lurking, an incontestable crippled-mother power which could capture and choke me. . . . I had to keep myself sharp-tongued and cynical, arguing and deflating. Eventually I gave up even that recognition and opposed her in silence. (20)

Although recognizing the vulnerability and the impulse to self-preservation behind her teenage rejection of her mother's "reading" of Flora's tale, the adult narrator nonetheless judges her former self harshly, immediately undercutting the sympathetic presentation of her adolescent self that she has just written: "This is a fancy way of saying that I was no comfort and poor company to her when she had almost nowhere else to turn" (20).

Still, this unsparing, mature judgement on her younger self does not keep the narrator from relating that self's competing construction; in scornful contrast to her mother's wistful evocation of unfulfilled potential, the adolescent daughter "didn't think that I could have written a novel but that I would write one. I would take a different tack." As if anticipating the narrator's literary practice in "Meneseteung," she tells us, "I saw through my mother's story and put in what she left out" (20). The narrator then provides an account of her own youthful imaginings, which lead to an altered ending in which Flora emerges as a Presbyterian witch who gets her comeuppance in a lurid gothic finale.

The mature narrator of "Friend of My Youth," however, now rejects the competition of codas that she has just sketched, seeking instead a more dispassionate and deeper comprehension of their conflict: "What made Flora evil in my story was just what made her admirable in my mother's—her turning away from sex" (22). Moving beyond guilt and self-recrimination, the narrator meditates on the different worldviews inherent in their different exegeses, seeing in them attitudes beyond conscious, individual choice: "My mother had grown up in a time and in a place where sex was a dark undertaking for women. She knew that you could die of it" (22). Indeed, within the mother's story, Ellie *does* seem to have died of it (though by a logic that is clearer morally than physiologically).

> So she honored the decency, the prudery, the frigidity, that might protect you. And I grew up in horror of that very protection, the dainty tyranny that seemed to extend to all areas of life. . . . The odd thing is that my mother's ideas were in line with some progressive notions of her times, and mine echoed the notions that were favored in my time. This in spite of the fact that we both believed ourselves independent, and lived in backwaters that did not register such changes. (22–23)

Her meditation concludes with a stunning image for the *Zeitgeist*: "It's as if tendencies that seem most deeply rooted in our minds, most private and singular, have come in as spores on the prevailing wind, looking for any likely place to land, any welcome" (23). Words of remarkable generosity and humility, which enable the narrator to transcend the mother–daughter competition for narrative authority through an understanding of the wider context of their conflict.

The narrator does not, however, bring her story to a close on this note of understanding and wisdom. Like the narrator of "The Ottawa Valley" in *Something I've Been Meaning to Tell You*, she pushes beyond the easier ending, adding yet another coda to the Grieves story. The mood of harmony as well as the competing codas that precede it are now displaced by the narrator's revelation that years later her mother received a letter from "the real Flora" (23), telling of her move to town and her clerking job in a store and, in an inversion of roles, offering sympathy to the mother for her debilitating illness. Flora's letter leads the narrator to memories of her stricken mother's inability to get beyond writing the beginnings of letters (one of which started with "Friend of my youth") and of her "impatience with [her mother's] flowery language, the direct appeal for love and pity" (24).

Inevitably, the adolescent's impatience becomes guilt when recalled by the adult narrator. But the guilt is addressed by a circuitous route, which imperceptibly leads back to the opening dream. Although at the time of Flora's letter and her mother's illness the narrator "had lost interest in Flora," she has "thought of her since," imagining a happier ending to her story. In the narrator's more recent speculations, Flora is no longer the hateful, sex-rejecting witch of her youthful fantasies; her new, alternative ending springs Flora loose from her predictable stoic fate and the rigidities that defined and confined her in her mother's tale. The older narrator re-creates the formerly alien Flora as someone with whom she might even discover affinities. She spins an open-ended fantasy of Flora's progressive liberation, in which Flora, now working in a store, "might have had to learn about food blenders or chain saws, negligees, cosmetics, even condoms" (24). Each image suggests another, leading to a Flora who might "get a permanent, paint her nails, put on lipstick," or even "go on holidays ... [and] eat meals in a restaurant ... where drinks were served. She might make friends with women who were divorced. She might meet a man" (25).

From this fantasy of open-ended possibility, the narrator slips into a more personal one: "I might go into a store and find her." Immediately recognizing the impossibility of doing so ("She would be dead a long time now"), she nonetheless persists: "But suppose I had gone into a store—perhaps a department store" (25)—where she imagines meeting Flora, wanting to tell her that she knows her story, even "trying to tell her. (This is a dream now, I understand it as a dream)" (25–26). Whether or not we hear an echo here of the opening sentence of "The Ottawa Valley"—"I think of my mother sometimes in department stores" (*Something* 227), the dream of meeting a transformed Flora clearly echoes the opening dream of "Friend of My Youth" and quickly merges with it as the narrator now conflates the two long-dead women. When the dream-Flora responds to the narrator's claims with a mocking smile, "weary ... of me and my idea of her, my information, my notion that I can know anything about her," the narrator recognizes that "Of course it's my mother I'm thinking of, my mother as she was in those dreams, saying, It's nothing, just this little tremor; saying with such astonishing light-hearted forgiveness, Oh, I knew you'd come someday. My mother surprising me" (26).

But the surprise surprises further by not being altogether pleasurable. Seeing her mother's "mask, her fate, and most of her affliction taken away," the daughter, though "relieved" and "happy," is also "disconcerted":

> I felt slightly cheated. Yes. Offended, tricked, cheated, by this welcome turnaround, this reprieve. My mother moving rather carelessly out of her old prison, showing options and powers I never dreamed she had, changes more than herself. She changes the bitter lump of love I have carried all this time into a phantom—something useless and uncalled for, like a phantom pregnancy. (26)

In springing Flora loose from her fixed role in the mother's story, the narrator has also opened the way for her mother to get loose from "her old prison"—her illness and the narrator's fixed memories of her[3]—which in turn places the daughter in a new position. For with her new freedom and independence, the dream-mother also seems to have got loose from the narrator's knowledge and control. That this "turnaround," which destabilizes all that has preceded it, should prove disconcerting as well as "welcome" forces us to ponder why a part of the narrator suddenly seems to prefer the rigid and demanding mother. Why does she feel "cheated" at having to relinquish "the bitter lump of love"—presumably, the guilt with which she has lived for so long? (The lump is also an image that, within the story, looks back to Ellie's "growth" and unsuccessful—phantom?—pregnancies[4] and, elsewhere in the collection, forward to Barbara's lump in "Oranges and Apples.") Is it that by transforming her mother's story into narrative the narrator has automatically opened it up to the possibility of other directions that threaten the rigidity of her own mechanisms for dealing with the past? Or is it due to the threatened loss of narrative control once she begins to give free reign to her fantasies?[5] Or does her sense of being tricked and cheated point, as Carol Shields suggests, to a painful recognition of the fundamental unknowability of the mother, "her steadfast resistance to the notions of others" (22)?[6] In any case, as the mother is imaginatively freed from her prison, the narrator reveals needs and potentialities that we (and she) see for the first time. Perhaps most intriguingly, the destabilizing fantasy calls into question the truth value and the stability of any narrative, either imagined or remembered, reminding us that, as both memory and storytelling are constructions, creative acts, their content is always, in some sense, problematic and open ended. There is always another way of coming at the same material.[7]

The mother in the closing dream of "Friend of My Youth" may seem reminiscent of the mother at the end of "The Ottawa Valley," who is "indistinct," whose "edges melt and flow" (*Something* 246). But while in the earlier story the mother "weighs everything down, . . . has stuck to me as close as ever and refused to fall away" (246), the self-sufficient dream-mother of "Friend of My Youth" eludes the narrator's grasp, seeming simply to slip away. Ultimately, her getting loose is experienced as more unsettling than liberating. Hence, while the narrator of "The Ottawa Valley" understands the final "purpose" of her (narrative) "journey" as an effort to "get rid" of the mother (246), the narrative of "Friend of My Youth" appears, instead, as an effort to recapture the mother, to bring her back.

The daughter's desire to recapture the mother in "Friend of My Youth" suggests another function of the daughter's tale. I have looked at the Grieves story as a site of competition between mother and daughter for narrative (and hence moral) authority. Additionally, though, we can see the story as a collaborative effort, even a kind of *hommage* to the mother, whose early illness and death perhaps prevented her from fulfilling her potential. In "Winter Wind," the daughter relates that her mother's "vocal cords were partly paralyzed" and that "Sometimes I would have to act as her interpreter, a job that made me wild with shame" (*Something* 195).[8] In the later "Friend of My Youth," the daughter finds a different, more affirmative, way to give a more permanent voice to the mother whose own voice was prematurely silenced.

Munro, of course, has always been interested in the process of story-telling, and her stories abound with fragments of stories and contradictory versions of characters and events. *Friend of My Youth*, however, viewed in its entirety, shows a newly focused interest in the construction of collaborative, shared narratives.[9] In addition to the complex title story, this interest is nota-ble in the two other stories that directly treat a mother–daughter relation-ship—"Meneseteung" and "Goodness and Mercy." Before turning to them, however, we should dwell a moment longer on the destabilizing dream as well as on the fantasy that introduces it and the unexpected affinities that this fantasy suggests, for they illustrate motifs that reverberate throughout the collection. Just as the mother "moving . . . out of her old prison" points to characters in other stories who get loose from the bonds of predictable narra-tives, so too the narrator's fantasy of meeting an altered Flora and her desire to construct a happier ending for a woman whose fate has been presented to her as sealed in inescapable resignation or gloom are echoed in the impulses of other female protagonists in the collection.

In "Five Points," Brenda refuses to accept as final the dismal end for the adolescent Maria on which Neil's story from his past concludes. (After steal-ing money from her parents' cash register to pay boys to have sex with her, Maria was "sent to a place for young offenders" [*Friend* 40].) Brenda doggedly wants to know "what happened to Maria. . . . The story won't leave Brenda alone," and she goes on to imagine a more generous conclusion: "Well, maybe she got married. . . . Lots of people get married who are no beauties. . . . She might've lost weight and be looking good even" (42). Brenda's insistence on pushing beyond the known ending of Maria's incarceration to more open-ended possibilities provides the occasion for her first fight with her lover, Neil. Although it is not clear that his account of Maria's humiliating sexual need is intended to humiliate the attractive, sexy Brenda, her insistent desire to see Maria get loose from Neil's confining narrative shows an instinctive identification with the pathetic young woman whom she knows only from her lover's story.

A female protagonist's recognition of affinity in unexpected quarters and her impulse to write a more open ending through which an appar-ently dead-ended woman can get loose from a presumed foreclosed destiny reappear in "Hold Me Fast, Don't Let Me Pass." Having met the beautiful young Judy, whose illegitimate daughter, Tania, seems to confine her to a long dreary future looking after an isolated semi-invalid, Hazel speculates aloud (to Antoinette, Judy's older and successful rival for Tania's father), "It must be a lonely life for her," adding, "She might like to get married" (97). Just as Nell in "Five Points" rejects Brenda's hopeful scenario for Maria, so too Antoinette dismisses Hazel's generous thoughts about a happier future for Judy. And, like Brenda, Hazel refuses to back down: "It doesn't matter so much nowadays.... Girls have children first and get married later. Movie stars, ordinary girls, too. All the time" (97).

As suggested earlier, it is not only characters and narrators within the stories who offer liberating endings to foreclosed plots presented to them in interpolated tales; the characters themselves also get loose from expected, constricting story lines.[10] For example, Hazel is not simply the sympathetic imaginer of a more open future for Judy than her limiting circumstances might suggest but also someone who, years earlier, "broke open the shell of her increasingly doubtful and expensive prettiness; she got out"; even though she remained in a dreary marriage, she found a way to take "hold of her life" (82). In *Friend of My Youth*, unlike most of the earlier collections, some female characters are able to get loose from confinement—Hazel and Brenda, also Barbara of "Oranges and Apples"—even though they remain within their flawed marriages. (It is perhaps puzzling, but an example of the force of optimism, that both Brenda and Hazel, who have not exactly found marriage liberating themselves, should nonetheless construct it as such for others in their imagined narratives). At the same time, we also see the situation more familiar to Munro readers of a woman breaking free from her marriage,[11] described in ways that tie in with motifs present elsewhere in the collection. Joan in "Oh, What Avails," heeding the call of "a person not heard from in her marriage, and perhaps not previously heard from in her life" (199), "feels herself loosed" and "knows that she cannot go back to the life she was living or to the person she was before" (200). Georgia in "Differently," who similarly discovers that she "contained another woman" (233), is seen as confuting more conventional expectations familiar in literature (and in life): "you would have thought that after such scourging she'd have scuttled back into her marriage.... That was not what happened" (241). In "Wigtime," the divergent youthful paths of Anita and Margot seem early to cast them as contraries in a traditional good woman/bad woman dichotomy, but their later choices invert and then effectively dissolve this opposition (a staple of more predictable plots). The story ends with their renewed friendship, allowing Margot to tell of her frequent friendly visits to the now institutionalized ex-wife whom she has displaced. A similar rejection of clear divisions between recognizable types of women is present in "Hold Me Fast, Don't Let Me Pass" in the feelings of female loyalty and solidarity with which Hazel responds to both her dead husband's former lover, Antoinette, now respectable hotel owner and *soi-disant* widow, and the publicly stigmatized Judy.

"Meneseteung" is another story in which a protagonist gets loose from narrative expectations engendered by familiar, predictable plots, while it, too, presents unexpected affinities among three dissimilar women. Moreover, if, in Virginia Woolf's much-quoted words, "a woman writing thinks back through her mothers" (127), then this story of a female narrator seeking to recover a forgotten woman writer of the past may also be read as a version of the mother–daughter drama. Such recoveries have become a frequent subject of both fiction and historical research for contemporary women writers. Moreover, here, as in "Friend of My Youth," the narrator's treatment of material from a (literary fore)mother may be viewed as both competition and *hommage*.[12]

"Meneseteung" opens with a discussion of Almeda Joynt Roth's book of poetry *Offerings*, and excerpts from that volume provide epigraphs for each of the story's six sections. At the same time, the researching writer of "Meneseteung"—more successfully than the adolescent narrator of "Friend of My Youth" who "saw through ... [her] mother's story and put in what she left out" (20)—portrays a denser and imaginatively richer world than that suggested by the pretty, sanitized poetry of her nineteenth-century foremother. Moving from Almeda's book of verse to her world in the second section of the story, the narrator, aided by old issues of the local *Vidette*, evokes a raw frontier town in which "Cows are tethered in vacant lots or pastured in back yards, but sometimes they get loose. Pigs get loose, too, and dogs roam free. . . . Animals . . . leave horse buns, cow pats, dog turds that ladies have to hitch up their skirts for," young rowdies trundle a drunken Queen Aggie all over town in a wheelbarrow, "then dump her into a ditch" (54), and Almeda's bedroom window overlooks the disreputable Pearl Street at the edge of the swamp, to which "No decent woman ever would ... [walk]" (56). Implicitly underscoring the greater authenticity of her re-creation of Almeda's world, the writer reminds us that "The countryside that she [Almeda] has written about in her poems actually takes diligence and determination to see. Some things must be disregarded. Manure piles ... and boggy fields ..." (61).

The various texts uncovered by the narrator—Almeda's poems, with her author's introduction and photograph, supplemented by *Vidette* entries—suggest a character recognizable from familiar plots: first, the decorous nineteenth-century maiden poetess, modest, if not downright apologetic, about her literary ventures, a baker of "fancy iced cakes and decorated tarts" (58); next, the not entirely over-the-hill spinster, embarking on a romance with her neighbour, Jarvis Poulter, presumably hoping for the closure of the marriage plot. The final *Vidette* entry fits Almeda into yet another female plot, that of the increasingly eccentric old maid who meets an ignoble end. Navigating among the "facts" and "documented" innuendo (supplied by the author of "Meneseteung"), however, the narrator enables Almeda to get loose from these familiar plotlines,[13] inventing for her a story of far greater drama and an inner life of far wider imaginative scope than any that one could hope to find in the pages of the *Vidette* or in the work of a nineteenth-century poetess.

The crucial imagined scene of the audible "ball of fire rolling up Pearl Street, shooting off sparks," followed by sounds of "a woman . . . being beaten" (63) and the imperfectly glimpsed grappling figures at Almeda's back fence, with their "confused . . . gagging, vomiting, grunting, pounding" and the "choking sound of pain and self-abasement, self-abandonment," suggest to Almeda that she has witnessed "the sound of murder" and pose the question of her personal responsibility—"What is to be done, what is she to do"?[14] Although her immediate response is that "she must go out into the yard" (64), she succumbs to the medically (patriarchally) prescribed "nerve medicine" (62) and falls asleep. Waking, she imagines "a big crow sitting on her windowsill" and telling her, "Wake up and move the wheelbarrow. . . . [S]he understands that it means something else by 'wheelbarrow'—something foul and sorrowful" (64). While Almeda's gloss on wheelbarrow is certainly apt, if the narrator has found the account of Queen Aggie's treatment in the *Vidette*, then might not Almeda have read it there too? Additionally, a wheelbarrow is used to cart away rubbish, but the woman's body "heaped up" at the back fence is neither rubbish nor ready to be carted away, though it appears to Almeda's horrified gaze in dehumanized, brute animal—and vegetable—terms: "a bare breast let loose, brown nipple pulled long like a cow's teat, and a bare haunch and leg, the haunch showing a bruise as big as a sunflower. The unbruised skin is grayish, like a plucked, raw drumstick" (65). Fearing that her hesitation has been responsible for the woman's death, Almeda hastily summons Jarvis, who "looks down at" the body and "nudges the leg with the toe of his boot, just as you'd nudge a dog or a sow." In response, sustaining its closeness to brute animal life,

> The body heaves itself onto all fours, the head is lifted—the hair all matted with blood and vomit—and the woman begins to bang this head, hard and rhythmically. . . . As she bangs her head, she finds her voice and lets out an openmouthed yowl, full of strength and what sounds like an anguished pleasure. (66)

Whether or not we accept Dermot McCarthy's description of this woman as "Life itself in all its obscene splendor" (7),[15] she certainly serves as a graphic reminder of the animal nature of human—if not specifically female— life. After his encounter with the beaten, bruised woman and the dishevelled, agitated Almeda, Jarvis may still wish to preserve the fiction of two types of women, though he now "speaks to her [Almeda] in a tone of harsh joviality that she has never before heard from him" (67). Almeda, however, consciously or unconsciously, recognizes her bond with this other woman,[16] hitherto so remote from her fenced-in world and representing all that has been excised from her poetry, and Jarvis's contemptuous treatment of *her* signals the end of Almeda's romantic interest in *him*.

In a series of interlocking images, the blood that has congealed in the woman by the fence begins to flow in Almeda, as her menstrual flow merges with the grape juice overflowing its container, and both merge with the flow of words in her mind, staining the kitchen floor boards with a "stain [that] will never come out" (70). Almeda's newly recognized kinship with the other woman has irrevocably changed and stained her. The "little jars of grape jelly" that Almeda has planned as "fine Christmas presents, or offerings to the sick" (62), are like her earlier literary "*Offerings*"—discrete units, attractively packaged and carefully contained. But Almeda and her new vision can no longer be contained so neatly. Like the genteelly crocheted roses in her tablecloth, which she soon imagines escaping into "floating independence" (70), Almeda has got loose from her previous moorings. Resembling another nineteenth-century fictional woman poised to rebel against patriarchal confinement, who obsessively watches the patterns of the wallpaper, seeing figured in these domestic surroundings her own imprisonment and then a promise of her escape,[17] Almeda "[surrenders] to her surroundings," watching the "garlanded wallpaper," curtains, floral carpet, and "sideboard spread with embroidered runners and holding patterned plates and jugs":

> For every one of these patterns, decorations seems charged with life, ready to move and flow and alter. Or possibly to explode. Almeda Roth's occupation through the day is to keep an eye on them. Not to prevent their alteration so much as to catch them at it—to understand it, to be part of it. (69)

As the "glowing and swelling" in Almeda begin "to suggest words . . . a flow of words" (69), she has a Whitmanesque vision of "one very great poem that will contain everything," including "the obscene racket on Pearl Street and the polished toe of Jarvis Poulter's boot and the plucked-chicken haunch with its blue-black flower" (70). Judging that the violence of climate and life can be "borne only if it is channelled into a poem," she decides that

> the name of the poem will be—it *is*—"The Meneseteung." . . . No, in fact it is the river, the Meneseteung, that is the poem—with its deep holes and rapids and blissful pools under the summer trees

and its grinding blocks of ice thrown up at the end of the winter
and its desolating spring floods. (70)[18]

As the story has progressed, the narrator has gradually seemed to lose herself in Almeda, moving into her mind and shedding the cool detachment
of the first section, with its almost pedantic observations about masculine
and feminine rhymes. But here a glaring cliché suddenly reminds us of the
distance between Almeda and the narrator, through whose mediation we
have been reading her story, as we are shown Almeda's vision in what must
surely be her own words: "Almeda looks deep, deep into the river of her
mind and into the tablecloth, and she sees the crocheted roses floating" (70).
Almeda is presented as a foremother who is granted a vision that, due to the
limitations of her time, place, and culture, she lacks not simply the courage and the encouragement but also the adequate linguistic resources—the
language—to express. Unlike the woman by the fence, Almeda does not,
finally, find her voice. Yet while her all-embracing cosmic vision remains
unwritten, the narrator's imagined rendering of decisive moments in Almeda's life and thought constitute her own "offerings" to a literary foremother.
The narrator's story can be viewed as a collaborative creation in which a
more privileged literary daughter gives voice to a disadvantaged predecessor
who did not, ultimately, succeed in finding her own.

The final scene, as in "Friend of My Youth," brings us back to the frame.
The narrator now distances us from Almeda through the *Vidette*'s report of
her ignominious end, allowing us to draw ironic parallels between this account
and the earlier accounts of Queen Aggie and the woman by the fence. But
though we are brought back to the narrator as researcher, the detachment of
the first section is gone. Looking for Almeda's gravestone, the narrator pas-
sionately begins "pulling grass and scrabbling in the dirt with my bare hands"
(73), seeking to affirm her conjecture that the "Meda" mentioned in one of
the poems is indeed Almeda Roth, author of the poems. The narrator on her
hands and knees in the dirt (how else can we envision the scene?) suggests
by her posture her own closeness to the animal life that she has imagined
Almeda recognizing in herself on seeing the woman by the fence. Thus, the
narrator's identification with Almeda is completed by her own final bodily
identification with this other, unnamed woman.[19]

At the same time, there is a certain play in this frantic search, for the
narrator's bold leap of imagination does not lie in her intuition that Meda
was Almeda's nickname. The Almeda Roth who has come to interest the
narrator (and us) is no longer primarily the Almeda Roth of the early book
of poems and of the *Vidette* accounts but the author of the wholly imagined
poem that remains unwritten—though the story that we have just finished

reading may be seen as a prose approach to it. No sooner has the narrator prided herself on "scraping the dirt off gravestones, reading microfilm, ... seeing this trickle in time, making a connection, rescuing one thing from the rubbish" than she concedes radical doubt: "I may have got it wrong. I don't know if she ever took laudanum. Many ladies did. I don't know if she ever made grape jelly" (73). These final sentences, added after the published *New Yorker* version, may be seen as part of Munro's increasingly characteristic refusal of definitive closure, and in light of issues raised earlier in this essay the disclaimer provides another example of a character escaping authorial control. But, of course, it is not the "facts" of laudanum or grape jelly that are in question, any more than whether Almeda was called Meda in her family. The narrator's apparent concern for historical accuracy is belied—even ignoring for a moment the fundamental fictionality of Almeda Roth—by the "fact" that even the (constructed) "record" gives no justification for the crucial events of the fracas on Pearl Street, the woman by the fence, the voice of the crow, and, indeed, all of Almeda's vibrant inner life in response to these experiences, including her unwritten poem. However, because the "record"—*Offerings*, the *Vidette*—*has been* invented, we cannot help but return at the end to the implied author behind the narrator who can never be wholly erased from our consciousness. So we are left with a series of refracted and related women, a sisterhood encompassing the invisible author, the narrator, Almeda/Meda, and the other woman.

Whereas "Meneseteung" presents a daughter generously reaching out across the gulf of historical time to resuscitate a forgotten foremother, "Goodness and Mercy" reworks the mother–daughter drama as a wish-fulfilment idyll. In contrast to Maddy's ten-year vigil caring for a mother whose "bizarre" disease inflicted "such unnecessary humiliation" on her daughters in "The Peace of Utrecht" (*Dance* 195), or the "decade or more" during which "the paralyzing disease" held the mother in "Friend of My Youth" "in its grip ... before her death" (*Friend* 3), the companionable ocean voyage of Bugs and Averill (for which Averill has generously paid with "money left to her by the father she had never seen" [156]) lasts a mere ten days. Behind the figure of the "charming" (160), witty Bugs, minimizing her illness, continuing to jest, uncomplainingly absenting herself gradually from one meal or social occasion after another, yet still able to sing "with unimpaired—or almost unimpaired—sweetness" (167), we may see the shadows of other ailing mothers, far less attractive and easy to love: the mother in "The Peace of Utrecht," barely able to articulate, who demanded the love of her daughters "without shame or sense" (*Dance* 199), or the mother in "Friend of My Youth," who, with her "direct appeal for love and pity," refused to "withdraw with dignity, instead of reaching out ... to cast her stricken shadow" (*Friend* 24). And, unlike the daughter-narrator in the earlier story left to lament that "the resources of love we had were not enough, the demand on us was too great" (*Dance* 199), or the daughter-narrator in the later story, who "was no comfort and poor company to her [mother] when she had nowhere else to turn" (*Friend* 20), Averill is unwavering in her devotion to her dying mother, the loving and dutiful daughter—except in her own eyes, as we learn when the captain tells "her perfectly secret story" aloud (177). Here Averill's story itself seems to get loose: "She had made it, and he had taken it and told it, safely" (178). For in telling it "safely," the captain, "alert to everything on the ship" and the embodiment of "peaceable authority" (166, 167), acknowledges her hidden fantasies and absolves her from guilt.

"Goodness and Mercy" hovers at the border of magic realism. The captain's wisdom and his knowledge of human nature may, of course, suffice to let him know that even a love as true and freely given as Averill's must have its ambivalent, dark side. Still, the story shared by Averill and the godlike captain seems to emerge as a mysterious collaboration, one that stands out from the collaborations between women that we have been looking at. Told by the captain, then amended (with his acceptance) by Averill, who recognizes it as her own, it slips loose from any fixed form, changing through successive versions in her fluid imagination and ultimately proving capable, through the captain's authority and participation, not only of absolving her from guilt but also of legitimizing the plenitude of her desires even in the face of loss and death.

The daughter's ambivalent feelings for the mother, implicit in the combination of competition and *hommage* in "Friend of My Youth" and "Meneseteung," are revealed here by the presence of the secret, liberating death wish that Averill harbours for Bugs alongside her profound love and solicitude. Except perhaps in Averill's free-floating fantasies or in the grace with which Bugs is dying, neither woman can be said to get loose from expected roles, escape authorial control, or discover surprising bonds with other women. Rather, "Goodness and Mercy" may be viewed as an idyllic replay of Munro's albatross story, creating a charmed space that corresponds to the "thing she [Averill] always felt, when her mother sang. The doors flew open, effortlessly, there was a lighted space beyond, a revelation of kindness and seriousness. Desirable, blessed joy, and seriousness, a play of kindness that asked nothing of you" (168). Unlike the mother's generous words in the opening dream of "Friend of My Youth," whose "transparent . . . hopefulness [and] too easy . . . forgiveness" the daughter is forced to deconstruct (3), Bugs's "gift" (168), though first presented as lasting only as long as her singing, seems endorsed at the end by "the captain's offering" (179). Within the idyllic space created by the story, Averill "is absolved and fortunate" (179), and the hope expressed in her hymn—"Goodness and Mercy all my life/Shall surely follow me" (169)—

almost seems attainable. But Munro never wholly abandons her ironic edge. Underscoring the tenacity of the bond between daughter and mother, Averill first marries one man "chiefly because Bugs would have thought the choice preposterous" and then a second, who, with his "flippant and ironical manner," "either charmed people or aroused their considerable dislike" (179)—just like the flippant and ironic Bugs, whom people either consider "charming" or "can't stand" (160)—a sure indication of the daughter's abiding loyalty to the first friend of her youth.

## NOTES

1. On metamorphosis, change, and fluid boundaries, see Irving, who treats them as properties of *female* nature. On Munro's refusal of definitive closure, see Crouse; and Hoy 18–19. A number of critics observe that the self in Munro is shifting and multiple. See, for example, Blodgett 12, 68, and passim; Hoy 17; Stead 151–53; and Thacker 156.

2. Speaking of her mother in another interview, Munro says of "The Peace of Utrecht" that "The first real story I ever wrote was about her" ("Alice Munro" 215).

3. See also Carrington 187–88; and Stead 156. Earlier in "Friend of My Youth," the narrator writes of her mother's becoming "busy with her own life and finally a prisoner in it" (19).

4. See also Redekop 215; and Stead 156.

5. This fear would fit nicely into Carrington's thesis that "the most central and creative paradox of Munro's fiction is its repeated . . . attempt to control what is uncontrollable" (5).

6. Dermot McCarthy writes of the mother's affirming "her own impenetrable otherness" (12).

7. This suggests more radical doubt than is implied by the question in "Winter Wind"—"how am I to know what I claim to know?" (*Something* 201)—or than "the difficulty of getting to the truth," which W.R. Martin has described as a focus of *Lives of Girls and Women* and "The Progress of Love" (179). It leads into "the vexatious question of the nature of reality" (Hoy 12) and of Munro's relation to postmodernism and metafiction, which have been treated with increasing frequency by critics. Linda Hutcheon, for example, identifies Munro as a "postmodern metafiction writer" (45 and passim), while Stephen Regan comments on her willingness "to harbour intense doubts about the representational value of fiction and yet to persevere in the creation of something that is true to life" (124–25).

8. Also see "The Peace of Utrecht" (*Dance* 195, 199).

9. Katherine Mayberry discusses the development of the "communal cooperative narrative" in *The Moons of Jupiter* (though she locates it first at the end of *The Lives of Girls and Women*) (59). The kind of collaborative narrative that I am describing in *Friend of My Youth* is similar to, but not identical to, the narrative cooperation that she describes in the earlier books; our views of the impulse behind such narratives also differ somewhat. In a parenthetical remark, Mayberry does mention "Friend of My Youth" as an example of this "new configuration of narrative," but she does not elaborate (64).

10. Munro's rejection of anything like "a traditional plot" has become a basic premise of Munro criticism. See, for example, Mathews.

11. For example, Rose in *Who Do You Think You Are?* and Isabel in "White Dump" in *The Progress of Love*. The situation recurs in the recent stories "The Children Stay" and "Jakarta."

12. McCarthy 1 and Redekop 227 also speak of Almeda as foremother and offer various Canadian examples of this kind of recovery.

13. See McCarthy: "the 'plot' of the story is the project of freeing this imaginative ancestor from the patriarchal stereotype" (4).

14. McCarthy 20; Redekop 255; and Stead 159 all see "wrath" in Almeda's last name, Roth. Perhaps we can also see the Early Middle English "ruth," whose first definition in *The Shorter OED*, is "the quality of being compassionate; pitifulness; compassion, pity."

15. For Redekop, "this body is a parody of Mother Earth" (224).

16. See also Stead 161.

17. In Charlotte Perkins Gilman's *The Yellow Wallpaper*, the heroine obsessively watches movements behind the wallpaper, seeing there a woman behind bars struggling to get out. After "helping" the kindred woman by ripping off wide swaths of the wallpaper, she imaginatively merges with this phantom as she seeks her own escape.

18. More than twenty years ago, Munro wrote of the "short river the Indians called the Menesetung [sic] and the first settlers ... called the Maitland land," which flowed past her father's land. Rising in spring to cover the flats, thus earning the nickname "the Flood," "shallow and tropical" in summer, and filled with myriad varieties of plants and fish, it offered a comprehensive image of the variegated abundance of ordinary experience: "We believed there were deep holes in the river. . . . I am still partly convinced that this river—not even the whole river, but this little stretch of it—will provide whatever myths you want, whatever adventures. I name the plants, I name the fish, and every name seems to me triumphant, every leaf and quick fish remarkably valuable. This ordinary place is sufficient, everything here is touchable and mysterious" (Munro, "Everything").

19. While this scene has rightly been viewed as echoing the end of "The Stone in the Field" in *The Moons of Jupiter*, it may be more instructive to contrast the narrator's passionate "scrabbling" in "Meneseteung" with the narrator's rational decision in "The Stone in the Field" not to bother walking over to the rock pile.

## WORKS CITED

Blodgett, E.D. *Alice Monroe*. Twain's World Authors Series, Canadian Literature. Boston: Twain, 1988.

Carrington, Ildikó de Papp. *Controlling the Uncontrollable: The Fiction of Alice Munro*. DeKalb: Northern Illinois UP, 1989.

Crouse, David. "Resisting Reduction: Closure in Richard Ford's *Rock Springs* and Alice Munro's *Friend of My Youth*." *Canadian Literature* 146 (1995): 51–64.

Gilman, Charlotte Perkins. *The Yellow Wallpaper*. 1892. New York: Feminist, 1973.

Hoy, Helen. "Alice Munro: 'Unforgettable, Indigestible Messages.'" *Journal of Canadian Studies/Revue d'études canadienne* 26.1 (1991): 5–22.

Hutcheon, Linda. *The Canadian Postmodern: A Study of Contemporary English-Canadian Fiction*. Studies in Canadian Literature. Toronto: Oxford UP, 1988.

Irving, Lorna. "Changing Is the Word I Want." MacKendrick 99–112.

MacKendrick, Louis K., ed. *Probable Fictions: Alice Munro's Narrative Acts.* Downsview, ON: ECW, 1983.

Martin, W.R. *Alice Munro: Paradox and Parallel.* Edmonton: U of Alberta P, 1987.

Mathews, Lawrence. "*Who Do You Think You Are?* Alice Munro's Art of Disarrangement." MacKendrick 181–93.

Mayberry, Katherine J. "Narrative Strategies of Liberation in Alice Munro." *Studies in Canadian Literature/Études en littérature canadienne* 19.2 (1994): 57–66.

McCarthy, Dermot. "The Woman Out Back: Alice Munro's 'Meneseteung.'" *Studies in Canadian Literature/Études en littérature canadienne* 19.1 (1994): 1–20.

Munro, Alice. "Alice Munro." *Canadian Writers at Work: Interviews with Geoff Hancock.* Toronto: Oxford UP, 1987. 187–225.

———. "The Children Stay." *New Yorker* 22 and 29 Dec. 1997: 90+. (Rpt. and rev. in Munro, *Love* 181–215.)

———. *Dance of the Happy Shades.* 1968. Toronto: McGraw-Hill, 1988.

———. "Everything Here Is Touchable and Mysterious." Weekend Magazine [supp. to Globe and Mail] 11 May 1974: 33.

———. *Friend of My Youth.* 1990. Toronto: Penguin, 1991.

———. "Jakarta." *Saturday Night* Feb. 1998: 44–60. (Rpt. in Munro, *Love* 79–117.)

———. *The Love of a Good Woman.* Toronto: McClelland, 1998.

———. *The Moons of Jupiter.* 1982. Toronto: Penguin, 1986.

———. *The Progress of Love.* 1986. Toronto: Penguin, 1987.

———. "The Real Material: An Interview with Alice Munro." With J.R. (Tim) Struthers. MacKendrick 5–37.

———. *Something I've Been Meaning to Tell You.* 1974. Toronto: Penguin, 1990.

———. *Who Do You Think You Are?* 1978. Toronto: Penguin, 1991.

Redekop, Magdalene. *Mothers and Other Clowns: The Stories of Alice Munro.* London: Routledge, 1992.

Regan, Stephen. "'The Presence of the Past': Modernism and Postmodernism in Canadian Short Fiction." *Narrative Strategies in Canadian Literature.* Ed. Coral A. Howells and Lynette Hunter. Philadelphia: Open UP, 1991. 108–34.

"Ruth." *The Shorter OED.* 3rd ed. 1973.

Shields, Carol "In Ontario." *London Review of Books* 7 Feb. 1991: 22–23.

Stead, Kit. "The Twinkling of an 'I': Alice Munro's *Friend of My Youth.*" *The Guises of Canadian Diversity/Les Masques de la diversité canadienne.* Ed. Serge Jaumain and Marc Maufort. Amsterdam: Rodopi, 1995. 151–65.

Thacker, Robert. "'So Shocking a Verdict in Real Life': Autobiography in Alice Munro's Stories." *Reflections: Autobiography and Canadian Literature.* Ed. K.P. Stich. Ottawa: U of Ottawa P, 1988. 153–63.

Woolf, Virginia. *A Room of One's Own.* 1929. Ed. Morag Shiach. Oxford: Oxford UP, 1992.

JUDITH McCOMBS

# Searching Bluebeard's Chambers: Grimm, Gothic, and Bible Mysteries in Alice Munro's "The Love of a Good Woman"

Like her 1992 story, "A Wilderness Station," Alice Munro's 1996 "The Love of a Good Woman" is a concealed murder mystery whose luminous, disturbing power emanates in great part from her transformations of Grimm's Bluebeard tales, compounded with other Grimm tales, Gothic romance, and Bible myths. Both stories are masterpieces of Munro's realism, simultaneously archetypal and documentary, revealing people's lives in exact and mythic detail. People's "lives," as she wrote in *Lives of Girls and Women*, are "dull, simple, amazing, and unfathomable—deep caves paved with kitchen linoleum" (210). Both "Wilderness" and "Love" are set in Walley, a small Ontario town whose name suggests a walleye with a skewed or wider vision; in both a brutal Bluebeard murder is revealed in secret by a woman who may be crazed or lying. In both stories elusive clues, illuminations, allusions, and archetypes lure the reader to search the Bluebeard's chambers of storytelling, sex, and death.[1]

"The Love of a Good Woman" opens with an objective yet image-laden and resonant description of things preserved for "the last couple of decades" in the local historical museum of Walley, Ontario; these include a red box of optometrist's implements that once, the label tells us, "belonged to Mr. D. M. Willens, who drowned in the Peregrine River, 1951. It escaped the catastrophe and was found, presumably by the anonymous donor, who dispatched it to be

From *American Review of Canadian Studies* 30, no. 3 (Autumn 2000): 327–48. © 2000 by *American Review of Canadian Studies*.

a feature of our collection" (3). There follows a description of Willens's ophthalmoscope, with its large and small top disks that "could make you think of a
snowman," its lenses and "hole to look through," handle and electric batteries;
then of his retinoscope, with its column from which "a tiny light is supposed to
shine," and its flat glass face that "is a dark sort of mirror. Everything is black,
but that is only paint.... [W]here the optometrist's hand must have rubbed
most often, ... you can see a patch of shiny silver metal" (3–4).

This present-time prologue is both overture and, we will later be able to
see, conclusion to Munro's Bluebeard and Bible mysteries. Here is the clue
that will solve the murder mystery: the red box that "escaped the catastrophe" and was anonymously "dispatched" some twenty years later. Here are the
intimations of a gender and otherwise-transformed Bluebeard tale to come:
the victim, the red chamber-box, the hole he looked through. Here are the
archetypal images from myth and Bible myth that structure Munro's setting and theme. The "snowman" suggested by the ophthalmoscope's disks is a
winter man who will give way to the story's flowerings of spring and summer,
childhood and adulthood; and, simultaneously, the "snowman" warns us of
snow jobs—in the socially accepted story of Willens's drowning, and in the
Bluebeard stories to come.

The "dark sort of mirror" is, as Dennis Duffy has pointed out, St. Paul's
glass through which we now see darkly (183–84; 1 Corinthians 13:12). The
tiny light that "is supposed to shine" evokes Christ's Sermon on the Mount
("Let your light so shine before men, that they may see your good works,"
Matthew 5:16), and the hymn Protestant children are taught to sing ("This
little light of mine, I'm gonna let it shine"). On the level of the murder mystery, the blackness that "is only paint," except where Mr. Willens's hand
rubbed, so that "a patch of shiny silver" can be seen, hints at the sexual rub-
bings that will lead to murder and dark, cover-up paint. On the mythic and
Bible mystery level, the same image intimates that out of our blackness and
rubbing, shining patches of illumination will come, when we learn to see not
darkly but clearly.

* * *

Munro's Bluebeard archetypes come primarily from two Grimm's tales,
"Fitcher's Bird" and "The Robber Bridegroom." The essential Grimm's
characters are three: the Bluebeard serial killer, who compels or lures maidens to his isolated dwelling; the dismembered victim maidens; and the surviving clever bride who by daring, trickery, lies and storytelling saves herself
and ruins Bluebeard.

In "Fitcher's Bird" the Bluebeard is an evil wizard, or fitcher, who with
his magic touch carries off a first sister, then a second, then a third, giving

each in turn an egg to carry always and keep spotless, and a key to a forbidden chamber. Curiosity leads each sister in turn to open the forbidden chamber, where she finds a chopping block and axe, and a bloody basin full of dismembered bodies. Frightened, each of the first two sisters lets her egg slip into the basin; when she cannot wash the telltale blood from the egg, the wizard drags her to the bloody chamber and chops her into pieces. The third, clever sister puts her egg away, explores the forbidden chamber, and heals her two dismembered sisters by gathering and putting in order their severed parts. Tricked by her lies, the wizard loses his power; the clever bride compels him to carry his gold and her sisters home, while she prepares his house for a wedding feast. She places a flower-decked skull in the garret window, and greets the wizard and his friends disguised as a wondrous bird, singing of the young bride: "'From cellar to garret she's swept all clean / And now from the window she's peeping, I ween'" (219–20). When they go inside, her kinsmen lock the doors and burn them all.

In Grimm's "Robber Bridegroom" the clever bride feels "a secret horror" of her rich betrothed, and marks her way to his dark forest house with peas and lentils (200). Exploring all his empty house, she finds a caged bird who sings "'Turn back, turn back, young maiden dear / 'Tis a murderer's house you enter here'" (201). In the cellar an old, old woman warns "you will keep your wedding with death," for the robber bridegroom and his men "are eaters of human flesh" (201). Hidden behind a hogshead by the old woman, the bride sees the cannibal robbers kill and dismember another maiden, whose cut-off finger with a gold ring on it springs "up in the air" and lands in her bosom (202). When the robbers fall asleep, the bride and old woman help each other escape to her father's mill. At the wedding feast, the bride tells as if it were a dream her story of the singing bird, the old woman, the murder, and then the dismembering of the other maiden, following each of these four revelations with the tag line, "My darling, I only dreamt this," and at the climax producing the cut-off finger with its ring (204). So her father's guests send the robber and his crew to execution.

These Grimm's Bluebeard tales, then, are thrilling sex-and-death versions of the archetypal fairy-tale quest, where a young person goes out into the world, is tempted and threatened by evil, and must use courage and trickery to triumph. Other Bluebeard versions may be found in Perrault's "La Barbe bleüe," with its greedier bride and telltale bloodied key to the forbidden chamber, and the English tale of "Mr. Fox" (Opie 133–46). An asexual, childhood version may be found in Grimm's "Hansel and Gretel," with its cannibal witch and clever Gretel, who tricks the witch into the oven and rescues her brother, Hansel. An animal version may be found in "The Three Little Pigs," where a fairy-tale fox gets tricked and boiled by the clever pig, who then rescues his brother and sister; and in the very similar nursery tale, where a wolf eats the two stupid pigs, but is tricked and boiled by the third, clever pig.

Grimm's Bluebeard tales are often read as warnings to women to beware rapacious men and to keep their eggs clean, by remaining virgins or faithful, obedient wives; both "Fitcher's Bird" and "The Robber Bridegroom," however, clearly show the advantages of daring, lying, acting, and storytelling (see Bettelheim 299–303 and Wilson 259–62). And although these tales have been read as sexual polarizations of evil men versus innocent women, in the end good men and clever bride cooperate to destroy the Bluebeard: the bride's kinsmen and her society's executioners have the necessary power; the clever, daring bride has the trickster-hero role. And, in the animal versions as well as the human ones, it is the hungry, devouring Bluebeard, or witch, fox, or wolf who is never portrayed as a victim, only as a villain who has to lose possessions and power, and end up justly burnt or executed, roasted or boiled.

* * *

Although Munro's four main characters are fully made, fully believable inhabitants of her 1951 Huron County, Ontario, their stories rework much older archetypes, in which the dismembered Grimm elements are brought to life again, reversed, and recombined. The two men, Mr. Willens and Rupert Quinn, are each a Bluebeard and a Bluebeard's victim. Rupert's dying wife, Mrs. Quinn, and her home nurse, Enid, are each a victim and a clever bride; Mrs. Quinn is also something of a female Bluebeard or Atwoodian Robber Bride.

We know Mr. D. M. Willens as a drowned victim before we know him as a Bluebeard character; the first two of the story's four sections only hint at his ladykilling ways. A short, hairy, unattractive optometrist in small-town Walley, Mr. Willens is a minor sexual predator who roams the countryside making house calls; sometimes, Mrs. Willens tells the authorities, he gets "held up" overnight (30). The name Willens suggests *will ends, will lens, willing*; the full name, D. M. Willens, may be a rough anagram for *demon*. The D. may hint ironically and pathetically at a first name of David, which means beloved.

Our first glimpses of Mr. Willens come by way of the three young boys who in the spring of 1951, we are told omnisciently, find his body caught in his car in the river, like a muskrat drowned in a trap.[2] They see his arm in its "hairy" sleeve pushing up through the car's open roof panel like a "dark and furry ... big animal tail" (6). That description, a bestial, phallic image, suggests the wolf's tail in children's storybook illustrations for "Little Red Riding Hood."[3] The boys "picture" the Mr. Willens they know as a "grotesque" brassy-haired, caterpillar-eyebrowed "cartoon character," short and thick, large of shoulder and head, who in death as in life seems "crammed into his little [foreign] car as if it was a bursting suit of clothes" (7, 6)—a sort of animal, troll, or cramped giant—or overgrown child. His marriage is childless; Mrs. Willens is a harsh-voiced, androgynously dressed, "lumpy little woman" and a renowned, generous, shear-carrying gardener, whose house-high forsythia seems like a vision of joyous fertility and sexuality from Katherine Mansfield or Virginia Woolf: "it sprayed yellow into the air the way a fountain shoots water" (23).[4]

Enid, the thirty-seven-year-old home nurse who, with her widowed mother, lives next door to the Willenses, knows Mr. Willens as a bridge partner who with "jokey gallantry," offers her chocolates or a pink rose "to make up for his own inadequacies as a partner" (50, 41). Munro's sexual pun is obvious; her subtler pun contrasts the limited romantic possibilities among the Bridges of Huron County with the idealized love affair between a lonely farmwife and a photographer in the American *The Bridges of Madison County*.[5] Whether the Willens marriage is sexless as well as childless, and whether Mrs. Willens knows about his tomcatting, we cannot know: separately and together, the Willenses keep up the appearance of vigorous and reasonably happy lives.

Not until the third section of Munro's story, when on 9 July 1951 the dying Mrs. Quinn tells her home nurse, Enid, what happened in her front room, can we clearly see Mr. Willens's death that spring as no accident, no hushed-up suicide, but a Bluebeard-imaged murder. In Mrs. Quinn's deathbed narrative, Mr. Willens becomes an electrified magic-wand version of Grimm's magic-touch wizard, peering into her eye through the hole in his battery-powered ophthalmoscope while he kneels like a clumsy, off-balance suitor to grope her bare leg. And Mrs. Quinn, like a mesmerized victim bride, cannot stop him because she has "to concentrate on keeping still" (57). This house call (which may have been arranged by telephone) happens at a time when her husband "was supposed to be cutting wood down by the river" (57).

But, almost immediately in Mrs. Quinn's narrative, her groping lady-killer lover becomes a helpless victim, "down before he knew it," bashed to death in a Bluebeard killing chamber (57). Rupert, her husband, sneaks in on the two of them when Mr. Willens's hand was on her bare leg: Rupert jumps on the kneeling Mr. Willens from behind "like a bolt of lightning. . . . Rupert banged his head up and down on the floor, Rupert banged the life out of him" (57). Like the severed gold-ringed finger flying through the air in Grimm's "Robber Bridegroom," everything "flew out of" Mr. Willens's knocked-over box. When Mrs. Quinn turns Mr. Willens over, "to get him right side up," he is dead or near death; his eyes are neither open nor shut, and dribbly "pink stuff," like the froth on boiling-down strawberry jam, "com[es] out of his mouth" (57). Although there is no sign that Mrs. Quinn intends to kill the battered Mr. Willens, it is quite possible that he does literally drown when she turns him over: "he made a sound. . . . *Glug-glug* and he was laid out like a stone" (57–58).

The Willens-Quinn foreplay was "the same game every time" (62), Mrs. Quinn says; that she builds her tale to four Bluebeard–female romance climaxes of helpless female passivity and increasingly rapacious male lust—first Mr. Willens's groping, then his dead foot nudging, then his dribbly kissing, then his battering sexual attack—may echo the four-times repeated passive female disclaimers ("My darling, I only dreamt this" [204]) with which the Grimm storytelling bride exposes the evil Robber Bridegroom.[6] And, in a perverse echo of the Fitcher's bride who brought her dismembered sisters back to life, Mrs. Quinn's tale does bring her battered lover back to lustful, demon-lover life: even dead he was still a "horny old devil," with "his dead old foot" nudging her between the legs as she helps Rupert carry him out (59). Her description of their kissing sounds like an unaroused woman's—or child's—disgust with an impotent or incontinent lover—or with a wolf's or wolf-child's grabbing and devouring: he was a "dribbly," "dirty old brute," "sucking and chewing away at her lips and her tongue and pushing himself up at her and the corner of the [dark red optometrist's] box sticking into her and digging her behind" (60). And each time Mrs. Quinn, "so surprised" and trapped, is helpless as Yeats's high-art Leda with the Swan (60). The symbolically dismembering climax of their Bluebeard coupling was supposed to happen after he'd got "his fingers slicked" inside her and packed up his "looker thing" and she'd asked how much she owed for today? "And that was the signal for him to get her down and thump her like an old billy goat . . . to knock her up and down [on the bare floor] and try to bash her into pieces. Dingey on him like a blowtorch" (62).

Mrs. Quinn's tale, then, like that of her precursor Annie Herron in "A Wilderness Station," is a recognizable but radical transformation of the Grimm Bluebeard tales: Munro's triangle involves one woman and two men, rather than one man and what are essentially two women, the victim and the clever hero; and Munro's essential roles are divided, doubled, shared. Each of the three characters in Mrs. Quinn's killing chamber is some kind of killer and some kind of victim, is basher and bashed and, with genders transcended, some kind of Bluebeard and dismembered or clever maiden. Rupert, after "bang[ing] the life out of Mr. Willens, goes to pieces mentally (57). Shocked and incoherent, he puts Mrs. Quinn"; knocked-over chair right side up, then just sits there; then jumps up, and tries to fit "everything in right" in Mr. Willens's knocked-over red-plush-lined optometrist's box (58). Acting like the hapless Fitcher's brides who cannot wash the red blood from their eggs, and also like the clever bride who puts their dismembered parts in order, Rupert puts things right, and yet cannot put things right. Like a thwarted, overgrown child, he sits bashing himself, "pounding on his knees" and "banging his big flat hands" (58).

It is Mrs. Quinn who, like the clever bride healing her sisters, or the practical Lady Macbeth standing by her man, puts the incoherent killer back together—once she sees that he is not going to attack her. Munro has indicated that what fascinated her in the true murder story that stands behind "Love" is the "sudden switch from sex to murder to marital cooperation . . . one of those marvelous, unlikely, acrobatic pieces of human behavior" ("Contributors'" 443). If we read again slowly, and go beneath the overriding rhythms of Mrs. Quinn's salacious murder tale, we can see how the "sudden switch" begins nonverbally, in what child psychologists call parallel play: he jumps on Mr. Willens, she jumps up from the chair, knocking it over. He sets the chair right side up, she gets Mr. Willens "right side up" (a position which may finish what her husband started in killing Mr. Willens) (57).[7] Rupert then sits in the chair where his wife had sat, jumps up as she did, sits again, and pounds himself. Then, trying to spare them both, she covers up Mr. Willens's bloodied head with a tablecloth.

Soon the couple switch into step-by-step, verbal, complementary cooperation: she says to bury him and suggests where, he asks where can they bury his car; she "thought of him sitting in his car" in the river, he "thought up the rest of what to do" (58–59). She gets the keys to the car from the still-warm body and gives them to Rupert; together they carry out the body. Then, honoring the traditional female-indoors and male-outdoors division of labor, she cleans up inside while he drives Mr. Willens's car and body to a nearby little-used road that dead-ends at the river, and pushes them in. Rupert walks back home and tells his wife he did the job in his sock feet, to avoid leaving identifiable tracks; she tells him he "must have got [his] brains going again" (61). Both husband and wife, however, are more shaken than they realize, for both leave the telltale dark-red, red-plush-lined box out in plain sight on the front room table, like the Grimm's telltale bloodied egg; Mrs. Quinn finally sees it, many days after the murder, and hides it, in one place and then another; she will not tell where.

Like a Fitcher's victim bride or a Lady Macbeth, Mrs. Quinn tries to erase the telltale blood stains: she scrubs her shoes and the stained floor of the front room and burns the bloodied cloth with which she had covered Mr. Willens's smeared face; she burns her own front-smeared blouse; she paints over the still-stained front-room floor with leftover ugly brown paint. Then, like the Grimm's victims and Lady Macbeth, she goes to pieces: it was the smells of the burning cloth and of the paint that began her fatal sickness, she tells Enid. But, as we can infer from an earlier section of Munro's story, it is more likely that Mrs. Quinn is dying of kidney failure because, as Rupert's nosey, righteous sister suspects, Mrs. Quinn took pills to abort a fetus—probably, as Dennis Duffy has argued, Mrs. Quinn thought the fetus was Willens's child (182).[8] This aborted fetus would be a literal equivalent of Grimm's dirtied, bloodied egg.

* * *

Part of the disturbing power of Mrs. Quinn's salacious Bluebeard murder story is that it is formed from, and brings to shocking life the Grimm and Gothic elements in what we already know from the second section of Munro's story. Rupert Quinn is a big, shy, hardworking farmer. About thirty-seven now, he apparently married late, and "never had any kind of girlfriend before" he met a pretty, fair-haired, green-eyed girl who said she was an orphan from Montreal (33). Rupert was then working alone in the bush up north, and she was working as a chambermaid or something in a hotel, Rupert's sister tells Enid. As a young schoolboy, Rupert had been romantically "teased and tormented" by Enid and her girlfriends, who mocked his name to make him blush (33); later, as bright, studious seniors, Enid and Rupert had formed a shy, tenuous friendship. The name Rupert suggests both rube and the seventeenth-century hero/exile Prince Rupert, nephew to Charles of England and third son of an exiled Bohemian king, who became a Royalist cavalry leader known for his fiery charges, a general, an exile, an admiral—and the first governor of the Hudson's Bay Company. Rupert now keeps some distance from his dying wife. Though he seems concerned he also seems wary, paying her brief, late visits; he sleeps and eats at his sister's, who arranged this ostensibly to spare Enid, and he has to work later and later in the fields to save the rain-threatened crops that have ripened weeks early in the summer's heat wave. Some evenings, while his dying, drugged wife sleeps in the front room, Rupert sits quietly with Enid in the kitchen, sharing the newspaper's headlines and crossword puzzle, much as the two had shared schoolwork in their senior year. As Duffy points out, the two are already "cohabiting" like an "old married couple" (176–75).

Should Rupert be seen as a Bluebeard who brought a young orphan to his lonely farmhouse, then trapped her in the chambers of murder and abortion? And now, as she lies dying in the next room, quietly courts a replacement bride? Shy, wary Rupert is subtly but repeatedly associated with woodsmanship, chopping, and hatchets—in the bush up north, supposedly chopping wood the morning of Mr. Willens's visit, volunteering to cut back the berry canes from the road. Is Rupert a bride-dismembering Bluebeard? Or a rescuing huntsman who came out of the woods to save his Little Red Riding

Hood, first from orphanhood and later from a "wolf," Willens? A Prince-in-exile, who would hack through the thorns of the "Sleeping Beauty" story that Enid reads his daughters, to bring love to a lonely orphan or an unawakened, virginal nurse? For us and for Enid, the archetypes arouse possibilities of death and desire, making shy Rupert a demon lover and Gothic hero/villain who might, like Brontë's Mr. Rochester, be hero, or villain, or victim of a bad, mad wife.

Throughout Munro's story, what we are told of Rupert and Mrs. Quinn is limited to and colored by what Enid sees, hears, and thinks, as selected, arranged, and reported by Munro's Joycean omniscient-subjective narrator, who shows us only Enid's thoughts. What Enid knows of Mrs. Quinn begins with suspicion, and soon gets worse. A green-eyed, once-pretty young woman, the dying Mrs. Quinn claims to be twenty-seven, though Enid would have thought her older. Rupert's sister, the childless Mrs. Olive Green, who covets the Quinn children and who Enid sees as bent on "sniffing out rampant impurity" (38), doubts Mrs. Quinn's Montreal-orphanage story and says she wrecked her kidneys by taking pills "for a bad purpose"—that is, an abortion (32). We learn Mrs. Quinn's first name only after her death, when Enid notes that it is Jeannette, which sounds French-Canadian. Munro's story may seem merely to follow Enid's professional courtesy in referring to her patient as Mrs. Quinn; but the surname pairs Mrs. Quinn and Mr. Willens as unknowable, death-bound, corrupt Gothic elders, in opposition to the younger-seeming, nascent couple, Enid and Rupert. This effect must be deliberate, as it takes some maneuvering to have Rupert never once use his wife's name.

In this story called "The Love of a Good Woman," the good nurse Enid sees Mrs. Quinn as a disturbingly bad and unloving woman. Poisoned and deformed by the wastes of her own body, suffering pain and torment, scarcely able to eat or drink or keep warm, often unable to bear light or sound, Mrs. Quinn resents her husband, her children, and Enid. She mocks Rupert's brief, late visits, complaining to Enid that he, Enid, and everyone think her better dead, and that he goes to other women after seeing her. When Enid says that as far as she knows, Rupert goes to his sister's house after his visit, Mrs. Quinn throws the words back at her: "As far as you know. But you don't know much'" (36). She seems to Enid to be "without shame" in her vulgar sexual talk and in opening her legs to be washed (35). She doesn't want to see her seven- and six-year-old daughters, whom she has raised "wild as little barn cats," without manners or prayers (34). Her housekeeping is filthy and without order. She rejects Enid's offer of a minister or priest—"Do I look like a Mick?'" with a slur that calls to mind Rupert's and his sister's round, snub-nosed, "'potato-Irish'" faces (54, 32). When Rupert comes early to visit his wife, because he will be away for two days at a stock auction, with the doctor's approval, eavesdropping Enid hears "Mrs. Quinn weakly laughing," and hears—or mishears—a vileness in that laughing, and then sees a shocked-looking Rupert come out of her room (56).

Enid, the thirty-seven-year-old home nurse who was Rupert's classmate, finds herself losing a contest of wills with this "doomed, miserable young woman" who seems filled with "spite and venom" (38, 36). Enid has been a compassionate, dedicated, hardworking, self-sacrificing home nurse for sixteen years, since she was twenty-one; she chose this calling as a way "to be good, and do good," but "not necessarily in the orderly, customary, wifely way" (41)—and to honor her father's dying wish that she foreswear hospital work, which he thought would be sexually coarsening. Celibate, or perhaps androgynous, Enid is known among patients and doctors as an "angel of mercy" (52), a gentle, generous female healer who spends most of her earnings on needy patients' children. Her name, Enid, is almost an anagram of deny; her namesake, "Enid the Good" in Tennyson's *Idylls of the King* (Book 4, line 963), is an exemplary long-suffering good woman whose love redeems her unjust and cruelly mistrustful husband.[9]

Against Mrs. Quinn's vulgar sexuality, her bitter mockery, her repudiations of conventional comfort, Enid feels her goodness and vocation fail. Reproaching herself, but increasingly unable to "conquer her dislike of this doomed, miserable young woman," Enid sees "a willed corruption" in Mrs. Quinn's diseased body, sees its nipples as "malignant-looking" and its teeth as "pathetic [and] ferretlike" (38). Worse still, Enid senses that Mrs. Quinn knows her revulsion, and "made knowing it her triumph" (39). Though naïve, repressed Enid consciously "didn't know why this was happening" (38), her shocked revulsion involves not only righteousness and prudery, but also sexual rivalry with Mrs. Quinn—as Munro's puns and juxtapositions make clear. Enid offers Rupert capable fuse-changing and calm candlelight against Mrs. Quinn's darkened room and weak, shocking laughter; mannerly Christian mothering of his children and orderly housekeeping against neglect, disorder, and filth; companionably shared crossword puzzles against cross, mocking words. The scene where Rupert gives Enid crossword clues of exotic foods— "'Manioc?'" "'Cassava?'" is immediately juxtaposed with Enid seeing Mrs. Quinn as "more capricious daily about her food," because the dying woman asks for but cannot eat simple foods when Enid has prepared them (48–49).

Beneath Mrs. Quinn's sufferings and mockery, and Enid's revulsion, are the Grimm Bluebeard patterns of a young orphan carried off by an older, foreign man to a lonely farmhouse where, her egg bloodied by a second man who is an ophthalmoscope-wielding wizard, she sickens and lies dying. Friendless and luckless as the substitute victim-bride in Grimm's "Robber Bridegroom," Mrs. Quinn is not healed by any stronger sister: instead, her husband's sister, like a bad Queen Mother, snoops around, keeps the Prince at her house, and plots to carry off the children; while Enid the good healer and Sleeping Beauty/self-imprisoned Rapunzel becomes a Grimm True Bride bent on reclaiming her first, tenuous bond with Rupert, and ministers to the dying first, False Bride with increasing hostility.[10]

Underneath the Grimm True Bride/False Bride struggle, and the *Jane Eyre* female Gothic mad wife story is, of course, an Electral story: a primal triangle of a good, strong daughter supplanting a bad, worn-out mother, and claiming the father for herself. Enid may be older than Mrs. Quinn, but Enid is fresh, full-breasted, virginal, and childlike; Mrs. Quinn is diseased and finished, her abdomen "swollen," her breasts shrunk to "malignant-looking," "dried-currant nipples" (35, 38). Under the Grimm and Gothic stories there is also, here and elsewhere in Munro, the story of a daughter's anger, fear, and desertion of a sick, pregnant, or dying mother: see especially the autobiographical "The Peace of Utrecht," with the sisters' guilty rejection and resentment of "Our Gothic Mother" dying in a back room (200); and "Images," the early Bluebeard story that is the first sketch and germinal core of "Love's" essential Grimm and Gothic elements.

Sleeping on a couch in her patient's room, hearing Mrs. Quinn's "harsh and angry breathing," Enid wakes from shameful dreams of herself "trying to copulate with utterly forbidden and unthinkable partners"—babies, bandaged patients, "her own mother" (50–51). These dreams are obscene versions of Enid's daylit life where, honoring her father's deathbed wish, she meets only such partners: she washes Mrs. Quinn's exposed genitals, "do[es] without a man," and "tak[es] her father's place" in bridge games with her widowed mother and the Willenses (34, 41). In these dreams Enid's life is both corrupted and awakened by Mrs. Quinn's shameless, vulgar sexuality—and by Enid's own consciously denied attraction to Rupert. Afraid to sleep, Enid tries reason and religion, but her "hopeful and sensible" Protestant faith gives way to the cynical despair she hears from Mrs. Quinn: life's loveliness seems to lead to "animal horrors," and Enid's dedicated goodness seems despised foolishness (51–52). Seeking "to be penitent," Enid finds a female Protestant way; she gets up and works quietly "through the night," cleaning and restoring to order the filthy kitchen cupboards, trying to save the neglected "good house" (52–53).

In these dreams, as in the parts of Mrs. Quinn's subsequent Bluebeard story that cunningly amplify Enid's own thoughts of the shocked Rupert and the gallant Mr. Willens, the dying woman's sexuality, anger, and despair invade Enid's conscious and unconscious mind; as Coral Ann Howells says, Mrs. Quinn "becomes Enid's dark mirror" (152). It is as if the two women were secret sharers—or as if Jane Eyre were made the sister's keeper of Sandra M. Gilbert and Susan Gubar's Madwoman in the Attic, forced to sleep in her chamber, dream her vileness, wake to her despair. Or as if Mrs. Quinn were a trapped, amateur version of Margaret Atwood's Grimm-based Robber Bride, a malicious storyteller who preys on lonely, repressed good women, evoking their sexual and forbidden shadow sides; and Enid a professional version of Atwood's gentle would-be healer, Charis.[11]

\* \* \*

The fourth and final section of Munro's story shows us, in evocative and tantalizingly cryptic flashes of illumination, the Grimm, Gothic, and Bible-imaged crises through which Enid passes in the three sleepless nights and days after she hears Mrs. Quinn's shocking Bluebeard story—interior crises, known only to Enid and us, that determine the course of her and Rupert's lives, love, and salvation.[12] Troubled and unsure after the first sleepless night, Enid, in a scene that replays Rochester's resolution scene in *Jane Eyre*,[13] goes out into the "sopping wet" meadow and along a "clear" path to see the mist-hidden river, where a tied-up rowboat that the current "lifted and let fall" seems to tell her "something gentle and final. You know. You know" (63–64). What Enid knows is "What had happened"—but did it happen?—and "What to do about it" (63)—but are these statements clues, or further mysteries? How can we know?

Secretly resolved, Enid sets to work like a Grimm's True Bride sup-planting a ugly, luckless False Bride: knowing Mrs. Quinn will die after that "last" "wicked outpouring," Enid in "bountiful good spirits" lets her own "hair loose," suns her bare legs, and makes for the children special treats and memorable "holiday" games. While Mrs. Quinn's shrunken kidneys fail, Enid the good fairy godmother shows the children how to make, from bent-wire "bubble-wands" and soapsuds, "as large a shining bladder as possible." When the children scream with joy as they chase the shining bubbles, nurse Enid, who knows their mother's sensitivity to noise, "put[s] no restriction on the[ir] noise." Wanting the children to see the outcome of her plan, and "herself," "in a redeeming light"—but deciding that "nothing good" can come of their seeing their mother—Enid teaches them that you must always tell and "'be punished'" if you do a very bad thing, even if nobody knows, because if "'you are not punished you feel worse'" (64–66).

Insofar as she deems proper, Enid abandons her patient, "never sp[eaking] to her and never touching her hand, except with the cloth" (66).[14] Mrs. Quinn dies alone, her head "hanging over the side of the bed"; Enid gets "the body straightened out . . . and the bed put to rights before the doctor" comes (67). Like her partner the drowned Mr. Willens, whose furry and hairy-looking arm "got free" of the car (7), Mrs. Quinn has gone beyond propriety in death as in life: and Enid believes in putting things right.

Two days later Enid, resolved like Jane Eyre on Christian romantic sacrifice ("'your heart shall be the victim; and you, the priest, to transfix it'"),
and rapt like Saul in a blinding vision followed by three sleepless, fasting
days, returns to Rupert (Brontë 341; Acts 9:3–9). The funeral is over, Rupert's
childless sister has taken the children away, and Rupert comes to the door
with the "heavy, steady footsteps" of an unreadable hero/villain (69). Suddenly
awkward, Enid twice avoids "look[ing] into his face"; he seems "bewilder[ed]"
by her visit (69–70) until she takes refuge in talking about the shortening
days. Enid has transformed herself—powdered her face, French-braided her
hair, and dressed in what might be "the last clothes she would ever wear"
(70), dark green silk and matching green suede shoes. Green suggests her
naïveté and her fertility, in contrast to Mrs. Quinn's diseased browns and
blood-smeared reds; but green also links Enid to Rupert's other women—his
green-eyed wife, his sister Mrs. Green.

Seated at the table across from Rupert, facing Mrs. Quinn's shut door,
Enid almost forgets her secret mission. Enid has planned—we learn only
now—to risk her life to redeem Rupert: she will get him to row her out in the
river, ostensibly so she can get a picture of the willows; then tell him she cannot
swim, which is true; then ask him if Mrs. Quinn's story is true. If Rupert does
not deny the story, or drown her, as he could easily do, Enid will guide him,
"one step at a time," on the long journey of confession and jail, trial and punishment, with a pure, sexless, selfless "devotion . . . that is like love but beyond love"
(73). Is naïve, reckless, devoted Enid bound for redemption or death?[15]

Now, when she asks to be rowed out, Rupert says "'All right.'" But
Enid, distracted by Rupert's treating her as country people treat a visitor,
"foolish[ly]" asks a housewife's question—have the quilts been taken down
from the front windows? (73). Rupert offers to show her the room: "'It's all
right,'" Rupert says, "'Come in'" (73). The room is empty of bed and coffin;
the table that may have held Mr. Willens's dark-red box, that did hold Enid's
supplies, holds only flowers now; the tall windows are filled with light.

Rupert is silent; but Enid hears, "out of all the words that Mrs. Quinn
said in that room," the word "Lies"; and Enid asks herself whether such a
"detailed and diabolical" story could have been made up (74). Remembering
her own filthy, elaborate dreams in that haunted chamber, Enid answers, "yes"
(74). Then Rupert, the front room, lies and dreams call up the childhood
memory that will change Enid's life in an inner drama that Carrington calls
"the story's central act of moral acrobatics," more central than the Quinns'
switch from sex and murder to cooperation (168).

Once, when Enid was four or five, so young that she did not know the
word for breasts, and called them fronts, Enid saw her father "behind his
desk with a woman on his knee," her clothing unbuttoned, the tip of her

bare breast "disappearing into Enid's father's mouth." Enid told her mother that "'One of her fronts was stuck in Daddy's mouth. . . . Like an ice-cream cone.'" The grown-up Enid can still see what she saw as a child, the "mound of vanilla ice cream squashed against the woman's chest and the wrong end sticking into her father's mouth." Enid's mother had pulled out her own dull, floppy breast to persuade Enid that it was all a silly dream, too silly to tell Daddy; and Enid as a child came to believe her mother, because ice-cream cones "were never so big" (74–75).

Now the scales fall from Enid's eyes, as they did from Saul's (Acts 9:18), and she sees clearly that the remembered scene is no childish dream, but a shocking truth: her father was toying with a woman, was nursing for sexual pleasure in an adulterous dalliance. Celibate, self-sacrificing Enid, with her "big udders," has nursed home patients instead of ever nursing a baby with her milk, or nursing a man for pleasure (36). But now it is as if a fairy-tale curse had been lifted, and Enid is freed, by seeing clearly her father's sexual coarseness and her mother's silencing complicity, from the "deathbed prom- ise" her father had exacted: Enid had given up her almost-completed nurse's training, and the hospital career and wider life that would have followed, because her father thought that "the familiarity [hospital] nurses had with men's bodies" would make a woman sexually "coarse" (40, 39).

Freed also from her mother-judging pride and her reliance on good works alone, the self-denying "angel of mercy" Enid opens her heart to a Joy- cean, human charity (52; cf. 1 Corinthians 13, Tindall 32) as she sees clearly now "an entirely different possibility" for her life: if she keeps silent about the murder, if she "collaborat[es] in a silence, what benefits could bloom. For others, and for herself" (75–76). The protagonist of Joyce's "A Painful Case," reseeing his life, saw too late that "venal and furtive loves" were love, and that his solitary righteous life made him an "outcast from life's feast" (*Dubliners* 146). But Enid sees in time to recant, inwardly, the "melodramatic fate" in which she had been inwardly "glorying" (76, 75).[16] She weeps with relief, and thinks she sees that Rupert too has wept.

"'I don't know what I was thinking of,'" she tells Rupert; "'I can't walk down to the river in these shoes'" (76). Rupert, reenacting the Cinderella shoe-test, finds in an old storage bin a pair of discarded boots for Enid to wear—not Mrs. Quinn's, which would be too small for Enid's big feet. When Rupert sets the boots before her, the freed Enid is aroused by his smell, and welcomes "something new and invasive about the smell of a body so distinctly not in her power or under her care" (77). But Enid, like the Grimm and Perrault Bluebeard brides and Jane Eyre, is also powerfully aroused by the prospect of hidden chambers: Rupert's neglected house "would have plenty of bins, drawers, shelves, suitcases, trunks, crawl spaces full of things that it would be up to Enid to sort out," to save and label, restore or send to the dump (77). Enid has taken Mrs. Quinn's bait: if there is a hidden, dark-red chamber in some hidden chamber, Enid will find it. Like a victorious True Bride or a Fitcher's Bride ("'From cellar to garret she's swept all clean'"), Enid will make this house into her realm, "a place that had no secrets from her and where all order was as she had decreed" (Grimm 219, "Love" 77).

"'See can you walk,'" says Rupert, and Enid can. Walking in what may be his boyhood boots, Enid follows Rupert into the cows' meadow as he chops at "the big fleshy thistles" with his hatchet, "to clear their path" (77). Sleeping Beauty/Rapunzel/Little Red Riding Hood Enid, compelled now by a vision of a different, secretly collaborative redemption, thinks that her earlier despair "had to seem childish to her now" (77). But is hero/villain Rupert the rescuing woodsman-Prince, and the agrarian Adam to this secretly knowing Eve—or the dangerous "bolt of lightning" killer (57) of his wife's Bluebeard story?

Following Rupert and his hatchet, Enid moves through clear, sunlit air and through clouds of bugs "no bigger than specks of dust . . . yet . . . together in the shape of a pillar or a cloud," as if she were moving towards a divinely Promised Land (78; Exodus 13.21). The "almost night" of the path under trees holds wild, post-Edenic, Darwinian obstacles of swelling roots and dangling vines; but opens into the "flash of water," "the trees still decked with light," and the oracular rowboat she had seen before, that holds her fate, still "riding in the shadows, just the same" (78).

Enid soon loses sight and sound of Rupert when he goes into the willow bushes to find the hidden oars. Alone, Enid goes "to the water's edge, where her boots sank into the mud a little and held her" (78)—compare Jane Eyre who, after discovering Rochester's secret lies, despaired: "'the waters came into my soul; I sank in deep mire; I felt no standing'" (340; Psalm 69, 1–2). Enid is about to submit herself to Conrad's "'destructive element,'" but she cannot rely on "'the exertions of [her] hands and feet'" to make the depths keep her up (*Lord Jim* 214)—she cannot swim. In the story's final lines, Enid can still hear Rupert if she tries, but like the bride-to-be at the end of Joyce's "Boarding House," Enid is at the fateful moment more tempted by reverie than reality: if she concentrates on the boat's "slight and secretive motion, she [can] feel as if everything for a long way around had gone quiet" (*Dubliners* 84; "Love" 78). Rupert remains hidden and unknown, to Enid and to us; and inwardly questing Enid has slipped once more into a secret vision that opens her to love, or to death.

* * *

We can know what happened in the murder chamber and thereafter only by returning to the prologue and considering the dark-red optometrist's box of

Mr. D. M. Willens, that "escaped the catastrophe" of his 1951 drowning, and was found and anonymously dispatched to the local historical museum in Walley, which opened "a couple of decades" ago, in the 1970s (3). That the optometrist's dark-red box "escaped the catastrophe" surely means that it escaped undamaged—not battered, not stained, not water-marked or mud-died as it would have been if it had gone into the river with Mr. Willens and his car in the spring of 1951.[17] "For the last couple of decades" the dark-red box has been a silent witness, like the severed finger or the bloodied egg of the Grimm Bluebeard tales, to the truth of Mrs. Quinn's story.

Enid did survive to marry Rupert, then, and to search in all his hidden chambers till she found the dark-red telltale box where Mrs. Quinn had hid it. (And, let's face it, being married to shy, "withholding" Rupert would be much enlivened by the dangerous mystery of his Bluebeard, hero/villain past [32].) Then, like the first Mrs. Quinn, Enid neither threw the dark-red box into the river nor sent it to the dump: she kept it, "sav[ed] and labell[ed]" as she "decreed" (77). Perhaps Enid waited until Rupert died; perhaps until Mrs. Willens died. Or perhaps she waited only until there was a right place to put the saved red box—in the new museum in Walley.

## Notes

An earlier version of this paper was presented at the ACSUS convention, Pittsburgh, PA, 17–21 November 1999.

1. I am indebted to Ildikó de Papp Carrington's authoritative explication of Munro's intensities, allusions, metaphors, "documentary realism," splits and "seismic shifts," in the 1989 *Controlling the Uncontrollable*, quoted page 4. For walleye, see Carrington, "Double-Talking" 78–79, 87.

2. Just before they find Mr. Willens, Cece Ferns and the two other boys talk of trapping muskrats; when they peer hard to see Mr. Willens's pale, drowned hand riding "tremulously and irresolutely, like a feather" in the water (7), that image reworks what the child narrator of Munro's early Bluebeard story, "Images," saw when she peered hard at the drowned muskrat "waving at the edge of the water, like . . . a dark fern" in her father's trap (36). Thus, sees fern becomes Cece Ferns.

In character, setting, archetypal images, and themes, Munro's 1968 story "Images" is prototype for the 1996 "The Love of a Good Woman." The child narrator of "Images," who learns in flashes something of the adult mysteries of birth and death, sex and violence, who treasures the electrifying thrill of a longed-for Blue-beard terror coming true, and then kept secret, prefigures the childlike home nurse who is the protagonist of "Love," Enid, as well as the three boys hesitating between childhood and adulthood. The vulgar, bossy home nurse of "Images" prefigures both the foul-mouthed Mrs. Quinn and the take-charge nurse Enid. The bedrid-den, unwelcoming, pregnancy-swollen mother of "Images," and the grandfather who lies dying in the dark and stifling-hot front room while she awaits the birth, pre-figure the swollen, dying Mrs. Quinn in her dark, hot, blood-haunted front room. Both the muskrat-killing, secret-keeping father, and the semi-crazed man with the hatchet who comes through the riverbank bushes towards him, prefigure the wary, withholding, hatchet-bearing Rupert. In addition, James Joyce's story from *Dubliners*, "An Encounter," where young boys encounter adult lust and brutality, stands behind Munro's "Images" and is reworked in the boys' section of "Love"; but Munro, unlike Joyce, uses Bluebeard themes in both stories. J.R. (Tim) Struthers and Walter Martin have each discussed Munro's connections to Joyce.

3. See, for example, the wolf of Little Red Riding Hood, whose furry tail protrudes from his human clothes, in Zipes 248–49, 252–53, illustrations by Walter Crane 1870, unknown n.d., John B. Gruelle 1914, and for Encyclopedia Britannica Films, Inc. 1968; the 1870 Crane wolf is reproduced as the cover of the Opies's *Classic Fairy Tales*. In the Grimm's "Little Red-Cap," after the familiar story where the girl and her grandmother are saved from the wolf's belly by the huntsman, and the wolf dies with stones in his belly, there is another, shorter version, where grandmother and granddaughter cooperate to trick a second greedy wolf into falling into the grandmother's great trough, where he, like Mr. Willens, "was drowned" (143).

4. The tall, quivering, blossoming pear tree in Katherine Mansfield's 1918 "Bliss" helps awaken a childlike young woman to her own bisexual desires. Mrs. Ramsay, in Virginia Woolf's 1927 *To the Lighthouse*, "pour[s] erect into the air a rain of energy, a column of spray [ . . . that is a male-nourishing, deliciously fecund] fountain and spray of life" (58); see Annis Pratt's explication of Mrs. Ramsay's nurturing, androgynous eroticism, 144–46. Munro's story is also about awakening sexuality, in the boys, Rupert, and her protagonist Enid; Enid's awakening and shameful, lustful dreams will be in part androgynous.

5. In "Save the Reaper," which is the fourth story in Munro's *Love of a Good Woman*, the temporarily reunited mother and daughter watch a videotape of *The Bridges of Madison County*; its simpler true-love story contrasts with their divided and unfulfilled yearnings (149).

6. Carrington, however, finds Mrs. Quinn's narrative unreliable, because her passivity is unconvincing and because Mr. Willens's lust changes and gets worse in each of the four times Mrs. Quinn tells it ("'Don't Tell'" 165). I agree that Mrs. Quinn is boasting to the naïve Enid, but I find that Mrs. Quinn's passive disclaimers and four increasingly salacious climaxes serve her storytelling purposes—to increase the shock, thrill, and horror.

7. In Munro's 1996 *New Yorker* story, Rupert "set the chair right side up" (130); in Munro's 1998 book version, Rupert "set the chair up" (57).

8. Mrs. Quinn's taking abortifacient pills, as Rupert's hostile sister suspects, is the only sufficient cause of her fatal illness mentioned in the story. The medically knowledgeable Enid avoids confirming the sister's suspicions, but does not contradict them. While it is true that the unmaternal Mrs. Quinn might not want more children, she would have a much stronger motive to abort a child fathered by the short, dark, hairy Mr. Willens, who looks quite unlike her tall, light-skinned husband.

9. Another namesake, Robert Thacker has suggested to me in conversation, is the sexually-repressed Enid Royce in Willa Cather's *One of Ours*. Thacker has discussed Munro's use of Cather's fiction.

10. For the Rapunzel syndrome, in which a woman imprisons herself in internalized walls, see Atwood's *Survival* 209–10. The best known of Grimm's True Bride versus False Bride tales is "Cinderella"; "The Robber Bridegroom" can also be read as a True versus False or substituted Bride. Grimm's less-known "Maid Maleen" is closest to Munro's story: there, after seven years in a Rapunzel tower, a

loving maiden reclaims her curiously forgetful Prince from the ugly false bride in his bed. Grimm's "Brother and Sister," "The Three Little Men in the Wood," "The Goose-Girl," "The White Bride and the Black Bride," and "The True Bride" are also True versus False Bride tales.

11. Designed as a vampirish female equivalent of the Grimm cannibal robber bridegrooms, Atwood's modern Robber Bride, Zenia, is a con-artist predator who delights in wrecking the lives of good women, by gaining their trust and friendship, then stealing their goods and men. Like Atwood's Robber Bride, Mrs. Quinn is a foreigner of suspect, unverified origins, an openly sexual and defiant woman, and a gifted storyteller. Munro's sickroom struggle between Good Enid and Evil Mrs. Quinn strikingly reworks Atwood's duels between Zenia and the gentle Charis, who has repressed her abused, dangerous childhood self and renamed herself after 1 Corinthians 13.13, *charity* (*Robber Bride* 303). Charis tries and fails to heal the cynical, lying, supposedly dying Zenia; but false Zenia does awaken true Sleeping Beauty/Rapunzel Charis to orgasm and conception. Munro's story reverses Atwood's True Bride/manstealing False Bride romance to have the bad storyteller's man quietly drifting towards the good Sleeping Beauty. The creative and competitive metamorphoses between Munro's and Atwood's Muses go back decades, and at times involve Bluebeard elements (McCombs 1997, 1999).

12. As Robert Thacker has pointed out, Mrs. Quinn dies on Munro's birthday, 10 July (conversation). The autobiographical link would seem to be that Enid's rebirth, which involves her abandoning a diseased and dying mother, begins on that date (62–67).

13. Like Rochester walking in his "'dripping'" "'wet garden'" after a desperate night of his wife's maniac curses, gazing at blue water and "'clear prospects'" while the voice of Hope tells him he can leave his dishonorable wife, and have her cared for in secret, and be free to form a new tie (354), Enid in the wet meadow sees a "clear" path that, we later learn, parallels Rochester's: apparently the first wife's "wicked outpouring talk" justifies Enid secretly "absent[ing] herself," insofar as proper, from that wife's care, and seeking a new bond (63–64, 66).

14. In Munro's earlier "A Wilderness Station," the main character, Annie Herron, similarly withholds touch from her brutal, dead Bluebeard husband: as she washes his body she keeps "the rag between my hand and his skin" (208).

15. As Carrington points out, Enid's camera-boat-drowning scenario resembles the camera-drowning-murder scenario in Dreiser's 1925 *An American Tragedy* ("'Don't Tell'" 159–60, 166). A less similar drowning test of love, between two lovers who have murdered the wife's husband, occurs near the end of Tay Garnett's 1946 film, *The Postman Always Rings Twice*: there the widow persuades her lover to swim out with her to the point where she cannot get back without his help; proving his love, he helps her back. As Howells points out, *Postman* is a possible source of Mrs. Quinn's story (151–52). If Munro saw the film, she would have been quite interested in the lightning-like depiction of the short circuit that coincidentally strikes just as the adulterous, murder-minded wife hits her unsuspecting husband on the head.

16. Compare Jane Eyre's secret heroism as she confronts the dangerously angered Rochester: "I felt an inward power, a sense of resolution, which supported me. The crisis was perilous; but not without its charm: such as the Indian, perhaps, feels when he slips over the rapids in his canoe" (347).

17. Though I am indebted to Carrington's admirable explication of Enid's childhood memory, and much else, I cannot agree that Mr. Willens's box could

have gone into the river and been washed up—or that Cece Ferns, whose hideaway cannot even keep cardboard safe over the winter, could have been hiding it there for years and years (see "Love" 3, 30; Carrington 168–69).

## WORKS CITED

Atwood, Margaret. *The Robber Bride*. Toronto: McClelland and Stewart, 1993.

———. *Survival: A Thematic Guide to Canadian Literature*. Toronto: Anansi, 1972.

Bettelheim, Bruno. *The Uses of Enchantment: The Meaning and Importance of Fairy Tales*. New York: Vintage, 1977.

*The Bridges of Madison County*. Dir. Clint Eastwood. 1995.

Brontë, Charlotte. *Jane Eyre*. 1847. Ed. Michael Hulse. Köln, Ger.: Könemann, 1997.

Carrington, Ildikó de Papp. *Controlling the Uncontrollable: The Fiction of Alice Munro*. DeKalb: Northern Illinois University Press, 1989.

———. "'Don't Tell (on) Daddy': Narrative Complexity in Alice Munro's 'The Love of a Good Woman.'" *Studies in Short Fiction* 34 (1997): 159–70.

———. "Double-Talking Devils: Alice Munro's 'A Wilderness Station.'" *Essays on Canadian Writing* 58 (1996): 71–92.

*The Complete Grimm's Fairy Tales*. Trans. Margaret Hunt; rev. James Stern. New York: Pantheon, 1944.

Conrad, Joseph. *Lord Jim*. 1900. Ed. John Batchelor. Oxford: Oxford University Press, 1983.

———. "The Secret Sharer." 1912. *The Portable Conrad*. Ed. Morton Dauwen Zabel. New York: Viking, 1947. 648–99.

Dreiser, Theodore. *An American Tragedy*. 1925. New York: Signet, 1994

Duffy, Dennis. "'A Dark Sort of Mirror': 'The Love of a Good Woman' as Pauline Poetic." *The Rest of the Story: Critical Essays on Alice Munro*. Ed. Robert Thacker. Toronto: ECW, 1999. 169–90.

Gilbert, Sandra M., and Susan Gubar. *The Madwoman in the Attic: The Woman Writer and the Nineteenth-Century Literary Imagination*. New Haven: Yale University Press, 1979.

*Holy Bible*. King James Version. Cleveland: World Publishing, 1945.

Howells, Coral Ann. *Alice Munro*. Manchester, England: Manchester University Press, 1998.

Joyce, James. *Dubliners*. 1914. New York: Modern Library, 1926.

Mansfield, Katherine. "Bliss." 1918. *The Short Stories of Katherine Mansfield*. 1937. New York: Knopf, 1961. 337–50.

McCombs, Judith. "'From Listening to the Stories of Others, We Learn to Tell Our Own': Southern Ontario Gothic in Alice Munro's 'Wilderness Station' and [Margaret Atwood's] *Alias Grace*." *Margaret Atwood Society Newsletter* 22–23 (Fall/Winter 1999): 32–33.

———. "Munro's and Atwood's Bloody Chambers: Epistolary Structure, Storytelling, Grace Notes and Grimm Archetypes in 'A Wilderness Station' and *Alias Grace*." Paper presented at the biennial meeting of the Association for Canadian Studies in the United States, Minneapolis, MN, 22 November 1997.

Munro, Alice. Contributors' Notes. *Prize Stories 1997: The O. Henry Awards*. Ed. Larry Dark. New York: Anchor, 1997. 442–43.

———. "Images." *Dance of the Happy Shades and Other Stories*. Harmondsworth, Middlesex, England: Penguin, 1968. 30–43.

———. Introduction to the Vintage Edition. *Selected Stories*. By Munro. 1996. New York: Vintage, 1997. xiii–xxi.

————. *Lives of Girls and Women.* 1971. New York: Signet, 1974.

————. "The Love of a Good Woman." *The Love of a Good Woman.* New York: Knopf, 1998. 3–78.

————. "The Love of a Good Woman." *New Yorker* (23 and 30 December 1996): 102+.

————. "The Peace of Utrecht." *Dance of the Happy Shades and Other Stories.* Harmondsworth, Middlesex, England: Penguin, 1968. 190–210.

————. "Save the Reaper." *The Love of a Good Woman.* New York: Knopf, 1998. 146–80.

————. "A Wilderness Station." 1992. *Open Secrets.* Toronto: McClelland and Stewart, 1994. 190–225.

Opie, Iona and Peter. *The Classic Fairy Tales.* New York: Oxford University Press, 1974.

Perrault, Charles. "Bluebeard." ["La Barbe bleüe." 1697.] Trans. Robert Samber. 1729. *The Classic Fairy Tales.* Iona and Peter Opie. New York: Oxford University Press, 1974. 133–41.

*The Postman Always Rings Twice.* Dir. Tay Garnett. 1946.

Pratt, Annis. *Archetypal Patterns in Women's Fiction.* Bloomington: Indiana University Press, 1981.

Tennyson, Alfred Lord. *Idylls of the King.* 1859–72, 1885. *The Poems and Plays of Alfred, Lord Tennyson.* New York: Modern Library 1938. 433–664.

Thacker, Robert. "Alice Munro's Willa Cather." *Canadian Literature* 134 (1992): 42–57.

————. Conversation with author, Pittsburgh, PA, 18 November 1999.

"The Three Little Pigs." *The Green Fairy Book.* Circa 1892. Ed. Andrew Lang. New York: Dover, 1965. 100–05.

"The Three Little Pigs." *The Three Little Pigs and Other Favorite Nursery Stories.* Cambridge, MA: Candlewick, 1991. 82–93.

Tindall, William York. *A Reader's Guide to James Joyce.* New York: Noonday, 1959.

Wilson, Sharon Rose. *Margaret Atwood's Fairy-Tale Sexual Politics.* Jackson: University Press of Mississippi, 1993.

Woolf, Virginia. *To the Lighthouse.* New York: Harcourt, Brace, 1927.

Yeats, W. B. "Leda and the Swan." *The Collected Poems of W. B. Yeats.* New York: Macmillan, 1959. 211–12.

Zipes, Jack. "A Second Gaze at Little Red Riding Hood's Trials and Tribulations." *Don't Bet on the Prince: Contemporary Feminist Fairy Tales in North America and England.* 1987. Ed. Zipes. New York: Routledge, 1989. 227–60.

JANET BEER

# Short Fiction with Attitude: *The Lives of Boys and Men in the* Lives of Girls and Women

There have been many discussions of Alice Munro's 1971 volume of interlinked stories, *Lives of Girls and Women*, in the context of its generic identity.[1] Andrew Gurr in his essay 'Short Fictions and Whole-Books' sees 'inherently novelistic impulses'[2] in the organization of the text and Coral Ann Howells, in a capacious discussion of its form, describes it as, amongst other things, a '*Bildungsroman* with a decentralised narrative structure'.[3] The story of Del Jordan's progression from childhood into adolescence into young womanhood becomes our intimate possession as Munro draws her readers into the smell and taste of the vulnerability, ignorance, and venality that is girlhood in the confused and confusing years of the 1940s and 1950s through a series of narratives linked not chronologically but topographically. What I intend to focus on in this essay, however, is not the sweep of the whole but the detail of the individual narratives and, in particular, the way in which Munro writes about men; in other words I will be privileging the autonomy of the individual stories over the unifying factors in the volume. I would argue that it is in the telling of the tales of the men who variously feature in this text that the most powerful generic affiliations to the short story form are demonstrated; in the stories contained within Del Jordan's overarching narrative the lives of boys and men can be read.

From *The Yearbook of English Studies*, vol. 31, North American Short Stories and Short Fictions (2001): 125–32. © 2001 by Modern Humanities Research Association.

Alice Munro has talked about her fictions being fundamentally concerned with looking at 'what people don't understand. What we don't understand. What we think is happening and what we understand later on'.[4] Whilst
this is actually a subtle description of the fruitful tensions generated by the
retrospective cast of the narrative style, which combines the insights of the
mature writer with the adolescent subject, it is also an accurate assessment of
the manner in which the text is engaged in the portrayal of the disaggregation
of white male identity from the centre of the action. Story after story delin-
eates the end of male exclusivity, whether in the role of pioneer, breadwinner,
intellectual, or suitor; and this is so imminent a phenomenon that no one
is quite alert to the reverberations and implications. The complications that
arise from the use of the retrospective view (into which obsolescence is built)
highlight, with the greatest clarity, the fact that the status quo, the world of
'Masculine self-centredness' (p. 30) is in the process of being superseded. As
Munro describes it in a prefatory note, this is a text which is 'autobiographical in form but not in fact' and women are shown throughout to be emerging from contingency, no longer peripheral to the central thrust of a certain,
seamless narrative or forced to speak lines already scripted for them. The
men are the bit-players, featuring in single episodes rather than informing
the whole, and reduced in status by being made subject to judgement. Uncle
Craig, in common with Uncle Benny, Jerry Storey, Mr Chamberlain, Garnet
French, Naomi's father, Del's own father and brother, is shown at peace in
complacency, misguidedly secure in a value system which is rapidly becoming obsolete. The rapidity of social change is reflected in the accumulated
detail of people's lives in Munro's fictional small town—shifts of allegiance
both large and small, intergenerational conflicts, alterations in the balance
of power between the sexes—but these are not to be found in Uncle Craig's
meticulous recording of births, deaths, and marriages: 'He did not ask for
anybody in the family to have done anything more interesting, or scandal-
ous, than to marry a Roman Catholic (the woman's religion noted in red ink
below her name)' (p. 31). Rather, they are made manifest by disruptions of
another kind, disjunctions between what is said and what is understood, what
is acknowledged and what is resisted.

The organization of the text into episodes deemed to be significant by
the mature narrator reinforces a larger sense of the dislocation of socially
accepted structures of authority. For example, the narrator's estimation of
Jerry Storey combines the adolescent with the adult voice, fusing Del's teenage instincts with the insights of the mature woman writer: 'I felt in him what
women feel in men, something so tender, swollen, tyrannical, absurd; I would
never take the consequences of interfering with it; I had an indifference, a
contempt almost, that I concealed from him' (pp. 193–94). The figurative lan-

guage here could be understood to be referring to Munro's estimation of the inappropriateness of the imperatives of the conventional novel form to communicate her chosen subject as much as to the potential physical and intellectual tyranny of the phallus, of male egocentricity. One of the most important things that the particular organization of *Lives of Girls and Women* allows is the fracturing of any preconceptions that the story of a young woman's teenage years must incorporate a natural or inevitable movement toward the married state or attainment of romantic love or that there is any one dominant chord in the woman's life. There is a concomitant effect achieved by the episodic structure, however: it highlights the marginality of the male players; as straightforward narrative chronology is refused so too is the status quo and, indeed, existing hierarchies of male influence.

Alice Munro most obviously expresses the difference between the generations, between the lives of Del and her mother, Ada, in her treatment of sexuality and the conflict between the academic and the social life as it afflicts girls. Del's mother has ambitions for her daughter which centre on the leaving of the small town, the development of the life of the mind rather than the life of the body; all her own frustrations are channelled into the hope and expectation that her daughter will have a different type of existence, driven by intellectual rather than physical imperatives. Del is aware that there are choices available to her which were not on offer to her mother and this is made clear when her mother's story is retold in terms of the struggle she had in order to be educated, emphasizing her constant urge toward self-improvement. Ada Jordan's story most closely approximates to a nineteenth-century narrative of a woman's life; there is no ending for her except in marriage and children. Her life ambition is to become independent but she cannot quite make the full journey towards autonomy and never escapes the consequent feeling of failure, a failure which finally sends her to bed, defeated by the ruin of her best laid plans to guarantee her children's escape from the provincial by equipping the region with encyclopaedias, spreading 'Knowledge' (p. 64) from house to house in order to make up for the fact that her own mother threw away the only chance of an education she had had by squandering money on bibles, sending Ada out to distribute them 'to the heathen' (p. 75) when she possessed neither shoes nor gloves of her own.

No such sense of failure afflicts Del's maiden Aunts; they rest easily and, indeed, expansively, in their contingency, celebrating the division between men's and women's lives, talking up Uncle Craig's trifling achievements, making even his abstentions into matters to be venerated: 'He could have been elected to the legislature. He could have been in the cabinet, if he'd wanted' (p. 38). Their married sister, however, suffers 'from varicose veins, hemorrhoids, a dropped womb, cysted ovaries, inflammations, discharges, lumps and stones in various places [ . . . She is] one of those heavy, cautiously moving, wrecked survivors of the female life, with stories to tell'. Defined only by her female organs and their malfunctions, Aunt Moira tells the other side of the story to that rehearsed in traditional women's fiction; the married woman is the casualty, not the spinster sisters, she is to be pitied rather than the pity being reserved for those without men. They 'jump up so quickly [ . . . and] still smelled fresh and healthy' whilst she has a 'gynecological odor' and gives 'off rumbles of complaint, involuntary and eloquent as noises of digestion or wind' (p. 40). The kind of plot that has produced Aunt Moira would have Del becoming the woman that Garnet French wants her to be; the wife who would be baptized into her husband's church, who would accept the conditions of life on the edge, subsistence with his extended family, years of childbirth and domesticity at its most basic. Del's final refusal of subjection: 'I felt amazement, not that I was fighting with Garnet but that anybody could have made such a mistake, to think he had real power over me' (p. 234), is the refusal of this particular female role; this female *bildungsroman* ends in authorship and exile not in love and marriage. The short stories that tell of men's lives here, however, end in stasis, with a funeral, with failures of imagination, refusals to change and even regression, as in the case of Del's brother: 'There was Owen, living out on the Flats Road, saying "turrible" and "drownded" and using Uncle Benny's grammar, saying he wanted to quit school' (p. 237).

Del's account of her teenage years is articulated as a series of engagements with male authority; this authority comes in various guises but it is always refuted, not only in terms of plot but also in terms of structure. Throughout the volume the generic injunctions of the novel form are heard: there is a unity of setting, of concerns, of characters, and, of course, of narratorial voice, but there is also closure; there are regular interruptions to the narrative flow that usually signal the termination of a masculine influence or presence. For example, 'Heirs of the Living Body' not only gives an account of the funeral of Uncle Craig, it also despatches, without mercy, his life's work to a watery grave; 'Lives of Girls and Women' sends Mr Chamberlain off masturbating into the sunset but closes on Del's resolution: 'Men were supposed to be able to go out and take on all kinds of experience and shuck off what they didn't want and come back proud. Without even thinking about it, I had decided to do the same' (p. 174); and in 'Baptizing', whilst apparently carrying out a conventional lament for her lost love, Garnet French, Del immediately undercuts the pathos generated by any such performance by condemning Tennyson's 'Mariana' as 'one of the silliest poems I had ever read', therefore satirizing it as an appropriate model but acknowledging all the while her own self-reflexivity: 'I said it with absolute sincerity, absolute irony' (p. 238).

It is often the case that short stories treat the lives of those who are, for some reason, marginal or marginalized in society and Munro gives this a radical spin by showing her women moving towards the centre, whether the metropolitan centre or the narrative centre. It is the men here who are in retreat towards an increasingly irrelevant hinterland, bound rather than liberated by the limits (often self-imposed limits) of their stories. The lives of men are expressed as secondary, their words, bloated and redundant like Uncle Craig's sodden regional history, steeped in complacency. The elegant, though ruthless, precision of Del's comment as Craig's work is found to be ruined highlights the difference between the eloquence of the emerging female voice as it is opposed to the old veneration of the simple fact of 'men's work' (p. 32); 'I thought of them watching the manuscript leave the house in its padlocked box and I felt remorse, that kind of tender remorse which has on its other side a brutal, unblemished satisfaction' (p. 62). Craig's manuscript is carried out in much the same way as his body, in a box from which 'he himself was wiped out' (p. 58). There is no man or boy in this story sequence whose language is sufficient either to communicate or endure; Naomi's father speaks in biblical warning notes, Uncle Benny veers between cliché and sensation, Mr Chamberlain's language is, literally, cocksure, his exhibition serving only to emphasize the surreal incongruity between his own estimation of his importance and his actual influence. 'Boo!' he says, as he reveals his pride and joy to Del; 'Quite a sight, eh?' is his post-masturbatory valediction, words which leave Del untouched, her attention being elsewhere: 'The landscape was post-coital, distant and meaningless' (p. 167). She projects onto the natural world the anti-climax which is expressive of both her own and Fern's unsatisfactory dealings with Mr Chamberlain.

Munro is charting the decline of the male language, and the paucity or inadequacy of the masculine word is exemplified in a number of ways. Mr Chamberlain is concerned enough about the words he once wrote to Fern to enlist Del to sneak around her room looking for any trace of old promises. Fern, however, has destroyed his words, whilst deeming it worthwhile to keep a chain letter, crude illustrations of the sexual organs, sagas centring on a variety of birth-control techniques, and some smutty verses. Del's father retreats further and further into silence, restricting the number of books he reads to the few beside his bed, using them as sleep inducers, mind quieteners, not stimulants: 'He never talked about what he read' (p. 227).

A central part of the narrative in the longest story in the volume, 'Baptizing', is consumed by the issue of a spreading, contaminating male silence; with the single exception of Jerry Storey, whose IQ disqualifies him from full participation in small or large-town life, the men who feature here are associated with failure of expression, with inarticulacy. As Del grows away

from Jerry and the compulsion to shield herself from the rival claims of love
and sex with 'tangible' A grades which, as she says, were 'stacked around me
like barricades, and if I missed one I could feel a dangerous gap' (p. 192),
so she becomes aware of the silence or wordlessness gathering around her
sexual being. As the A becomes meaningless, unworthy of her attention, she
becomes incapable of registering anything but the physical; as her mother
bombards her with possible subjects for academic pursuit she acknowledges:
'Such words would not stay in my head' (p. 228). Del describes the changes in
her sexual knowledge and experience in a manner which is at once self-possessed and self-conscious but her account of the frequency and fullness of her
love-making with Garnet is followed by the single line paragraph: 'We never
spoke a word, to each other, about any of this' (p. 226). Such physical obsession
can exist only in a place where language is denied entry; Del cannot afford to
hear the words he actually speaks: even as he reaches climax he admits only to
thinking about fixing 'that muffler' (p. 232). The words when they are actually
spoken are so disappointing, so affronting that Del must remove them from
their status as forms of expression that might require a response.

Substantial shifts are being recorded in the organization of the lives of
both men and women, brought to the surface in the narrative by moments
of realization signalling recognition of the true condition of the conventions
that continue to bind male expression of the woman's life: 'Owen had half
a bottle of beer. When I asked for some my father said, "No, your mother
wouldn't like it." Uncle Benny said, "No good ever come of any girl that drunk
beer." That was what I had heard Garnet say, the same word' (pp. 226–27).
Garnet's syntactic contiguity with Uncle Benny can only be ignored for so
long and the identification of their likeness is one of a number of moments of
cognition that will lead Del back from her obsession. It is not to aggrandize
such moments of illumination to call them epiphanies, and, moreover, epiphanies which, in prompting gender-specific moments of recognition, force the
negation of men as enduring influences. Similarly, the behaviour of women
whose sole ambition lies in the pursuit of the marriage plot (Naomi and her
'well-groomed' office mates), who are so absorbed by the matter of 'diets,
skin-care routines, hair-shampooing methods, clothes, diaphragms' that their
limitations prompt Del not to imitation but to an acute realization of her
own peculiar status as a girl without the power of 'sustained attention' to her
appearance. 'Love is not for the undepilated' (pp. 176–77), she reflects. The
only insightful words Garnet does speak, 'You think you're too good for it' (p.
234), are the ones that bring Del back to her sense of the world beyond: 'The
future could be furnished without love or scholarship.' For the duration of the
love affair she has suspended time and reason, moving in a narrative enacted
in defiance of the 'Real Life' (p. 238) time-frame which is re-invoked, supply-

ing the closing words to the story, and thus consigning Garnet French to the lumberyard of history.

Munro is careful to weigh the balance between the opinion of the child Del and the adult narrator on the subject of her mother, but Ada's voice is a powerful, definite presence in the text in contrast to the silence, the wilful opinionlessness of her husband. The scepticism, even fond contempt with which Del treats her mother's pronouncements is again a feature of the tension between the adolescent and the mature narratorial voice but, in spite of this, it is Ada to whom the task is given to make the most forcible expression of the new order: 'There is a change coming I think in the lives of girls and women. Yes. But it is up to us to make it come. All women have had up till now has been their connection with men. All we have had. No more lives of our own, really, than domestic animals' (p. 173), whilst the change itself is given to Del to enact, if not exactly in the way her mother had intended.

In her essay, "'Heirs of the Living Body': Alice Munro and the Question of a Female Aesthetic' Barbara Godard poses the question: 'How to write as a woman?' in the context of Munro's exploration of 'the special problems stereotypes have created for the woman artist'.[5] Whilst I would not dispute the productiveness of Godard's line of enquiry I would want to turn it around somewhat and re-apply it to an exploration of the male stereotypes Munro unlooses in this short story sequence. Women's roles are demonstrably changing, and whilst Ada still inhabits a world where the woman is fighting to free herself from stereotype and the familiar figure of the young women in search of a husband, any husband, is busy furnishing her bottom drawer, Del herself is bewildered by stereotypical assumptions made about her, whether by magazine articles, her mother, Mrs Storey, or Garnet French. The men here, however, are without doubt articulated as a series of stereotypes: from village idiot to town boffin, middle-aged flasher to religious maniac, local history bore to Southern gothic recluse. Their role in the larger narrative is transformative, they are catalytic to changes in Del's life, not necessarily because they have taken an active role but often because what they are or what they do enables her to understand things in a different way and to leave them behind. They are, in many ways, functions of the individual short stories and, in the end, merely representative figures, albeit figures imbued with significance through the subjectivity of the narrative voice.

Howells talks about the 'unscripted spaces' (*Alice Munro*, p. 36) which are everywhere in the narrative, in human as well as physical geography, and it is these spaces that metaphorically encode the central thrust of the narrative. Stories lie upon stories here palimpsestically, glimpsed through cracks and fissures in the landscape and the memory; as Del breaks away from Garnet so she 'repossessed the world' (p. 236); as she composes her novel in her head, featuring 'Caroline', a Canadian Blanche Dubois, her fictional town is 'lying close behind the one I walked through every day' (p. 244). The oft-quoted line from the final story, 'Epilogue: The Photographer': 'People's lives, in jubilee as elsewhere, were dull, simple, amazing, and unfathomable—deep caves paved with kitchen linoleum' (p. 249), marries the generic with the specific, the mundane with the fantastic, the natural with the manufactured, the stability of all and each threatened by these contiguities but also made rich and resonant. The short story in generic terms is often precipitous: it verges on the lyric, it verges on the novel but these are not necessarily negative comparators; here, the short story fruitfully and deliberately points in the direction of both more condensed and more extended narrative methods.

Munro's technique compresses signification, as in the retrospective view which adds layers of meaning, and the dominant metaphors in the text confront our understanding of both narrative and geographical space. She exploits the potential the short story offers to glide between surface and depth, fantasy and reality, compression and expansion; the organization of *Lives of Girls and Women* offers definitive endings whilst dealing comprehensively in the impossibility of taking down 'every last thing, every layer of speech and thought, stroke of light on bark or walls, every smell, pothole, pain, crack, delusion, held still and held together—radiant, everlasting' (p. 249). The mighty realist enterprise is interrogated as perhaps impossible to accomplish; instead Munro works with the domestic revelation, with Bobby Sherriff on his toes like a ballet dancer, suggesting, as Howells notes, 'alternative worlds which challenge each other as different representations of reality' (p. 31). Munro offers the crisis of recognition or the moment at which change becomes inevitable as well as the larger topography and thereby forges powerful connections between worlds: inner contemplative worlds, exterior physical worlds, as well as the kind of twilight world occupied by Bobby Sherriff.

Munro in her writings and rewritings of Jubilee is working with the regional, employing a form that has traditionally been associated with the telling of the lives of girls and women and as Lynette Hunter says: 'The serial form may prove helpful to the regional voice, may enable the communication of history through strategies of cumulative background'.[6] The regional history being communicated here is substantially women's history in the sense that the organizational principles of women's lives, both in fiction and in fact, are shown in the process of tumultuous change but, at the same time, the lives of men and boys are seen to be atrophying into a deadening provinciality: the men are all confined to the small town, white male identity being predicated on waste, violence, and lack of ambition.

In this text Munro appropriates the generic conventions she needs from the short story to support the telling of the lives of boys and men whilst also bending them into the service of the overarching narrative of the lives of girls and women. Del Jordan's account of her growing up is destabilized by breaks in the narrative chronology, but such disruptions are mirrored by equivalent breaks with male authority and especially with male language. Del's story is expressed through a complex set of aesthetic tensions between past and present perspectives, between different layers of experience, and even reality and surreality, but still coheres as a whole. The stories of the men who pass in and out of her life are contained by the structure of the individual short story, by their representative role, their marginality (both in social and geographical terms), and their function as adjuncts to the main thrust of the narrative.

## Notes

1. *Lives of Girls and Women* (1971; repr. London: Penguin, 1982).
2. In *Narrative Strategies in Canadian Literature* ed. by C.A. Howells and L. Hunter (Milton Keynes: Open University Press, 1991), pp. 11–18 (p. 17).
3. *Alice Munro* (Manchester: Manchester University Press, 1998), p. 33.
4. Graham Hancock, 'Alice Munro Interview', *Canadian Writers at Work* (Toronto: Oxford University Press, 1987), p. 201.
5. In *Alice Munro: Saying the Unsayable*, ed. by Judith Miller (Ontario: University of Waterloo Press, 1984), pp. 43–49.
6. *Narrative Strategies in Canadian Literature*, p. 4.

ROWLAND SMITH

# Rewriting the Frontier: Wilderness and Social Code in the Fiction of Alice Munro

In a well-known passage in *The Empire Writes Back*, the authors define one of the central problems in the literature of 'settler colonies' as that of the "relationship between the imported language and the new place."[1] This need to find an appropriate language to deal with the reality of new landscapes in settler colonies (such as those in North America, Australia and New Zealand, where Europeans formed independent societies out of colonies originally subservient to the metropolitan, colonial power) is of a different order from the cultural assertions of colonized societies in Africa and Asia. In those colonies, the differences between the indigenous culture and the imposed colonial culture were always obvious:

> Whatever the particular nature of colonial oppression in Africa or India, and whatever the legacy of cultural syncretism, the differences confronted as a result of colonialism were palpable [ ... ]. In the settler colonies, however, difference from the inherited tradition and the need to assert that difference were felt equally strongly. (136–37)

An interesting development of the need to assert the differences in settler realities is the possibility of later writers from those cultures re-investigating

From *Telling Stories: Postcolonial Short Fiction in English*, edited by Jacqueline Bardolph, pp.77–90. © 2001 by Rodopi.

the earlier, established models of settler myth. Do the long-established literary or cultural mythologies of settler difference adequately reflect the differing
realities of current writers in settler countries, even as they look back on the
settler past that has been inscribed as their authentic, non-metropolitan cultural identity?

The assumptions of settlers who first asserted a distinctly autochtho-
nous reality can be seen by later writers to be devices that obscure uncom-
fortable aspects of settler culture while highlighting what makes it different.
Edward Said has consistently argued that the way European explorers
and colonizers depict otherness is only partly an attempt to understand
or describe that different reality; it is also, invariably, an attempt to manage, contain, control it. Said discusses Western, colonizing habits of representation and the counter-assertions of colonized peoples about creating a
mythic, indigenous reality in opposition to that imposed on them. While
not directly related to the practices of settler cultures, his comments are
relevant to the non-belligerent attempts of early settler mythologizers (who
did not have to fight wars of liberation) to assert cultural independence.
Discussing the "constructions" of "insurgent 'natives' about their pre-colo-
nial past," he writes:

> This strategy is at work in what many national poets or men of
> letters say and write during independence or liberation struggles
> elsewhere in the colonial world. I want to underline the mobilizing
> power of the images and traditions brought forth, and their
> fictional, or at least romantically colored, fantastic quality.[2]

In discussions of the literary ethos of the settler culture of Canada,
representations of the wilderness or the bush, and refuge from them in concepts of survival or the garrison, are commonplace constructs. In *Strange
Things* (originally given as lectures at Oxford), Margaret Atwood links these
motifs to the practice of an equally celebrated Canadian cultural icon, Alice
Munro. Atwood discusses the mystique of the wilderness, particularly the
North, in Canadian imaginative writing. She discusses patterns of Canadian
reflection on the wilderness/North, and the different ways writers depict
either the malevolence or the neutrality of that vast expanse. In passing, she
comments on the difference between the perspective of male writers (with
their male protagonists) and that of female writers (with female protagonists): "If the North is a cold femme fatale, enticing you to destruction, is
it similarly female and similarly fatal when a woman character encounters
it?"[3] The continuing obsession with the North in the Canadian psyche is
one of her constant themes; it is this obsession that leads her to relate her

own interest in the wilderness motif to contemporary urban life. And it is to Alice Munro that she turns for oblique explanation of her own focus. Atwood writes:

> The fourth lecture is called "Linoleum Caves," a title suggested by a sentence in Alice Munro's *The Lives of Girls and Women*. "People's lives, in Jubilee as elsewhere, were dull, simple, amazing and unfathomable—deep caves paved with kitchen linoleum." I was intrigued by the contrast between the domestic linoleum and the natural and potentially dangerous cave, and in women-in-the-north stories there is often such a contrast—sometimes with the linoleum being the more treacherous feature. (4)

The surface ease of Atwood's writing is, as always, deceptively straightforward. The well-known passage quoted from Alice Munro introduces elements of the "amazing and unfathomable" alongside those of the "dull" and "the domestic"—all concepts that intrude with increasing urgency in Munro's later work. But it is Atwood herself who raises the question of which is the more "treacherous" or "dangerous"; domesticity (with "linoleum" suggesting a certain kind of economically strained, or at least not lavish, domesticity) or the wilderness—hostile or otherwise. And it is Atwood who typifies, as Canadian, Munro's trait of idiosyncratic juxtaposing or combining of the wild and the domestic; the tamed and the untameable; the decorous and the depraved. Atwood recalls a complaint made in Oxford by a young Canadian about her subject-matter for the Clarendon lectures:

> I should not be talking about the North, or the wilderness, or snow, or bears, or cannibalism or any of that [ ... ]. these things were of the past, and [ ... ] I would give the English a wrong idea about how most Canadians were spending their time these days. (5)

It was "the literature of urban life" that this particular young man thought Atwood should be discussing in Oxford in the 1990s. Atwood's reply—as a by-product—recognizes the unique quality of Alice Munro's imaginative perspective on modern urban life:

> I said I thought the English had quite a lot of urban life themselves, and that they didn't need to hear about it from me [ ... ]. Given a choice between a morning spent in the doughnut shop and a little cannibalism, which would you take—to read about, that is? Alice Munro of course could handily work in both—but as a rule? (5)

To posit as specifically Canadian an overriding awareness of the wilderness, or at least of natural hostility, is not far removed from familiar statements about survival or the garrison. The new element in Atwood's comments in *Strange Things* is the different uses to which male and female Canadian writers may put their common subconscious access to a mythology of the wild-at-the-door. Alice Munro seldom writes about the far North, but the settler origins of the culture she knows and explores form a substratum in her fiction. And the restrictions on her female protagonists of that early world are almost invariably more intense when created by humans than are those afforded by the roughing-it-in-the-bush motif of frontier literature.

The way the ethos of the past, whether distant or recent, permeates her protagonists' attitudes is a distinctive feature of her created world. And it is in this regard that her questioning is most consistent: how subjective are those memories and to what extent have they been sanctified as part of an imaginative need to create a special kind of mythologized experience of wilderness life in order to manage it and tame it emotionally?

Because her technique is often ironic, the bleakness in Munro's references to the distant frontier past can be muted in deadpan narration of events or customs. In "Meneseteung," the perspective moves between an almost celebratory, historical re-imagining of the growing prosperity of a frontier town and a straight-faced depiction of its human nastiness; the latter quality created implicitly in a narrative whose tone remains bland.

The spinster-protagonist, Almeda Joynt Roth, is an amateur poet whose derivative verses treat conventional subjects. The European context of a poem dealing with a gypsy encampment outside town typifies the conventional struggle of a colonial writer to find an indigenous topic, let alone an indigenous language. But mingled with such literary sources are elements derived from Roth's own experience—a poem by her depicts the children's game of making angel wings in the snow, an explicitly Ontarian experience, even if the Victorian manner of reflection is borrowed:

> White roses cold as snow
> Bloom where those "angels" lie.
> Do they but rest below
> Or, in God's wonder, fly?[4]

The sentiments may be borrowed, but the children's angels are indigenous.

A reflection on what is indigenous forms the topic of some of the protagonist's poems. "The Passing of the Old Forest" lists and describes the trees cut down in the original forest as well as providing "a general description of the bears, wolves, eagles, deer, waterfowl" (53). This is wilderness-writing in content, although the tone of all her poems is drawing-room poetic. An instinct to define the local is more pronounced in a companion piece, "A Garden Medley," which is a "catalogue of plants brought from European countries, with bits of history and legend attached, and final Canadianness resulting from this mixture" (53). Final Canadianness would be the goal of the most dedicated postcolonial settler-poet.

Almeda's interest in defining her connection to European roots exists side-by-side with an inability to create an indigenous style that is neither derivative nor romanticized. The title of the story itself, "Meneseteung," is taken from one of her poems, which epitomizes her penchant for mythologizing her environment. The narrator of the story gives this description of the poem: "'Champlain at the Mouth of the Meneseteung' [ ... ] celebrates the popular, untrue belief that the explorer sailed down the eastern shore of Lake Huron and landed at the mouth of the major river" (52). This is an example of Southwestern Ontario frontier myth. In it, the district's pioneering past is derived from the romantic voyage of a great European explorer, opening up its wilderness. The land of the noble adventurer is shared—through the use of the 'Indian' name of the river—with untroubled aboriginal people. From this idealized beginning, the later cosmetic historicizing of Almeda's nineteenth-century frontier town can develop.

The narrator of "Meneseteung" both speculates on life in Almeda's town and recounts the events recorded in contemporary issues of the *Vidette*. This mixture of the imagined ("perhaps petunias growing on top of a stump," 54) and the recorded ("I read about that life in the *Vidette*," 54) offers a shifting focus under the surface ease of the swiftly moving account of the ethos of the settler town, which explicitly resembles Northrop Frye's garrison:

> it's not going to vanish, yet it still has some of the look of an encampment. And, like an encampment, it's busy all the time— full of people [ ... ]. full of the noise of building and of drivers shouting at their horses and of the trains that come in several times a day. (54)

Here is the positive element of frontier myth: the wilderness driven back by human enterprise and determination. Mr Jarvis Poulter, the widowed businessman who interests Almeda, epitomizes the virtues of wilderness-into-profit; his salt-extraction enterprise is not only successful, but also uses technology to bring natural riches to the surface. In an area which is really "a raw countryside just wrenched from the forest, but swarming with people" (61), he embodies the official values of the settlement, and they have all the elements of Victorian puritanism and taboo that (as cultural baggage carried well into the twentieth century) provide the restricted ethos from which Munro's twentieth-century protagonists attempt to break free.

But the reality of the frontier town is two-sided. Human endeavour can be seen in heroic terms; the wilderness is receding, prosperity is evident, decorous social norms are being established. At the same time, there is a norm of atrocious behaviour. The list of accepted acts of viciousness is endless: "Strangers who don't look so prosperous are taunted and tormented [ . . . ]. Be on your guard, the *Vidette* tells people. These are times of opportunity and danger. Tramps, hicksters, shysters, plain thieves are travelling the roads" (55). Those who taunt and torment strangers are children, the boys of the town who "rove through the streets in gangs" and always pick on the weak or the socially unacknowledged ("strangers who don't look so prosperous," 54). The frontier idyll is at its least convincing in their treatment of the frailest in the encampment, its defenceless women: "one day they follow an old woman, a drunk named Queen Aggie. They get her into a wheelbarrow and, trundle her all over town, then dump her into a ditch to sober her up" (54). These elements of the settlement culture are presented in such a matter-of-fact manner that they appear on the surface to be part of the romance of imperial development.

Just as Almeda's penchant for romance disqualifies her from coming to terms with the raw side of life at the end of Pearl Street, so a romantic reading of these opening historical re-creations (by the narrator) of life in Almeda's town mask the rawness of the place; a rawness in which the town boys' treatment of Queen Aggie foreshadows their treatment of Almeda in old age when she has become a social oddity, conspicuously incapable of conforming to the decorum expected of her. In recording her death, the *Vidette* reports:

> She caught cold, after having become thoroughly wet from a ramble in the Pearl Street bog. (It has been said that some urchins chased her into the water, and such is the boldness and cruelty of some of our youth, and their observed persecution of this lady, that the tale cannot be entirely discounted). (72)

According to the narrator, who controls access to both imagined and recorded events, the latter account in the *Vidette* dates from the twentieth century (1903) rather than the nineteenth (1879 is adduced as the date of the near-miss with Mr Poulter). The change in mood is reflected in the disapproval of the behaviour of "our youth" in 1903, whereas the same behaviour has been neutrally recounted by the narrator in an imaginative re-creation of the frontier town in 1879. When Mr Jarvis Poulter's death is recorded in the *Vidette* of 1904, however, the celebration of the pioneer spirit of enterprise which he is seen to have epitomized is on a par with the implicit enthusiasm for the energy of the frontier town of 1879 in the narrator's account. He is described as

> one of the founders of our community, and early maker and shaker of this town [ ... ] [who] possessed a keen and lively commercial spirit, which was instrumental in the creation of not one but several local enterprises, bringing the benefits of industry, productivity, and employment to our town. (72)

By this time, the frontier virtues have been codified.

Almeda cannot cope with either the decorum of the town or the raw side revealed in a Saturday night squabble-and-fornication on Pearl Street. While her own house faces on Dufferin Street, which is a street "of considerable respectability" (55), her back gate opens onto Pearl Street, which degenerates block by block to the last "dismal" one: "nobody but the poorest people, the unrespectable and undeserving poor, would live there at the edge of a boghole (drained since then) called the Pearl Street Swamp" (55).

I will not belabour the obvious imagery of what the society "faces" and what it "backs onto," but it is worth pointing to the unrelenting nastiness in the presentation of the human values of the frontier town. The poorest people are unrespectable and undeserving, and that's that.

Human constructs defeat Almeda on both levels. She cannot digest the rawness of the Pearl Street scene (which Mr Poulter can move aside with his shoe) and she is entrapped in the straitjacket of official social decorum: for Mr Poulter to walk with her to church (as opposed to walking her home from church) would be a sign of "a declaration." Her retreat into the romantic fantasy world of her poems, seen as a "drawback, a barrier, an obsession in the young girl," becomes for the middle-aged woman a way to "fill her time." And what fills her verses is the myth-building fantasy of an early 'Canadianness' composed of plants and bears and a great explorer's visit to her part of the world, to the total exclusion of Pearl Street, the cause of her turning away from normal social life and her final dowsing in the bog.

As Atwood suggests, it is not the wilderness that is fatal in this experience of a woman on the frontier. A similar inversion of the relative safety offered by the wild or the pioneers in it occurs later in "A Wilderness Station." A reworking, from many viewpoints, of the tale of a colonial bride sent to a remote Ontario site in the mid-1800s, the epistolary narrative constantly captures—without authorial comment—the unthinking objectification of the young woman as commodity in the wilderness settlement. The wilderness *per se* is in fact relatively friendly to its bride. After her husband's murder (by his brother) she is safer—in her eyes—roughing it alone than remaining in contact with her brother-in-law, whose own guilt could be revealed by her.

It is not only the guilty brother who frightens the widow/bride, however. Even the friendly neighbours are a threat because of possible social censure. The shame of her position is an equally important element in her choosing the solitude of the wilderness over social contact with its settlers. Annie has been beaten, and does not want her past or present vulnerability exposed:

> Mrs. Treece came and tried to get me to go and live with them the way George was living. She said I could eat and sleep there, they had enough beds. I would not go. They thought I would not go because of my grief but I wouldn't go because somebody might see my black and blue, also they would be watching for me to cry. I said I was not frightened to stay alone.[5]

This is not the conventional plight of a woman widowed in the bush. The threat has in fact been turned inside out, and social life is the most menacing element in Annie's shocked condition. The point is made relentlessly. Annie stops sleeping in the house "where he could find me." She writes: "the flies and mosquitoes came but they hardly bothered me. I would see their bites but not feel them, which was another sign that in the outside I was pro-tected" (214). Those outside the immediate circumstances of Annie's plight can only explain her apparent abnormality in social terms. The conventional stresses of frontier life are judged to have affected her disposition. Letters from "good" males like the ailing Presbyterian minister in the region from which Annie flees, and the dutiful Clerk of the Peace in the village to which she flees, embody conventional attitudes toward women-on-the-frontier. The letter-writers cannot understand the nature of her plight and inscribe an inaccurate myth of frontier-woman problems as they fumble their way around the truth of her predicament. The bewildered Reverend McBain (who, as a male, is consumed by a frontier fever whereas Annie lives on to old age) ponders on her apparent insanity:

> It may well be that so early in the marriage her submission to her husband was not complete and there would be carelessness about his comfort, and naughty words, and quarrelsome behaviour, as well as the hurtful sulks and silences her sex is prone to. His death occurring before any of this was put right, she would feel a natural and harrowing remorse, and this must have taken hold of her mind [ ... ]. (203)

Mr James Mullen writes back with the views of a country doctor:

> His belief is that she is subject to a sort of delusion peculiar to
> females, for which the motive is a desire for self-importance, also a
> wish to escape the monotony of life or the drudgery they may have
> been born to. (205)

This rewriting of the wilderness myth is not an end in itself. Munro is
not merely re-interpreting the reality of settler culture. The plight of both
Annie and Almeda embodies the value-system underlying the reactions
of subsequent generations of Munro female characters to their parochial
world. That world may cease to be part of the wilderness, but as a settled
Victorian colony or a shabby-genteel mid-twentieth-century Dominion, or
the liberated, Trudeau-era 'world-class' province, its puritan roots, patriarchal and materialistic, inform the existential predicaments of Munro's
women.[6] When the irrational and the unpredictable erupt—with increasing frequency—into the lives of the protagonists in Munro's later volumes,
those flashes of quasi-insanity are almost without exception revealed in the
context of the suffocating conventions of either nineteenth- or twentieth-
century Ontario.[7]

Annie's temporary retreat into an outdoor life to escape the threats of
her society is seen as a kind of madness in the wilderness station. Almeda is
accepted as "odd" once she retreats from the twin nightmares of Pearl Street
and Mr Jarvis Poulter's respectable physicality. When Munro's contemporary
protagonists attempt to escape the confines of their society, they themselves
frequently see it as madness. The origins of this quite explicable turning to the
non-rational are what Munro reveals in her re-imagining of the settler roots
of their Ontario culture.

When she depicts the frenzy of contemporary, middle-class, professional
Ontarians, the frontier/colonial past is often juxtaposed with the swinging
present. In "Hard-Luck Stories," the choric comments of the narrator are
relevant to most of Munro's depictions of contemporary, middle-aged love-
wars. The hard-luck stories of the title are recounted by two women with a
male listener, after lunch in a country restaurant on a leisurely drive back to
Toronto from a librarians' conference in Ottawa. The tales involve sexual risk
and manipulation among lovers and ex-lovers. The professional status of the
trio and their educated, knowing talk over lunchtime wine are typical of the
liberated ethos of their Ontario. After lunch they stop at a country church:

> We walked around the graveyard first, looking at the oldest
> tombstones, reading dates and names aloud.

I read out a verse I found.
*"Afflictions sore long time she bore,*
*Physicians were in vain,*
*Till God did please to give her ease,*
*And waft her from her Pain."*
"Waft," I said. "That sounds nice."
Then I felt something go over me—a shadow, a chastening.
I heard the silly sound of my own voice against the truth of the
lives laid down here. Lives pressed down, like layers of rotting
fabric, disintegrating dark leaves. The old pain and privation.
How strange, indulged, and culpable they would find us—three
middle-aged people still stirred up about love, or sex.[8]

The seriousness of those colonial lives is obviously what is being con-
trasted with the flippancy of with-it sex-talk and practice in the present. And
the "indulged," "culpable" nature of the contemporary characters is reflected
in their determined flippancy. But that flippancy itself has its origins in a need
to break away from the "pain and privation" of a world of endurance and suffering.[9] In the midst of their smart, slightly tipsy discussion of hard-luck love
stories, the narrator has earlier revealed a different kind of truth; one that is
profoundly destabilizing, not flippant:

"There's the intelligent sort of love that makes an intelligent choice.
That's the kind you're supposed to get married on. Then there's the
kind that's anything but intelligent, that's like a possession. And
that's the one, that's the one, everybody really values. That's the one
nobody wants to have missed out on." (195)

The contrasting claims of conventional cultural expectation—for the
intelligent sort of love you're supposed to get married on—and the need to
break away from those expectations into unintelligent passion, form the subject of many of Munro's depictions of women's place in Ontario society. And
memories of the restrictions of past life flash into several of her protagonists'
ambivalent perceptions of their own connection to cultural environment. These
entail both their "culpable" frivolity and the need to strain against the straitjacket of social convention. Awe at the steadfastness of past life and respect for
shows of daring are reflected in the opening stories of *The Moons of Jupiter*. The
narrator's memories of visits from her urban cousins (from away) and to her
rural aunts (on neighbouring turf) make up her set of personal "connections."

my father's sisters scrubbed the floor with lye, they stocked the
oats and milked the cows by hand [ ... ]. That was their life. My

mother's cousins behaved in another way; they dressed up and took pictures of each other; they sallied forth. However they behaved they are all dead. I carry something of them around in me [ ... ] and the life buried here is one you have to think twice about: regretting. (35)

The first story in this duo is called "Connection," and the centrality of this concept is made explicit: "Connection. That was what it was all about. The cousins were a show in themselves, but they also provided a connection. A connection with the real, and prodigal, and dangerous, world" (6). The dangerous and prodigal—in the context of the story—are the natural opposites of the order and frugality of the aunts. The tug-of-war between these types of connection constitutes the cultural baggage of many of Munro's protagonists.[10]

Connection is indeed what it is all about in *The Moons of Jupiter*, as is its obverse: rupture and collision. For all the irrationality of motive and instinct revealed in *The Moons of Jupiter* tales, Munro constantly provides statements about the underlying need for connection, which in its turn provides identity and image.

Even the bizarre acts of several of her protagonists are examples both of unreason, the irrational, and of an insistent analysis of ways of finding connection. The stealing of her lover's cuff-link by the condescended-to Prue in the eponymous story is typical of the collection, in that the action is both unpredictably absurd and a transparent attempt to maintain connection of a kind. The "appalling rush of love and recognition" (226) in the dutiful, filial narrator in the title-story is an elegiac return (her father is dying in hospital) to what preoccupies Munro throughout the collection. In "Bardon Bus," the narrator, on parting with her lover, recalls:

our bags were packed and we were waiting for the taxi. Inside the bags our clothes that had shared drawers and closet space, tumbled together in the wash [ ... ] were all sorted and separated and would not rub together any more. (123)

And that concept is of a piece with her later, anguished comment: "I can't continue to move my body along the streets unless I exist in his mind and in his eyes" (126).

These observations are both charged and prosaic. Except for the theft of the cuff-link, there is little insane about them. Yet the other aspect of the connection offered by aunts and cousins—the capacity to yearn for, even celebrate, the dangerous and prodigal—is presented as a common feature in the sexual and cultural make-up of contemporary female characters in Munro's fiction. And the contemporaneity of that yearning is allied to a reaction against the proprieties and restraints of the past. This connection is made most explicitly in the title-story. The self-denying history of Flora, friend of the narrator's mother, is judged differently by daughter and mother. Jilted by her beau once her sister was pregnant by him, Flora is ditched once again when the sister dies and her former lover/brother-in-law marries the brassy nurse who attended his wife at the end. The contrasting reactions of mother and daughter to this history are explainable in terms of their shared cultural background:

> What made Flora evil in my story was just what made her admirable in my mother's—her turning away from sex [ ... ]. My mother had grown up in a time and in a place where sex was a dark undertaking for women [ ... ]. So she honored the decency, the prudery, the frigidity, that might protect you. And I grew up in horror of that very protection, the dainty tyranny that seemed to me to extend to all areas of life, to enforce tea parties and white gloves and all other sorts of tinkling inanities. I favored bad words and a breakthrough, I teased myself with the thought of a man's recklessness and domination. (22–23)

"Man's recklessness and domination," and the obsession with it, can, in Munro's fiction, become the corollary to both the "tinkling inanities" of "backwaters" and the "old pain and privation" of a frontier society. The narrator of "Friend of My Youth" has already made it clear that her interest lies in Robert—the villain in her mother's tale. And she explains that this is typical of her attitude towards men: "I expected nothing reasonable of them, only to be engulfed by their passion. I had similar thoughts about Robert" (22). Of course, obsessions like this are in themselves 'inane'; variants of the effect of backwater life, and yet as 'connected' to those backwaters and their limited options as the prudery of the recent past and the privation of the pioneering past.

Extravagantly complicated attempts to break away are remembered with amazement by several characters in *Friend of My Youth*. The language is consistently that of risk: "Joan thinks of her own history of love with no regret but some amazement. It's as if she had once gone in for skydiving" ("Oh, What Avails," 207); "I think we were just as vulnerable in some ways as the kids with their acid trips and so on, that were supposed to be marked for life. Weren't we marked—all of us smashing up our marriages and going out looking for adventure?" ("Differently," 222).

Just as the buried life of rural Ontario—with all its virtues of resolve and endurance—cannot be lamented, so too the insane moments of breakaway from the contrived decorum of a more recent past cannot provoke either total remorse or total relief. The possibility of having multiple attitudes towards one's own experience is insistently investigated in all of Munro's later books. The attitudes about which one can be ambivalent have not changed, however. The mixture of past restrictions and present follies, stifling social convention and non-rational reaction to it, is simultaneously present, as always, under the shadow of a dour frontier past.

## NOTES

1. Bill Ashcroft, Gareth Griffiths & Helen Tiffin, *The Empire Writes Back: Theory and Practice in Post-Colonial Literatures* (London & New York: Routledge, 1989): 135.

2. Edward W. Said, *Culture and Imperialism* (1993; New York: Random House/Vintage, 1994): 16.

3. Margaret Atwood, *Strange Things: The Malevolent North in Canadian Literature* (Oxford: Clarendon, 1995): 4. Further page references are in the text.

4. Alice Munro, *Friend of My Youth* (Toronto: McClelland & Stewart, 1990): 53.

5. Alice Munro, *Open Secrets* (Toronto: McClelland & Stewart, 1994): 214. Further page references are in the text.

6. Ildikó de Papp Carrington has an excellent discussion of Alice Munro's hesitancy to resort to an automatic use of the word patriarchal to describe the society of her youth. She deftly analyzes Munro's irony in using the phrase "anti-patriarchal rage" as an unthinking cliché used by two stereotypical feminists in the story "A Queer Streak" in *The Progress of Love*. Their capitalized phrases, "What is called Female Craziness is nothing but centuries of Frustration and Oppression," are seen to be used by Munro "to satirize their common 'anti-patriarchal rage' as a childishly simple-minded distortion of complicated facts" (178). Carrington, *Controlling the Uncontrollable: The Fiction of Alice Munro* (DeKalb: Northern Illinois UP, 1989): 177–79.

7. This analysis of apparent oddness or madness is not carried out in stereotypical fashion along the lines of the assertions of the two young women in "A Queer Streak." Munro's protagonists are not to be seen as typical madwomen in the attic.

8. Alice Munro, *The Moons of Jupiter* (Toronto: Macmillan, 1982): 196. Further page references to stories in this collection are in the text.

9. Ildikó de Papp Carrington discusses this scene in terms of narrative style, and the personal humiliations and judgements revealed by the use of a tale within a tale. "This split, in which the self-critical narrator recognizes the culpability of her own behaviour, is yet another illustration of the analogous functions of Munro's first-person and omniscient third-person narrators"; Carrington, *Controlling the Uncontrollable*, 155.

10. Lorraine York discusses the concept of connection in Alice Munro's work and the frequency as well as the variety of the appearances of the word in her fiction. She points to the centrality of the concept in *The Moons of Jupiter*, and argues that Munro investigates both family connections and connections with the past: "[in *The Moons of Jupiter*] he gives voice most strongly to the idea that art may be the most reliable means of forging an honest connection with the past" (142); York, "'Gulfs' and 'Connections': The Fiction of Alice Munro," *Essays on Canadian Writing* 35 (1987): 135–46.

CORAL ANN HOWELLS

# Intimate Dislocations: *Alice Munro,* Hateship, Friendship, Courtship, Loveship, Marriage

"On a bridge. This is a floating bridge."

Now she could make it out—the plank roadway just a few inches above the still water. He drew her over to the side and they looked down. There were stars riding on the water . . .

The slight movement of the bridge made her imagine that all the trees and the reed beds were set on saucers of earth and the road was a floating ribbon of earth and underneath it all was water. And the water seemed so still, but it could not really be still because if you tried to keep your eye on one reflected star, you saw how it winked and changed shape and slid from sight. Then it was back again—but maybe not the same one.

("Floating Bridge," 81–82)

Trying to figure out Fiona had always been frustrating. It could be like following a mirage. No—like living in a mirage.

("The Bear Came Over the Mountain," 317)[1]

A female figure in a dark landscape where everything is rocking on water and a man who sees his marriage as a mirage—what is illusory and what is real? And how do such subjective impressions of space relate to questions of identity in Alice Munro's latest short story collection, *Hateship, Friendship, Courtship, Loveship, Marriage*? For over thirty years Munro's stories have

---

From *Contemporary Canadian Women's Fiction: Refiguring Identities*, pp. 53–78, 210–12. © 2003 by Coral Ann Howells.

167

mapped the intricate social and emotional geographies of small-town com-
munities in Huron County in southwestern Ontario, where she was born
and brought up in the 1930s and 1940s, and to which she returned in the
early 1970s after twenty years away in British Columbia. Now she moves
regularly between home territory and the west coast, living part of the year
in one place and then in the other. Munro's new collection, like *The Love of a
Good Woman* (1998), reflects that movement backwards and forwards across
the geographical spaces of Canada and across time as well, for there is an
increasing emphasis here on elderly people (retired couples, recent widows,
old people in nursing homes) with an accompanying sense of individual lives
scrolling out over many decades. All this is familiar territory for Munro's
readers, and these latest stories resonate with echoes that go back to her first
collection, *Dance of the Happy Shades* (1968). As she said in an interview with
Peter Gzowski at the time of publication of this book in 2001, "I was afraid
people would say 'More of the same, more of the same.' And I felt, well I
don't care if they say that, I'm just going to do it."[2] Yet Munro's "revisitings"
(to borrow American critic Robert Thacker's word)[3] oddly combine familiarity with strangeness, for like the character in one of her early stories who
is asked if he is "back visiting old haunts," she might reply "Not visiting.
Haunting."[4] Though there is no suggestion of the supernatural or the psychic here (as there was in *Open Secrets*), there is a very strong sense of added
dimensions of vision, both in the collection as a whole and in the characters'
own subjective perceptions. The apparent unpredictability of individual lives
is shadowed by wider patterns beyond immediate apprehension, intimated
through literary allusions, through landscape, or through moments of retrospection and revelation, where what "looked like adventures . . . was all
according to script, if you know what I mean."[5] Every story contains seismic
shocks, identities are reinvented and relationships change over time, yet
through these fragmented narratives Munro introduces "powerful legendary shapes behind ordinary life" that appear to overlap with the anecdotal
present lives of her protagonists, just as they in turn experience moments of
slipping sideways between different dimensions of reality.[6] These intimate
dislocations point the way back to my opening questions, which could now
be reformulated as one question: How much might Munro's explorations
of identity be related to her characters' shifting locations within the textual
spaces of her stories?

    Munro's narratives are always geographically specific and place is fre-
quently a substantial support for her protagonists' sense of identity, as Gerald
Lynch argued in his recent study of Canadian short-story cycles, where he
commented on Munro's 1978 volume: "*Who Do You Think You Are?* is in fact
a supreme example of a contemporary story cycle of character wherein place

as small town, Hanratty, is recovered to play a definitive role in the formation of character, and, later, the affirmation of identity."[7] He goes on to suggest that this story cycle illustrates "the traditionally Canadian engagement with the question of individual and national identity in relation to place" (p. 160), and certainly in this most recent collection significant moments of realization and crisis are attached to specific places. Yet it is also true, as Lynch acknowledges, that within the environmental context Munro traces characters' shifts in subjective positioning over time as her stories open out into the spaces of memory and imagination. In *Hateship, Friendship, Courtship, Loveship, Marriage* written more than twenty years after *Who Do You Think You Are?*, there is a proliferation of characters through nine different stories as Munro looks into the complicated processes involved in growing up and growing older when identities appear to change at different times, in different places, in different relationships. Of course "place" is still important even if many of these stories are more concerned with departures than with returns home, though the abstract and malleable concept of "space" would seem better to accommodate the multidimensionality of Munro's representations of identity.

My critical understanding of space owes a great deal to Henri Lefebvre's masterly exposition in *The Production of Space*, where he explores the concept in theoretical and experiential terms, seeking to reconcile human space with physics, metaphysics, and ideology. Within this vast project, he speculates on the relationship between "mental space" (subjective inner space), "physical space" (the space occupied by human bodies and material objects and which would include geographical space), and "social space" (which incorporates social relations both individual and collective as well as social structures like families and towns and cities). It is his discussion about the connections between subjectivity and location that I have found most useful in my attempts to articulate the complexities of identity construction in Munro's latest fictions.[8] Indeed, Lefebvre's question about mapping social spaces might be easily translated into the challenge that Munro's stories pose for her critics: "How many maps, in the descriptive or geographical sense, might be needed to deal exhaustively with a given space, to code and decode all its meanings and contents?" (Lefebvre, p. 85). Lefebvre's depth model of multiple mapping, which effectively deconstructs a place into a series of overlapping spaces, would seem to provide a useful analogy for Munro's narratives, where her stories with their overlapping complexities plot identity not as single and fixed but as a series of alternative histories hidden within individual subjects' life stories. These are "identities always in process," and though Munro asserted recently "You're the same person at nineteen that you are at thirty that you are at sixty that you go on being" and "there is some root in your nature that doesn't change,"[9] her stories suggest a radical ambiguity as to where this core of self might be located when its figurings are always partial and changing. All her characters share the sense that life can be lived simultaneously in two different dimensions or experienced from two perspectives, with the result that her protagonists are not split subjects but pluralized subjects. The critical question is how Munro's stories manage to represent these dislocations and multiplicities within individual identity without her characters becoming estranged from the material spaces of their everyday worlds. As she once remarked, "We are the ones who impose the notion of succession on our lives. Perhaps this is how we avoid confronting what is fantasy and what is reality. That is, if it is ever possible to make a meaningful distinction between the two."[10]

Working with the conventions of realism, Munro begins by mapping her characters' identities through the traditional coordinates of age, gender, and social class, relationship to family and community or to region and place of origin. Though she revises these in multiple ways as connections with realism become more ambiguous, she does not engage directly with identity issues relating to nationality, race, or ethnicity. Such issues remain peripheral to the minds of the small-town Ontario citizens in the majority of her stories, whose attitudes might be summed up by the station master's comment in the first story of *Hateship, Friendship, Courtship, Loveship, Marriage* when a young woman wants her furniture sent by rail to a place out in Saskatchewan named Gdynia:

> "A lot of places out there it's all Czechs or Hungarians or Ukrainians," he said. It came to him as he said this that she might be one of those, but so what, he was only stating a fact.
>     "Here it is, all right, it's on the line." (p. 2)

Gdynia may be marked on the railway map, but he will take no responsibility for somewhere so far beyond familiar limits: "Towns out there, they're not like here."

For the station master an unfamiliar name on a map designates a blank space rather than a place, which raises questions around representation. How is a person's identity represented within the textual spades of Munro's stories, and how much of identity is constructed, as Stuart Hall suggested, "within, not outside, representation?"[11] Of course representation must play a substantial role in the way identities are perceived by the self-conscious subjects themselves as well as by others in a social context, but Munro is interested in hidden dimensions of the self that cannot be directly represented, though they constitute the complex layerings of individual subjectivity. She is fascinated by "the way people fall in and out of love, the way people twist things around, things that are ways that we all contrive our lives, I think ... to me they seem really extraordinary and things that I want to explore."[12]

Munro's concern is not exclusively with women, though her focus is predominantly on how female characters reexamine and revise their lives for she seeks, as she has always done, to "discover a possible space for the feminine imaginary," always so complicitously involved with and yet other than dominantly masculine discourse.[13] In all these stories relationships between men and women constitute the field in which "the feminine" is defined through varieties of resistance to masculine constructions, as each woman seeks not a room of her own but a space of her own where she can escape the constraints of expectation imposed upon her. Munro is still seeking for new ways of "saying the unsayable" and constructing "probable fictions,"[14] figuring out identities through narratives that reconstruct apparently stable surfaces as multidimensional spaces where characters are aware of slipping in and out of different subjective worlds while their bodies remain grounded in the physical spaces of the everyday.

Those slippages are eloquently suggested in my two opening passages—one from a feminine and one from a masculine perspective—to which I shall return briefly. The episode in "Floating Bridge" is set in a familiar Ontario landscape on the edge of a swamp where Jinny, a middle-aged woman dying of cancer, walks out on the bridge at night with a young man whom she has just met and finds a moment of release from pain and anxiety in that liminal space between the dark water and the reflected stars. There is slippage of a different kind in the mirage effect of the second passage when an elderly husband has a disconcerting flash of insight into his relationship with his wife who is now suffering from Alzheimer's Disease. While the first passage refers to a real landscape where sensory perception shifts into a moment of vision, the second passage is only a figure of speech, a provisional representation for something real, which like any mirage shimmers as an image in empty space.

In the first reflective moment, everything is floating and unstable as reality blurs into a mirror image of itself. The evidence of the senses is not to be trusted and Jinny's experience is one of continual movement with the rocking of the bridge and the vanishing then reappearing stars, while as she looks the real world becomes a floating world and then slides back into dimensions of rationality again. Jinny would like to solve the problem of where she is, not only in relation to physical space (which suddenly appears to be boundless and unfathomable) but also in relation to the "muddle" in her own mind. Is she under immediate threat of death as she had believed, or is she possibly in a period of remission as the doctor has just informed her? Her subjective perceptions of landscape reflect her psychological state as she wonders if the water is as still as it looks, and if the reflected stars are the same or not the same ones she sees at different times. There is a strong temptation to read this stunningly visual passage symbolically as an in-between space beyond normal life, separated from dry land and floating above the dark waters, or to interpret it through a Freudian model where a "manifest" dream content masks a "latent" content of anxiety, while those reflected stars may remind readers of the "star maps and constellations" in *The Moons of Jupiter* (1982) with their indecipherable patterns visible across the vast distances of the cosmos. It seems to me that all these interpretations are possible, though held as subsidiary meanings within the spaces of the text, where the floating bridge is a real topographical feature of the Sowesto landscape, which at the same time becomes a platform for what Dennis Duffy has described in another "near-visionary" moment as "an account of experience that redefines the nature of experience itself."[15]

A similar redefinition of experience is effected through the "mirage" in the second passage. Though far less elaborate than the first, it also encodes an image detached from reality, this time deconstructing an elderly husband's complacent assumptions about his long married life as he suddenly glimpses how it might be viewed from another perspective altogether, where everything turns strange.[16] As Lefebvre remarks, "Mirage effects can introduce an extraordinary element into an ordinary context" (p. 189) whereby what seemed clear and graspable shifts to become unreachable, delusory. A mirage is nothing but an optical illusion, when an image of something at a great distance or even invisible over the horizon appears in space, owing to the laws of reflection and reflection of light; there is something somewhere but it lies always beyond reach, or as Lefebvre explains it, "The mirage … is in some sense that which lies short of—and beyond—each part" (p. 181). It is Grant, the man who married Fiona because "she had the spark of life" ("Bear," p. 275), who suddenly sees his wife and their life together slipping away from him when he has to put her in a nursing home. Indeed, there has been a great deal in this marriage that was not transparent at all: Fiona has never known about Grant's many infidelities and he has never known what she really thought, in a relationship conducted on a bright surface of games and jokes where everything is something like the real thing, though there is always a dimension missing. (The phrase "something like that" is a recurrent emblem in this story.) Ironically, Fiona's dementia seems merely to exaggerate her elusiveness and Grant finds it impossible to believe that anything has really changed. Maybe she is only joking after all? "It would not be unlike her" (p. 291). Visiting her at the nursing home, he continually tries to remake Fiona in her old image, and it is an open question at the end whether enough of the old Fiona remains for him to go on doing this. Under what circumstances does a mirage disappear, leaving only empty space?

This last story in the collection ends appropriately with a "shimmer of signifiers," that evanescent cluster which underlay Jean Baudrillard's definition of seduction,[17] and seduction might be said to characterize not only the thematics of this story but also the appeal of the collection as a whole, which like Fiona's identity is always difficult to pin down. Though the stories are all concerned with different characters, there is a sense of patterning that makes it less like a collection and more like a sequence framed by the first and last stories and where all the others take up the same emotional and thematic resonances introduced in the title story.[18] The first story is named after a schoolgirls' game about romance and marriage that sketches what looks like a traditional sequence in a woman's life, though "hateship" introduces a disruptive element and it soon becomes apparent that the words of the game do not promise a predictable pattern but only a series of possibilities, which may occur in any random order. So it happens in the first story, where a young woman called Johanna suddenly leaves her position as an old man's housekeeper in small-town Ontario and goes out west to Gdynia to meet her "lover" as the result of a romantic correspondence forged by two schoolgirls. Instead of its turning into a disastrous joke, Johanna marries the man and they move to British Columbia where they have a son. However, that marriage happens offstage, and the final emphasis shifts back to one of the schoolgirls, who is suddenly dismayed by the "whole twist of consequence" unleashed by her invented letter narratives. What began as a game swings wide into spaces beyond her control so that she feels like the butt of somebody else's joke. Her sense of limited vision and artful contrivance is related here to the duplicitous powers of storytelling, as it is so many times in this collection—with the stories printed in newspapers or made up by a creative writer ("Family Furnishings"), with a satirical poem found in a dead husband's pajama pocket ("Comfort") or a disturbed young man's dream poem like an impression of "wet leaves" in "Post and Beam," and with the secret letters that a young wife tucks "under the elastic waistband of her underpants" (p. 267) in "Queenie" to prevent her jealous husband from finding them. The first story also functions as a metafictional commentary where female romantic fantasy is shown up as fabrication (as it is in "Nettles" and "What Is Remembered"), though possibly more significant is the sense of transgression when the schoolgirls' fantasy script is translated into a real-life narrative that produces a marriage and a child. That is not the end of the story however, for translation works both ways. When one of the girls hears the astonishing news about Johanna's baby she is doing her Latin homework at the kitchen table, and the words of Horace's Ode, which she is translating, take on a disturbing resonance, like a message from an ancient parallel world addressed directly to her across the centuries. Caught within the frame of an entirely different text, that girl is forced to review her childish prank so that she finds herself more deeply implicated in real-life events than she could ever have imagined. This sudden shift in perspective produces a moment of radical dislocation in mental space for the character and for the reader as well, jolting us into paying a different kind of attention to those "really extraordinary things" within everyday life that so fascinate Munro.

The first story with its emphasis on adolescent girls and young women might be seen as a kind of overture to a collection where all the other stories represent experience through middle-aged or elderly people's lives, so that the sense of arbitrariness and displacement is amplified within the wider temporal frames of retrospective knowledge or prospects of imminent death. In most of these stories loss seems inevitable, though that is alleviated by a surprising amount of laughter—laughing fits, giggles, and smiles of all kinds: silly smiles, absentminded smiles, sly charming smiles, and even a "swish of tender hilarity," while there are lots of games and jokes—word jokes, practical jokes, and other more ambiguous or possibly malicious jokes. As Magdalene Redekop alerted readers in *Mothers and Other Clowns*, jokes have always been an important feature of Munro's storytelling, with their potential to subvert carefully contrived structures of reason and social decorum in outbursts of irrationality, which reveal dimensions of absurdity within the seemingly normal.[19] Most memorable perhaps is Bobby Sherriff's gesture at the end of *Lives of Girls and Women*, which is a marvelous example of the mysterious power of a joke. As Del Jordan reports:

> Then he did the only special thing he ever did for me. With those things in his hands, he rose on his toes like a dancer, like a plump ballerina. This action, accompanied by his delicate smile, appeared to be a joke not shared with me so much as displayed for me, and it seemed also to have a concise meaning, a stylized meaning—to be a letter, or a whole word, in an alphabet I did not know.[20]

Whereas jokes in Munro's stories frequently offer a kind of pleasure in slipping sideways within familiar social spaces, others are much more ambiguous, being presented like Bobby Sherriff's in a coded language that seems to flaunt its duplicity. The question of jokes and their dislocating function will occur frequently in my discussion of particular stories, though it is also one of the techniques for producing the phenomenon of double vision or sideways slippage in this collection. Jokes undermine realism by exposing its limits as a mode of representation, challenging fixed notions of identity by gesturing toward what is unacknowledged, incomprehensible, or forbidden. Nowhere is this more apparent than in the last story, where Fiona's identity becomes fragmented as she succumbs to Alzheimer's Disease. It is the story of a wife's departure and a husband's bewilderment, but it is so full of jokes and games that in the end it shimmers like the mirage in my opening passage. The narrative is always slipping sideways between different places and periods of time, and the strange sly ending elides divisions between the present and the past (and possibly the real and the imaginary) as this woman suddenly makes a joke to her husband as she had always done. But is this just a momentary masquerade, and is her husband's reassuring response just a repetition of his old marital betrayals? Perhaps there are continuities in this marriage after all, where a joke is like a floating bridge rocking on unstable surfaces. The ending may also be a reminder that there are times when a joke is the only possible vehicle for representing a cluster of emotions too painful or too complicated to be described in any other way. Such jokes do not lose the mysterious power that Del perceived in Bobby Sherriff's gesture, though bewilderment may sometimes have a tragic rather than a comic resonance. This is the case in "Nettles," when a woman's romantic fantasies about an old childhood friend collapse in the face of his revelation of a terrible family disaster, revealing secrets lurking under the social surfaces of normalcy. Childhood memories and the realities of adulthood come into sharp collision as she remembers that his father was a well digger:

> "Mystery," he said. And again, "Well."
> That was a word that I used to hear fairly often, said in that same tone of voice, when I was a child. A bridge between one thing and another, or a conclusion, or a way of saying something that couldn't be more fully said, or thought.
> "A well is a hole in the ground." That was the joking answer.
> (p. 183)

Munro's narrative art is so complex that, having sketched the context for my inquiry, I have selected only four stories from this collection for detailed analysis: "Hateship, Friendship, Courtship, Loveship, Marriage," "Floating Bridge," "What Is Remembered," and "The Bear Came Over the Mountain." Any attempt to analyze the secrets of her storytelling as it weaves together networks of relationships across space and time is likely to end with something close to a "Well," though it is only through looking closely into the narrative mesh itself that we might hope to trace Munro's explorations of identities in process. That multidimensional concept of identity comes close to the concept of "meaning" in a Munro story as it is described by Carol Shields. "The meaning of a Munro story emerges from this complex patterning rather than from the tidiness of a problem/solution set-up or the troublesome little restraints of beginnings, middles and ends."[21] In turn, both "meaning" and "identity" in Munro bear a strong similarity to the concept of "truth," which Adrienne Rich spelt out in an essay on fiction and lies:

> There is no "the Truth," "a truth"—truth is not one thing, or even a system. It is an increasing complexity. The pattern of the carpet is a surface. When we look closely or when we become weavers, we learn of the tiny multiple threads unseen in the overall pattern, the knots on the underside of the carpet.
>
> That is why the effort to speak honestly is so important. Lies are usually attempts to make everything simpler—for the liar—than it really is, or ought to be.[22]

The title story, "Hateship, Friendship, Courtship, Loveship, Marriage," provides a programmatic overview of the collection as well as a word of guidance to readers on how to approach these stories. The traditional female destiny sketched out in the title is fulfilled in the narrative in unexpected ways, as a young woman goes out into unknown territory following a fantasy script through which she finds her new identity as a wife and mother. The story begins with the prospect of dislocation set uncompromisingly in a realistic small-town context as the young woman, Johanna, comes to the railway station to inquire about sending a load of furniture out west and also to buy a ticket for herself on the same train. She is represented as unglamorous, bossy, and determined, as unclassifiable as a "plain clothes nun" (p. 5). That is the point of view of the stationmaster who has never heard of Gdynia before, but there is another side to this story that begins to unfold when Johanna enters the feminine space of a ladies' dress shop, an incongruous figure surrounded by the glamour of full-length mirrors, taffeta evening gowns, and velvet trimmings. Though it would seem there is no possible fit between her clumsy body and the trappings of conventional femininity, the saleswoman cleverly finds a simple brown dress that gives Johanna her first glimpse of this new secret world. Appropriately enough at this point Johanna makes her surprising announcement, "It'll likely be what I get married in" (p. 9), which is all the more astonishing when we discover that her declaration, like her trip out to Saskatchewan with the furniture, is based not on certainty at all but on a romance conducted by letter where no wedding had ever been mentioned.

The story develops with constant shifts in narrative perspective between realism on the one hand and romantic fantasy on the other, though the fantasizing is not Johanna's but that of two schoolgirls, Edith and Sabitha, who forge a correspondence between Johanna and Sabitha's widowed father, Ken

Boudreau, who lives out in Gdynia. Johanna does actually write replies to "his" letters, but her letters are never sent and her own voice is obliterated in the girls' malicious game: "So then she falls in lo-ove," as indeed she does. There is a strong counterpoint between Johanna's developing narrative of desire and its realistic underpinnings, fleshed out by her loving care of Ken Boudreau's furniture from his first marriage, which is stored in her employer's barn and which she cleans and polishes: "It looked glamorous, like satin bed-spreads and blond hair" (p. 16). It is this furniture that always has to be taken into account and which provides the link between realism and romance when Johanna goes out west.

Her arrival in Gdynia is like entering a blank space; not only is there nobody to meet her but "there did not appear to be a town." Everything in that bare prairie landscape is so unfamiliar that she first of all mistakes Ken Boudreau's shabby hotel for a derelict family house, and when she does dis-cover the man himself naked in bed, the scene is in no way erotic: "The door of the bedroom at the end of the hall was open, and in there she found Ken Boudreau" (p. 42)—delirious with bronchitis. Johanna begins their relation-ship by taking command and nursing him back to health. The first thing she tells him is that she has brought his furniture, which was really the last thing he wanted. Boudreau is completely indifferent to this strange woman until he sees her bank account, "which added a sleek upholstery to the name Johanna Parry." Though the scenario is the opposite of romance in every way, ironi-cally Boudreau's words to Johanna when he is recovering echo the words in the forged correspondence earlier, so confirming her belief in his love for her though that letter "exchange" remains a secret part of Johanna's private fan-tasy life. Boudreau is a shiftless man as his past history reveals, though he has enough self-interest and sense as he lies on Johanna's freshly washed sheets to recognize her strength and devotion "like a net beneath him, heaven-sent, a bounty not to be questioned" (p. 49). Conversely, although she sees that he is weak, "another fine-looking, flighty person in need of care and manage-ment" like her beloved former employer Mrs. Willetts, these are qualities that provide Johanna with her chance of emotional fulfillment, "such a warm commotion, such busy love" (p. 51). Munro has deftly turned romance on its head, translating the dynamics of fantasy into real life while subverting the traditional gendered power relationship into celebration of a woman's managerial capacities and a man's gratitude for being rescued. Again, it is the furniture that codes in this link, as Johanna declares that they must sell the hotel and move to British Columbia, taking the furniture with them of course: "We have got all we need to furnish a home" (p. 50), a statement that Boudreau embroiders with thoughts of evergreen forests and ripe apples out in the Okanagan: "*All we need to make a home*" (p. 51).

The rest of Johanna's story of her changed identity as Mrs. Boudreau and mother of an infant son Omar remains untold in a space outside the text, for it happens in a location remote from the interests of small-town Ontario where the letter-writing frame story is set. Johanna's story of escape is one of the narratives embedded here that remains incompletely known, and of which only fragments are given, like pieces of supplementary information that engender radical reinterpretations. Back in Ontario, Edith still lives at home with her parents above their shoe shop, where she suffers from a clever girl's sense of alienation, which readers will remember from Del Jordan in *Lives of Girls and Women*: "And in a way, it seemed only proper that the antics of her former self should not be connected with her present self—let alone with the real self that she expected would take over once she got out of this town and away from all the people who thought they knew her" (p. 52).

Ironically, the news of Johanna's baby's birth is contained in the death notice of Johanna's old employer in the local paper, and it is that missing piece of information that Edith resents most of all. Try as she might to exonerate herself from responsibility for Omar's existence, it reminds her that the past cannot be shut off as completely as she had hoped. Moreover, the Horace quotation in her Latin homework challenges her image of herself as a "god-like arranger of patterns and destinies" (Munro's phrase to describe her own sense of power when as an adolescent she discovered the delights of storytelling),[23] as she is forced to contemplate the consequences of her letter-writing game in a wider frame of reference than she had ever imagined. It is one of those "vertiginous moments" to which Natalie Foy refers "when characters glimpse one of the parallel narratives" that intersect in their lives,[24] causing a tremor of subjective dislocation like a joke from the distant past that subverts any illusion of authority over the future: "You must not ask, it is forbidden for us to know ... what fate has in store for me, or for you—" (p. 52).

In "Floating Bridge" the action of the narrative is likewise suspended between past and future though for Jinny Lockyer, the middle-aged protagonist who is dying of cancer, there is no doubt of what fate has in store for her. In the shadow of approaching death the story moves from harsh sunlight to evening and nightfall, though the overall effect is not one of closure as might be expected but of an expanded perspective as Jinny stands on the floating bridge in a liminal space, overcome by "a swish of tender hilarity," contemplating her past and her future with equanimity. The poise of that near-visionary moment holds the structural and thematic complexity of this story in a delicate balance, and in my analysis I shall focus on how the narrative negotiates multiple spaces for representing a distinctively feminine subjectivity through landscape. Though the equivalence between the female body and landscape is a familiar trope in women's writing and one that Munro has used suggestively in other stories like "Oranges and Apples" and "What Do You Want to Know For?"[25] both stories about cancer threats, this revisiting presents no simple identification but a series of physical and emotional dislocations. Jinny moves backwards and forwards between past and present, always shifting between acquiescence and flight until she finds her moment of temporary freedom on the bridge at the end. This is the story of a good woman's resistance to her husband's persistent misconstructions of her identity through their long marriage, where Munro traces a particular kind of feminine anger that has always remained hidden and unsayable except in the disguised form of jokes and one failed escape attempt when Jinny got as far as the bus station and then came home again. That is the point where the story begins, with her departure and then a joke.

In this story, which is full of jokes of various kinds, it is interesting that the first joke, told by Jinny, relates to their marriage and to its threatened break-up, which never happened. As Munro remarked to Peter Gzowski, telling jokes was a popular literary genre in the place where she grew up:

> I don't know if they do that much any more. But it used to be sort of a habit when you went visiting, people one knew well, in Huron County. It meant that you didn't have to introduce conversation where people might not agree—politics and things like that. So you talked about the weather, and then as you relaxed, people began to tell jokes. And I very seldom had a good joke to tell ... It's a form of literary composition, but nobody feels it's literary, so anybody can become an expert at it.[26]

Evidently Jinny tells her joke "in company . . . many times," though why she should choose to make such an embarrassing topic into an amusing story for social occasions intrigues Munro's readers if not Jinny's listeners. How do we interpret the meanings coded into Jinny's joke, and why is it there as a flashback at the beginning of the story? This is where Freud's perspective on jokes is helpful for throwing theoretical light on the nature of jokes, or what in his investigations of the subject in *Jokes and Their Relation to the Unconscious* he calls "the problem of jokes."[27] Like Munro, Freud is of the opinion that jokes are a form of social communication designed to give pleasure to tellers and listeners in a licensed transgression of reason or decorum, while making visible hidden connections between words or incidents through shifts of emphasis: "a joke is developed play" (p. 238). Freud discusses verbal jokes and conceptual jokes though not practical jokes, arguing for strong similarities between the techniques of jokes and the dream-work in their processes of condensation and displacement, leading to the indirect representation of repressed materials, all of which are ways of saying the unsayable. Possibly his most revelatory comment in relation to Jinny's joke is the following: "A joke will allow us to exploit something ridiculous in our enemy which we could not, on account of obstacles in the way, bring forward openly or consciously: once again, then, the joke *will evade restrictions and open sources of pleasure that have became inaccessible*" (p. 147).

If all this sounds too far-fetched, it is worth remembering that Jinny's joke originated in a burst of anger and contempt at her husband Neal, a teacher at the Correctional Institute for Young Offenders, because he had joined a group of them in eating a cake she had just made for a meeting at their house, displaying a pattern of disrespect for his wife that the reader will come to see as characteristic of him. Apparently the only reason Jinny did not go ahead with her plan to leave was because of the graffiti messages written on the walls of the bus shelter, which terrified her with the possibility of becoming lonely and marginalized herself. "Would she be compelled to make statements on public walls?" (p. 53). Instead of graffiti, she makes her statement of rebellion against Neal's authority in the form of a joke, being the kind of person, a "Nice Nellie" as one of his friends spitefully calls her, "who finds criticism or aggressiveness difficult so long as they are direct, and possible only along circuitous paths."[28] Nevertheless, that joke foregrounded at the beginning signals a darker subtext to their marriage and provides a context for the puzzling mixed messages and habitual masquerades that constitute the multiple dimensions of Jinny's identity.

This is a story where a woman's hostility and discontent are so close to being inadmissible even to herself that it is quite difficult on a first reading to know what is central and what is marginal. "What is the important thing? What do you want us to pay attention to?"[29] Is Jinny's story of her cancer diagnosis and possible remission at the center of the narrative? Is it her husband's fascination with Helen their new home help, or their trip in the van to pick up Helen's good shoes from her caravan home out in the country? Is it the dynamics of this marriage itself with Jinny's mass of silent rebellious feelings littering her life like a pile of rubbish? Certainly all these strands are interwoven in a narrative whose dislocations suggest that this is a story that, like Jinny's joke, has a secret to hide. Only at the end with the view from the floating bridge do the seemingly random anecdotes fall into a pattern, as if this "barrage of human messages" like the graffiti on the walls of the bus shelter or the piles of letters and newspaper articles waiting to be put on disk in Jinny's front room, all sink to the status of insignificant background noise in the still landscape of the swamp. For most of the story readers find themselves in a position rather like Jinny herself: "The fact was that with so much going on and present events grabbing so much of her attention, she found it hard to take any view at all" (p. 58). Yet when read retrospectively, the apparently random sections and even their arrangement can be seen to take up the resonances of "Hateship, Friendship, Courtship, Loveship, Marriage," though with these varied emotional states deviously interwoven. Finally the reader is able to follow the clues both displayed and concealed in that first joke as the marriage is reconstructed from the disillusioned wife's perspective, though her husband is too busy even to notice. As the jangle of noise dies down, the reader is able to map a series of crisis points through which this woman's identity is represented, as the spaces for her self-figuring keep shifting from one form of domestic entrapment to another until she manages at last to find her glorious moment of escape.

Jinny's predicament might be understood through landscape after all, in the contrast between the freedom she experiences on the floating bridge at night and her evident distress during the heat of the day when she is subjected to her husband's incessantly nervous activity, driving pointlessly around town and then socializing with Helen's foster parents when all she wants to do is to go home. These different places provide a realistic context for Jinny's changing feelings, though it is also possible to read these spatial oppositions in gendered terms through a lens of feminist theory. I am thinking of Hélène Cixous's "Sorties" (the very title of which resonates through Jinny's deepest desires), where she lays out a suggestive paradigm of hierarchized relations between man and woman, which outlines the positions between husband and wife in this story:

> Activity / passivity,
> Sun / Moon,
> Day / Night ...
> Head / heart ...
> Form, convex ...
> Matter, concave ...
> Always the same metaphor: we follow it, it transports us, in all of
> its forms, wherever a discourse is organized ... The hierarchization
> subjects the entire conceptual organization to man.[30]

Of course in the story such diagrammatic representation is masked by realistic anecdote, though the pattern is absolutely consistent. Everything is dominated by Neal's activities, his decisions, and his friends, and even their home, which has been converted into an office for his good causes, is a male dominated space where Jinny serves as his secretary. In her bleaker moments she is aware that if circumstances changed, all the papers she is in charge of could easily be thrown out like a pile of useless rubbish. Jinny's resistance surfaces at unexpected moments, like the time when lying in bed she suddenly thinks of Neal's death and is shocked to find that what she feels is "the unspeakable excitement you feel when a galloping disaster promises to release you from all responsibility" (p. 58). Like the first joke, which no doubt she turns against herself in her retellings, so the disaster will be her own death and not his, but this obfuscation cannot hide her sense of the oppressiveness of his presence. This story is full of suppressed feminine rage though Jinny's anger is usually displaced on to other people associated with Neal, like the girl Helen who has for her "a disagreeable power" or like Matt, the grotesquely fat foster father whose purple navel "riding on his belly like a giant pincushion" provokes waves of nausea in Jinny. His shady joke about the pussy willow causes a rare outburst from Jinny, though ironically it has nothing to do with him directly. It is a symptom of her repressed anger against Neal and her doctor, neither of whom shows any sympathy for her condition, giving rise to one of those split moments when the subject inhabits two different worlds at once and the messages get confused. There is no confusion however, about her fierce silent criticism of Neal when she sees him playing his male power games with Helen in the van: "On his face there was an expression of conscious, but helpless, silliness. Signs of an invasion of bliss. Neal's whole body was invaded, he was brimming with silly bliss" (p. 65). This is the man who had not even listened when his wife tried to tell him about the doctor's diagnosis and her possible remission. Of course it is that anger which Jinny carries with her, even when she gains a space of solitude on Matt's farm. Refusing to accompany Neal into the caravan for a beer and a sociable conversation, she wanders off into a cornfield, but even here she is plagued by old resentments and the thought that after her death she will remain misunderstood: "Everyone was wrong ... When you died, of course, these wrong opinions were all there was left" (p. 72).

Only at the end when Jinny drives out to the floating bridge with the eighteen-year-old son of Helen's foster parents does she find a precious moment of freedom outside her "old, normal life," and it is a freedom associated with open spaces that might be read in Cixous's gendered terms as feminine. This is one of Munro's secret places hidden within a familiar landscape, reached by driving away from the farm and heading off on a dirt track, where daylight and heat gradually give way to cool darkness and the noises of the day are replaced by the sounds of frogs and lapping water. Jinny's experience is not that of a solitary spectator's rapture at the prospect of sublime landscape; instead it is closer to Aritha van Herk's description of a woman's experience of the prairie: "Landscape beckons escape: escapade."[31] Jinny is not alone, for Ricky the young man drives her out to the swamp and then he leads her on to the bridge, where first of all he shows her the stars reflected in the water and then he kisses her before they walk back the way they came. Though that kiss is an expression of casual intimacy, it is also a moment of intense mutual enjoyment:

> It seemed to her that this was the first time ever that she had participated in a kiss that was an event in itself. The whole story, all by itself. A tender prologue, an efficient pressure, a wholehearted probing and receiving, a lingering thanks, and a drawing away satisfied.
>     "Oh," he said. "Oh." (p. 82)

There is a strong inflection of the erotic in Jinny's sense of this fulfillment of her feminine identity, just as there is an odd freakish awareness (for the reader) of a parallel between her experience with Ricky as an enhanced version of Neal's silly infatuation with Helen. Yet it is also Jinny's moment of near-visionary experience, which "redefines the nature of experience itself,"[32] and where for the first time she is able to view Neal's foibles with a "lighthearted sort of compassion." Unlike the rest of the story, the ending is not infused with feminine anger but instead spells emotional liberation where binary oppositions become blurred like the stars reflected in the dark water. It is significant that this is a "floating bridge" where Jinny the older woman is standing with Ricky who is a young man less than half her age, so that neither she nor the reader is allowed to forget that her position is a very unstable one and that her transcendent vision is firmly located in relation to her suffering embodied self. There is no escape possible from the real world except through death, though the final words of the story do grant Jinny a moment of rejoicing with that "swish of tender hilarity, getting the better of all her sores and hollows, for the time given" (p. 83), thus making a joke against death itself.

"What Is Remembered" is also the story of a woman's escape from the dailiness of her marriage, but there is less doubt this time of where the center might be located. It is embedded in the space of female romantic fantasy, though it ends at a point beyond romance as Meriel, now an old woman, remembers her brief secret affair with a bush doctor early in her marriage, telling the story some time after the deaths of both the doctor and her husband. Munro is revisiting old haunts, for throughout her career she has traced the seductive maps of the feminine imaginary, showing how closely a woman's sense of identity is bound up with sexuality and desire that seems to defy age and experience. Meriel's story is situated within a long feminine tradition, marked by Munro from Del Jordan's teenage romance in "Baptizing" (*Lives of Girls and Women*), to adult women's fantasies in "Simon's Luck" (*The Beggar*

*Maid*) and "The Jack Randa Hotel" (*Open Secrets*), a process spelled out most explicitly in "Bardon Bus" (*The Moons of Jupiter*):

> Then I come back again and again to the center of my fantasy, to the moment when you give yourself up, give yourself over, to the assault which is guaranteed to finish off everything you've been before. A stubborn virgin's belief, this belief in perfect mastery; any broken-down wife could tell you there is no such thing.[33]

Nevertheless, those fantasies continue to engross the imaginative lives of older women like Louisa Doud in "Carried Away" (*Open Secrets*) who dreams of a man who died years before and who returns in a hallucinatory moment of "radiant vanishing consolations," and of younger women like Johanna Parry who secretly cling to "that preposterous hope of transformation, of bliss."[34] Munro remains fascinated by the dynamics of erotic fantasy, as she remarked in her Gzowski interview in 2001. Speaking of "Nettles" and "What Is Remembered" she managed to imply how the latter story is looking at romance from a new critical direction: "And the other story is about, of course, how our imaginations, how our fantasies can play such a terribly important role in our lives. Fantasies that never come true, but do come true in a way and then are misrepresented, and how we need these dreams to live by."[35]

What is remembered and forgotten only to be remembered years later, in this story that begins with a quotation taken from a newspaper and is then structured as a secret story about a woman's fantasy life hidden within the story of her real life? Who is Meriel, and how are her shifting subjective and social locations described within this text, which extends over a period of more than thirty years? The story opens in Vancouver with Meriel and her young husband Pierre at the funeral of his best friend Jonas, who died in a motor cycle accident up north, and it is at the lunch afterwards that Meriel, turning away from visions of the afterlife promised by the minister at the service, sees her husband speaking to the unknown bush doctor who had cared for Jonas after his accident. At that stage Meriel has no inkling that within a few hours time she and the doctor would come together in a passionate sexual relationship for one afternoon, which she would remember for the rest of her life. It is only when the doctor, who had driven her to visit an old family friend in a nursing home, makes the surprising offer to come in with her for the visit that she begins to understand the unspoken sexual chemistry between them, registered not consciously but entirely through the language of her body: "She had a sudden mysterious sense of power and delight, as if with every step she took, a bright message was travelling from her heels to the top of her skull" (p. 227).

Their visit to Aunt Muriel would seem like a digression though it turns out to be oddly complicitous with the romantic fantasy plot, for this almost blind old woman who sits smoking a cigarette while grotesquely wrapped in an asbestos cape, has an uncanny kind of second sight that unmasks their affair even before it has happened. Most disturbingly for Meriel, her much admired old friend changes before her eyes into somebody else, becoming "a suddenly strange old woman" who speaks with a new voice "not like any voice of hers that Meriel remembered." She tells them a story from her own youthful bohemian past in Vancouver, which uncannily foreshadows what will happen to them that very day. Perhaps Aunt Muriel is taking on the role of one of the Fates as she sits blindfolded by cataracts, remembering an erotic game that she once played in the dark, and wearing a blindfold: "Adventures. Well . . . It looked like adventures, but it was all according to script, if you know what I mean. So not so much of an adventure, actually" (p. 230). This strangely parallel narrative coming from somewhere in the past and interrupted by the old woman's violent coughing fits challenges the younger woman's willed innocence in an old sexual game whose rules are well known and to which she has already consented. Meriel dismisses all this as "salacious fantasy," as she would have to do in order to go on playing the game at all. Given the time frames of this story, the reader will be aware that Meriel is now the same age as Aunt Muriel was at the time of that last visit, a suggestive parallel that reminds us of the extraordinary number of proliferating stories which are interwoven with Meriel's—not only Aunt Muriel's story, but also the doctor's, Pierre's, Jonas's (none of which Meriel or the reader will ever know) as well as her own fantasy narrative in its different versions, which is at the center of the plot.

It is not so much the affair itself as how it is remembered and what this reveals about Meriel's double life that interests Munro most: "In fact, I'm never absolutely sure of anything, and that's probably why I write stories, because every story is an investigation for me."[36] After their one passionate afternoon together nothing else happens, for there are no dismaying twists of consequence here—at least not in the real world. Meriel never sees the doctor again and she returns to the familiar social spaces of her marriage, which ends only with Pierre's death thirty years later. Yet that affair retains all its vitality as the erotic subtext of her life, endlessly revisited in daydreams as the secret space beyond respectable domesticity where Meriel's other self, that fantasy self which confirms her sexuality and her desirability as a woman, continues to exist with "every cell in her body plumped up with a sweet self-esteem" (p. 239). What she remembers most clearly are her own words to the doctor at the beginning of their affair, which are a woman's words of surrender: "*Take me somewhere else*, not *Let's go somewhere else.* That is important to her. The risk, the transfer of power . . . The start for her—in all her reliving of this moment—of the erotic slide" (pp. 233–34), where "Yielding had been the order of that day" (p. 239). The doctor had taken Meriel to his friend's Kitsilano apartment, a "small, decent building, three or four stories high," though she deliberately reconstructs the memory of that place to fit in with her own romantic scenario: "Why did she conjure up, why did she add that scene?" Of course she is always adding to and revising her memories: "She would keep picking up things she'd missed, assailed by sudden recollections."

Meriel's addiction to her fantasy script represents a form of feminine creativity where she edits her own plot and rejects other plots like the tragic romance plot, "not the kind that anybody wrote any more" (p. 239), or Turgenev's plot in *Fathers and Sons* that she discusses with Pierre when he is dying. She would like to revise the romantic climax of that novel because she feels offended by Turgenev's distortion of the woman's position: "I feel it's just Turgenev coming and yanking them apart and he's doing it for some purpose of his own" (p. 236).[37] Meriel is resisting not only Turgenev's nineteenth-century discourse of femininity but also Pierre's late twentieth-century masculinist construction of a woman's identity: "When it was over she'd love him all the more. Isn't that what women are like? I mean if they're in love?" he asks. And Meriel, "cornered," still manages to answer, "No" (pp. 236–37). Her fantasy has an independent imaginative life of its own, proved by the fact that the news of the doctor's death makes no difference to her daydreams, "if that's what you could call them" (p. 238). Moreover, her fantasizing throws up a seemingly endless fund of memories, one of which surfaces only after Pierre's death, when she suddenly recalls not the goodbye between herself and the doctor at the ferry terminal but his parting words that were both a lie and a "kind and deadly caution" designed to keep her from making a serious mistake and losing her emotional balance. Their secret affair needs to remain in a space deliberately shut off from reality, which was exactly where the doctor was placing it for them both. Meriel recognizes the doctor's gesture of self-preservation, just as she is aware of her own survival mechanisms and the fact that "prudence" had always been her guiding principle, though in her case enhanced by romantic fantasy. Now an old woman casting a retrospective glance over her life, she quite coolly contemplates the doctor's ghost: "She wondered if he'd stay that way, or if she had some new role waiting for him, some use still to put him to in her mind, during the time ahead" (p. 241). After all, as Atwood remarked in *The Robber Bride*, "The dead are in the hands of the living," and Meriel is positioned here as the historian who is outside the event manipulating her own script. She offers perhaps unwittingly a savage anatomy of the narcissistic self-serving quality of romantic fantasy, which imaginatively reverses the dynamics of power in a sexual relationship while paradoxically guaranteeing its vitality as a crucial component of the feminine imaginary.[38]

As the last story in the collection, "The Bear Came Over the Mountain" resonates against the others as it traces the fragmentation of a seventy-year-old woman's identity through Alzheimer's Disease and the end of her marriage when she is placed in a nursing home. Alzheimer's would seem to be the test case for studying the relation between identity and memory, as this psychotic illness fractures connections while in the process revealing the multiplicities of a self, obliterating some layers of recent memory and uncovering other forgotten layers hidden in the past. In a strange way, this story represents another version of multiple mapping: "How many maps . . . might be needed to deal exhaustively with a given space, to code and decode all its meanings and contents?"[39] or in this case, how many narratives might be needed to map one person's identity and her shifting subjective locations over a lifetime? The story is told not from Fiona the woman's point of view but focalized through her husband Grant's perspective, with some commentary from an omniscient narrator. Beginning with a history of Fiona and Grant's life as a couple, it ends with the aftermath of marriage in a nursing home; the story is structured as a retrospective of their long married life, including the day Grant commits Fiona to the institution and an account of his regular visits to her over several months. It follows Munro's characteristically metonymic narrative construction, proceeding by an accumulation of fragments linked tenuously by associative processes through which a married relationship and a woman's loss of her social identity are figured out. Is the narrative suggesting that Fiona no longer has an identity, or does it merely indicate that the balance of her personality has altered, so that what look like dislocations or blanks in memory might be interpreted as relocations in a different area of subjective space?

Once again the reader is challenged by Munro's unsettling mixture of the familiar and the unfamiliar in a narrative set within a detailed realistic framework, which at the same time exposes the limits of realism with its glimpses of alternative realities, dream lives, secret lives, and a proliferation of subsidiary themes around one main event, that of Fiona's Alzheimer's and her removal to a nursing home. Seen through Grant's eyes, it might be read as a husband's narrative of loss and memory that circles around his wife's absence; but Fiona is not dead. She is still alive and now living in an institution from which he is shut out most of the time so that her life has become a mystery to him, as he is reminded on every visit. Confronted with the evidence of her changing identity and her new emotional relationship with a fellow patient called Aubrey, Grant is forced to consider how that affects his own relationship with his wife, so that his story of mourning slips into a different genre altogether as it assumes the configurations of a plot about marital infidelity and a husband's jealousy. Yet Fiona seems perfectly happy and without guilt in her new identity as Aubrey's close companion. Viewed from her perspective (which is only ever implied), this could be read as the story of a wife's escape through dementia from the prescripted plot of her married life. The narrative keeps all those possibilities in play through its sideways slippages into fragments of other remembered stories, defying resolution in a manner best described by Ajay Heble when he speaks of Munro's "awareness that for any utterance, for any claim to be inhabiting a particular realm of meaning, there are always potential levels of meaning, and alternative ways of formulating ideas and ordinary experiences."[40]

Fiona's residence at Meadowlake Nursing Home (or "Sillylake" as she had once jokingly named it) forms the center of Grant's narrative as he speculates endlessly on what is happening to her behind those closed doors. It is his recognition that he is now an outsider to her life that is the generative principle behind the stories he tells himself as he comes to realize that he does not know who she is or who she ever was. It is as if Alzheimer's has merely exaggerated the elusiveness that had always been her most seductive quality: "She's always been a bit like this" (p. 277). Grant finds it impossible to decide whether she has really changed or not, or whether she is playing a game to test his love and fidelity, "a game that she hoped he would catch on to. They had always had their games—nonsense dialects, characters they invented" (p. 277). However, he becomes increasingly bewildered by Fiona's behavior, for while she retains her social mask and always greets him with her "lopsided, abashed, sly, and charming smile" (p. 288), he can never be certain whether Fiona recognizes him or not: "He could not decide. She could have been playing a joke" (p. 291). Yet, as he reflects, it would have been a cruel joke and out of character. Despite the nurse's warning that with Alzheimer sufferers what is remembered and forgotten shifts from day to day, he persists in believing that Fiona is not lost to him, for he is a man who has always been slow to notice changes in his women—either in his female students in the 1970s or in his wife's present psychological condition. His visits become a torment to him as Fiona continues to treat him with a "distracted social sort of kindness that was successful in holding him back from the most obvious, the most necessary question" (p. 293). Does she remember that he is her husband of nearly fifty years?

Above all, Grant is tormented by jealousy as he is forced every visit to contemplate his wife's devoted attachment to Aubrey, an old boyfriend from her distant past, as the two of them unselfconsciously enact their parody of adolescent love at the card table and in the conservatory (and where else?). Grant is forced into a new role as voyeur and stalker of his own wife, "like a mulish boy conducting a hopeless courtship" or like "one of those wretches who follow celebrated women through the streets" (p. 296). While the nurses and other patients treat it as a joke, "That Aubrey and that Fiona? They've really got it bad, haven't they?" (p. 292) and the medical opinion would be that Fiona was not fully in control of her emotions, the sight of them together provokes Grant's furious anger and "a truly malignant dislike" of Aubrey. His jealousy is exacerbated by unease as Grant finds himself looking back through the spaces of memory to his own numerous secret affairs during the 1960s and 1970s, which he had always taken pride in concealing from Fiona under a masquerade of faithfulness: "He had never stopped making love to Fiona in spite of disturbing demands elsewhere. He had not stayed away from her for a single night" (p. 285). Now this complacency is shattered as Fiona's affair with Aubrey appears to him like an open demonstration of his own secret liaisons, just as in the past her jokey voices had "mimicked uncannily the voices of women of his that she had never met or known about" (p. 277). Meadowlake may be "short on mirrors" though Grant is forced to look at the reflection of his own past behavior, feeling increasingly "as if he were suffering some mental dislocations of his own" (p. 298). The nursing home starts to assume hallucinatory dimensions as Grant wanders around, getting lost in its labyrinthine passageways and always wondering if the different women he sees could be Fiona dressed up in somebody else's clothes. Tormented and confused, it would seem that Grant does not escape punishment for his infidelities but that Fiona all unwittingly (or wittingly, who knows?) is turning the tables and playing a cruel joke on him after all. Munro's readers may wonder if that is perhaps one of Fiona's remaining wifely functions: "Is this the last function of old women . . . making sure the haunts we have contracted for are with us, not one gone without?"[41]

The story loops backwards and sideways in unexpected directions, though it is Grant's perplexing relations with Fiona and his inability either to accept or to represent her changed identity that I shall focus on here. In the last episode when he visits Fiona, he has brought her a "surprise" though it is he who is surprised and not her. (The surprise is Aubrey whom Grant has brought back to visit Fiona, but she has already forgotten about him and he remains absent, presumably outside the door.) Suddenly Grant catches the look on Fiona's face, that of a woman marked with the indelible signs of Alzheimer's: "She stared at him for a moment, as if waves of wind had come beating into her face. Into her face, into her head, pulling everything to rags" (p. 321). Yet, despite these symptoms of decay, Fiona still retains some of her old "bantering grace" as she stand up and throws her arms about her husband in seeming recognition. She then makes one of her old word jokes, which is heart-breaking, not for its faint echoes of her former self but for the way it codes in her inarticulate fears and anxieties: "You could have just driven away," she said. "Just driven away without a care in the world and forsook me. Forsooken me. Forsaken" (p. 322). As Freud said of dreams, so too of jokes, "If we succeed in turning the dream into an utterance of value . . . we shall evidently have a prospect of learning something new and receiving communications of a sort which would otherwise be inaccessible to us."[42] The story ends with Grant's reply, "Not a chance,"which in its turn is an echo of his old duplicitous reassurances. It is as if this final scene is a replay of a relationship that has already vanished, where in the peculiar social spaces of Meadowlake, "people were content to become memories of themselves, final photographs" (p. 296).

Like Grant, the reader is left in a space of indeterminacy where Fiona's behavior is as mystifying as ever. What is going on in the mind of this woman who thinks today that she is in a hotel and about to check out? It seems like a real encounter between husband and wife, but is this genuine emotional warmth on Fiona's part or just in Grant's imagination? Does Fiona, who is wearing a bright yellow dress, which is not hers, resemble the yellow skunk lilies in the swamp that Grant observed driving home one day? She once told him that they were supposed to generate a heat of their own but that she doubted the truth of this statement: "She said that she had tried it, but she couldn't be sure if what she felt was heat or her imagination" (p. 316). Has Alzheimer's Disease at last cost Grant Fiona in a way that his marital infidelities never did, and is this loving embrace nothing but a mirage, or another of those "radiant vanishing consolations" that Munro sometimes offers?

It would seem that this last story offers a more complete version of the shifting locations through which identity might be represented though never defined in the multiple dimensions of Munro's narratives, just as it appears to figure the final episodes in that story of female destiny spelled out in the schoolgirls' word game at the beginning. With its own title based on a childish rhyme,[43] it confirms that promise of unpredictability coded into the opening game, in its artful arrangement of fragments that make up the narrative of a husband and wife's relationship over many years. Like most of the other stories in this collection it ends in the narrative present, this time marked by a joke and a moment of reconciliation, which may be nothing more than a simulacrum of reality. That indeterminate ending is so characteristic of Munro's stories, which are constructed like floating bridges across the spaces between what is real and may be imagined: "I wanted these stories to be open. I wanted to challenge what people want to know. Or expect to know. Or anticipate knowing. And as profoundly, what I think I know.[44]

## NOTES

1. Alice Munro, *Hateship, Friendship, Courtship, Loveship, Marriage* (Toronto: McClelland & Stewart, 2001). All further page references to the stories in this volume will be included in the text.

2. Peter Gzowski, "You're the same person at 19 that you are at 60: Interview with Alice Munro," *The Globe and Mail* (September 29, 2001). Focus F4–F5.

3. Robert Thacker, "Introduction: Alice Munro, Writing 'Home': 'Seeing This Trickle in Time,'" *Essays on Canadian Writing* 66 (Winter 1998): 1–20.

4. Alice Munro, *Something I've Been Meaning to Tell You* (1974) (Harmondsworth: Penguin, 1985), 13.

5. Alice Munro, "What Is Remembered," *Hateship, Friendship, Courtship, Loveship, Marriage*, 230.

6. Catherine Sheldrick Ross, "'At Least Part Legend': The Fiction of Alice Munro," in *Probable Fictions*, ed. Louis B. MacKendrick (Toronto: ECW Press, 1983), 112–36.

7. Gerald Lynch, *The One and the Many: English-Canadian Short Story Cycles* (Toronto, Buffalo, London: University of Toronto Press, 2001), 160. *Who Do You Think You Are?* is the Canadian title for the collection published in the United States and Britain as *The Beggar Maid*, obliterating this radical questioning of identity in its title.

8. Henri Lefebvre, *The Production of Space*. Translated by Donald Nicholson-Smith (Oxford, U.K. and Cambridge, U.S.A.: Blackwell, 2001). For a fuller exposition of Lefebvre's approach and methodology see 1–67. Other useful analyses of relations between geographical and psychological space may be found in K. Kirby, *Indifferent Boundaries: Spatial Concepts of Human Subjectivity* (London and New York: Guildford Press, 1996), 1–36, and C.A. Howells, *Alice Munro* (Manchester: Manchester University Press, 1998), 4–12.

9. Gzowski interview, F4.

10. P. Boyce and R. Smith, "A National Treasure: Interview with Alice Munro," *Meanjin* 54, 2 (1995): 222–32.

11. Stuart Hall, "Cultural Identity and Diaspora," in *Colonial Discourse and Post-Colonial Theory*, ed. P. Williams and L. Chrisman (New York and London: Harvester-Wheatsheaf, 1993), 392–403.

12. Gzowski interview, F4.

13. The phrase is Luce Irigaray's in *This Sex Which Is Not One*, trans. Catherine Porter (Ithaca and New York: Cornell University Press, 1985), 164.

14. My reference here is to the first two books of critical essays published on Munro in the early 1980s: Judith Miller, ed., *The Art of Alice Munro: Saying the Unsayable* (Waterloo, Ontario: University of Waterloo Press, 1984), and Louis MacKendrick, ed., *Probable Fictions: Alice Munro's Narrative Acts* (Toronto: ECW Press, 1983).

15. Dennis Duffy, "'A Dark Sort of Mirror': 'The Love of a Good Woman' as Pauline Poetic," *Essays on Canadian Writing* 66 (Winter 1998): 169–90.

16. Munro has been charting such glimpses of uncharted territory from the beginning. This phrase occurs at the end of the first story in her first collection, *Dance of the Happy Shades* (Harmondsworth: Penguin, 1983), 18.

17. Jean Baudrillard, *Seduction*, trans. Brian Singer (London: Macmillan, 1990), 90.

18. Though only *Lives of Girls and Women* (which was published as a novel) and *Who Do You Think You Are?* are true story cycles, many of Munro's collections are structured as sequences. See my chapter on *The Moons of Jupiter* in *Alice Munro* (Manchester: Manchester University Press, 1998), 67–74, and Natalie Foy, "'Darkness Collecting': Reading 'Vandals' as a Coda to *Open Secrets*," *Essays on Canadian Writing* 66 (Winter 1998): 147–68.

19. M. Redekop, *Mothers and Other Clowns: The Stories of Alice Munro* (London and New York: Routledge, 1992), 25–34.

20. Alice Munro, *Lives of Girls and Women* (Harmondsworth: Penguin, 1982), 250.

21. Carol Shields, "In Ontario: Review of *Friend of My Youth*," *London Review of Books* (February 7, 1991), 22–23.

22. Adrienne Rich, "Women and Honor: Some Notes on Lying" (1975), in *On Lies, Secrets, and Silence: Selected Critical Prose 1966–1978* (London: Virago, 1980), 185–94.

23. Alice Munro, "Author's Commentary," in *Sixteen by Twelve: Short Stories by Canadian Writers*, ed. J. Metcalf (Toronto: Ryerson, 1970). Quoted by Catherine Sheldrick Ross, *Alice Munro: A Double Life* (Toronto: ECW Press, 1992), 45.

24. Natalie Foy, "Darkness Collecting: Reading 'Vandals' as a Coda to *Open Secrets*," 149.

25. "Oranges and Apples" in *Friend of My Youth* (London: Vintage, 1991), 106–36, and "What Do You Want to Know For?" in *Writing Away: The PEN Canada Travel Anthology* (Toronto: McClelland and Stewart, 1994), 203–20.

26. Gzowski interview, F4.

27. Sigmund Freud, *Jokes and Their Relation to the Unconscious*. Penguin Freud Library, vol. 6 (London: Penguin, 1991), 137.

28. Ibid., 194.

29. Munro, *Friend of My Youth*, 216.

30. Hélène Cixous, "Sorties," in *New French Feminisms*, ed. E. Marks and I. de Courtivron (New York and London: Harvester-Wheatsheaf, 1981), 90–98.

31. "Women Writers and the Prairie: Spies in an Indifferent Landscape," in Aritha van Herk, *A Frozen Tongue* (Sydney: Dangaroo, 1992), 140.

32. Duffy, "A Dark Sort of Mirror," 170.

33. Alice Munro, *The Moons of Jupiter* (Harmondsworth: Penguin, 1984), 111.

34. Munro, *Hateship, Friendship, Courtship, Loveship, Marriage*, 6.

35. Gzowski interview, F4.

36. Ibid., F4.

37. This feminist critique of a nineteenth-century male plot bears interesting similarities to Aritha van Herk's critique of Tolstoy's *Anna Karenina*, in *Places Far from Ellesmere* (Alberta: Red Deer College Press, 1990), 131–39.

38. As if to underline the ongoing revisionary process of Meriel's romantic fantasy, Munro changed the ending of the story in this collection from its original published version in *The New Yorker* (February 19, 2001), 196–207, totally altering the emphasis of the final paragraph: "She wondered if he'd stayed that way, or if some other role had been waiting for him, up ahead."

39. H. Lefebvre, *The Production of Space*, 85.

40. Ajay Heble, *The Tumble of Reason: Alice Munro's Discourse of Absence* (Toronto: University of Toronto Press, 1994), 20.

41. Alice Munro, "The Peace of Utrecht," *Dance of the Happy Shades* (Harmondsworth: Penguin, 1983), 209.

42. Sigmund Freud, *New Introductory Lectures on Psychoanalysis*, Penguin Freud Library, vol. 2 (Harmondsworth: Penguin, 1977), 37.

43. What did the bear discover? "The other side of the mountain" is the enigmatic answer in the rhyme.

44. P. Boyce and R. Smith, "A National Treasure: Interview with Alice Munro," *Meanjin* 54, 2 (1995): 222–32.

# *Chronology*

| | |
|---|---|
| 1931 | Born Alice Laidlaw on July 10 in Wingham, Ontario, daughter of Robert Eric, a farmer, and Ann Clarke (Chamney). |
| 1949–51 | Attends University of Western Ontario on a scholarship. Marries James Munro, a bookseller, in December 1951. They move to Vancouver. |
| 1963 | Moves to Victoria, British Columbia, and establishes Munro Book Shop with her husband. |
| 1968 | Publishes first collection of short stories, *Dance of the Happy Shades*; receives Governor General's Literary Award. |
| 1971 | *Lives of Girls and Women* published. |
| 1974–75 | Publishes *Something I've Been Meaning to Tell You* in 1974. Writer-in-residence at the University of Western Ontario. |
| 1976 | Divorced. Marries Gerald Fremlin, a geographer and friend from her undergraduate days. Moves to Clinton, Ontario, a few miles from her childhood home. |
| 1978 | *Who Do You Think You Are?* published; receives Governor General's Literary Award. |
| 1980 | Writer-in-residence at the University of British Columbia for four months and at the University of Queensland in the autumn. |
| 1982 | *The Moons of Jupiter* published. |

1986        *The Progress of Love* published; receives Governor General's Literary Award.

1990        *Friend of My Youth* published.

1994        *Open Secrets* published.

1996        *Selected Stories* published.

1998        *The Love of a Good Woman* published; wins National Book Critics Circle Award.

1999        Publishes *Queenie: A Story*.

2001        *Hateship, Friendship, Courtship, Loveship, Marriage* published.

2003        *No Love Lost* published.

2004        *Vintage Munro* and *Runaway* published.

2006        *The View from Castle Rock* published.

# Contributors

HAROLD BLOOM is Sterling Professor of the Humanities at Yale University. He is the author of 30 books, including *Shelley's Mythmaking, The Visionary Company, Blake's Apocalypse, Yeats, A Map of Misreading, Kabbalah and Criticism, Agon: Toward a Theory of Revisionism, The American Religion, The Western Canon,* and *Omens of Millennium: The Gnosis of Angels, Dreams, and Resurrection. The Anxiety of Influence* sets forth Professor Bloom's provocative theory of the literary relationships between the great writers and their predecessors. His most recent books include *Shakespeare: The Invention of the Human,* a 1998 National Book Award finalist, *How to Read and Why, Genius: A Mosaic of One Hundred Exemplary Creative Minds, Hamlet: Poem Unlimited, Where Shall Wisdom Be Found?,* and *Jesus and Yahweh: The Names Divine.* In 1999, Professor Bloom received the prestigious American Academy of Arts and Letters Gold Medal for Criticism. He has also received the International Prize of Catalonia, the Alfonso Reyes Prize of Mexico, and the Hans Christian Andersen Bicentennial Prize of Denmark.

MAGDALENE REDEKOP is a professor at the University of Toronto. Aside from writing *Mothers and Other Clowns: The Stories of Alice Munro,* she is the author of several essays.

KATHERINE J. MAYBERRY is vice president for academic affairs at Rochester Institute of Technology. She is the author of *Christina Rossetti and the Poetry of Discovery* and *Everyday Arguments: A Guide to Writing and Reading Effective Arguments.*

GEORGEANN MURPHY is coordinator of the International Research Opportunities Program at the University of New Hampshire. She has published articles on Shakespeare.

AJAY HEBLE is a professor in the School of English and Theatre Studies at the University of Guelph. He is the author of three books and the founder and co-editor of *Critical Studies in Improvisation/Études critiques en improvisation*, a peer-reviewed online scholarly journal.

MARK LEVENE is an associate professor at the University of Toronto at Mississauga. He is the author of *Arthur Koestler* and was an advisory editor for *The Art of Short Fiction*, edited by Gary Geddes.

DEBORAH HELLER is retired from teaching humanities at York University. She is the author of *Literary Sisterhoods: Imagining Women Artists* and co-author of *Jewish Presences in English Literature*.

JUDITH MCCOMBS is the author of two books and numerous articles on Margaret Atwood. She also has written several books of poetry, such as *Against Nature: Wilderness Poems* and *Territories, Here & Elsewhere*. She teaches at the Writer's Center in Bethesda, Maryland.

JANET BEER has been a professor at Manchester Metropolitan University. She has published titles on Kate Chopin and Edith Wharton and edited the *Cambridge Companion to Kate Chopin*.

ROWLAND SMITH has been vice president of academics at Wilfrid Laurier University. He is the author of *Lyric and Polemic: The Literary Personality of Roy Campbell* and the editor of *Postcolonizing the Commonwealth: Studies in Literature and Culture* and other titles. He has contributed to book-length works and numerous periodicals.

CORAL ANN HOWELLS was a professor at the University of Reading, United Kingdom. She has written and lectured extensively on Canadian writing in English. She is the author of a book on Alice Munro, in addition to other titles, and is the editor of several works, including *Where Are the Voices Coming From? Canadian Culture and the Legacies of History*.

# Bibliography

Barber, Lester E. *Alice Munro: The Stories of* Runaway. *ELOPE: English Language Overseas Perspectives and Enquiries* 3, nos. 1–2 (2006): 143–56.

Becker, Susanne. *Gothic Forms of Feminine Fictions.* Manchester, England: Manchester University Press, 1999.

Beran, Carol L. "Thomas Hardy, Alice Munro, and the Question of Influence." *American Review of Canadian Studies* 29, no. 2 (Summer 1999): 237–58.

Carrington, Ildikó de Papp. "Where Are You, Mother? Alice Munro's 'Save the Reaper.'" *Canadian Literature* 173 (Summer 2002): 34–51.

Carscallen, James. *The Other Country: Patterns in the Writing of Alice Munro.* Toronto: ECW, 1993.

Charman, Caitlin J. "There's Got to Be Some Wrenching and Slashing: Horror and Retrospection in Alice Munro's 'Fits.'" *Canadian Literature* 191 (Winter 2006): 13–30.

Condé, Mary. "Fathers in Alice Munro's 'Fathers.'" *Journal of the Short Story in English* 41 (Autumn 2003): 93–101.

———. "Voyage towards an Ending: Alice Munro's 'Goodness and Mercy.'" In *Telling Stories: Postcolonial Short Fiction in English*, edited by Jacqueline Bardolph, pp. 59–66. Amsterdam, Netherlands: Rodopi, 2001.

Daniels, Cindy Lou. "Creating Fictionality: Re-Living Reality in Alice Munro's Fiction." *Eureka Studies in Teaching Short Fiction* 6, no. 2 (Spring 2006): 94–105.

Duncan, Isla J. "'It Seems So Much the Truth It Is the Truth': Persuasive Testimony in Alice Munro's 'A Wilderness Station.'" *Studies in Canadian Literature/ Etudes en Littérature Canadienne* 28, no. 2 (2003): 98–110.

Esplin, Marlene Hansen. "Revisions and Recontextualizations of Alice Munro's Short Fiction." *Eureka Studies in Teaching Short Fiction* 6, no. 2 (Spring 2006): 74–84.

Forceville, Charles. "Alice Munro's Layered Structures." In *Shades of Empire in Colonial and Post-Colonial Literatures*, edited by C.C. Barfoot and Theo D'haen, pp. 301–310. Amsterdam, Netherlands: Rodopi; 1993.

Garson, Marjorie; Alice Munro and Charlotte Brontë *University of Toronto Quarterly: A Canadian Journal of the Humanities,* 2000 Fall; 69 (4): 783–825.

Gerlach, John. "To Close or Not To Close: Alice Munro's 'The Love of a Good Woman.'" *Journal of Narrative Theory,* 2007 Winter; 37 (1): 146–58.

Godard, Barbara. "'Heirs of the Living Body': Alice Munro and the Question of a Female Aesthetic." In *The Art of Alice Munro: Saying the Unsalable,* edited by Judith Miller. Waterloo: University of Waterloo Press, 1984. 43–71.

Heble, Ajay. *The Tumble of Reason: Alice Munro's Discourse of Absence.* Toronto: University of Toronto Press, 1994.

Heller, Deborah. *Literary Sisterhoods: Imagining Women Artists.* Montreal, QC: McGill-Queen's University Press, 2005.

Hiscock, Andrew. "'Longing for a Human Climate': Alice Munro's *Friend of My Youth* and the Culture of Loss." *Journal of Commonwealth Literature* 32, no. 2 (1997): 17–34.

Houston, Pam. "A Hopeful Sign: The Making of Metonymic Meaning in Munro's 'Meneseteung.'" *North Dakota Quarterly* 52, no. 3 (Fall 1992): 79–92.

Howells, Coral Ann. *Alice Munro.* Manchester: Manchester University Press, 1998.

Jamieson, Sara. "The Fiction of Agelessness: Work, Leisure, and Aging in Alice Munro's 'Pictures of the Ice.'" *Studies in Canadian Literature/Etudes en Littérature Canadienne* 29, no. 1 (2004): 106–26.

Johnson, Brian. "Private Scandals/Public Selves: The Education of a Gossip in *Who Do You Think You Are?*" *Dalhousie Review* 78, no. 3 (Autumn 1998): 415–35.

Lilienfeld, Jane. "Shirking the Imperial Shadow: Virginia Woolf and Alice Munro." *Woolf Studies Annual* 10 (2004): 253–74.

Lynch, Gerald. "No Honey, I'm Home: Place over Love in Alice Munro's Short Story Cycle, *Who Do You Think You Are?*" *Canadian Literature* 160 (Spring 1999): 73–98.

Martin, Peggy. "'What a Pathetic Old Tart': Alice Munro's Older Women." *English Studies in Canada* 24, no. 1 (March 1998): 83–92.

May, Charles E. "Why Does Alice Munro Write Short Stories?" *Wascana Review of Contemporary Poetry and Short Fiction* 38, no. 1 (Spring 2003): 16–28.

McCaig, JoAnn. *Reading In: Alice Munro's Archives.* Waterloo, ON: Wilfrid Laurier University Press, 2002.

McCarthy, Dermot. "The Woman Out Back: Alice Munro's 'Meneseteung.'" *Studies in Canadian Literature* 19 (1994): 1–19.

McGill, Robert. "Somewhere I've Been Meaning to Tell You: Alice Munro's Fiction of Distance." *Journal of Commonwealth Literature* 37, no. 1 (2002): 9–29.

———. "Where Do You Think You Are? Alice Munro's Open Houses." *Mosaic: A Journal for the Interdisciplinary Study of Literature* 35, no. 4 (December 2002): 103–19.

Miller, Judith Maclean. "Deconstructing Silence: The Mystery of Alice Munro." *Antigonish Review* 129 (Spring 2002): 43–52.

———. "An Inner Bell that Rings: The Craft of Alice Munro." *Antigonish Review* 115 (Autumn 1998): 157–76.

———. "On Looking into Rifts and Crannies: Alice Munro's *Friend of My Youth*." *Antigonish Review* 120 (Winter 2000): 205–26.

Morgenstern, Naomi. "The Baby or the Violin? Ethics and Femininity in the Fiction of Alice Munro." *LIT: Literature Interpretation Theory* 14, no. 2 (April/June 2003): 69–97.

Phelan, James. "Judgment, Progression, and Ethics in Portrait Narrative: The Case of Alice Munro's 'Prue.'" *Partial Answers: Journal of Literature and the History of Ideas* 4, no. 2 (January 2006): 115–30.

Ross, Catherine Sheldrick. "Alice Munro: A Double Life." Toronto: ECW, 1992.

Somacarrera, Pilar. "Exploring the Impenetrability of Narrative: A Study of Linguistic Modality in Alice Munro's Early Fiction." *Studies in Canadian Literature/Etudes en Littérature Canadienne* 21, no. 1 (1996): 79–91.

Soper-Jones, Ella. "Wilderness Stations: Peregrination and Homesickness in Alice Munro's *Open Secrets*." *Wascana Review of Contemporary Poetry and Short Fiction* 38, no. 1 (Spring 2003): 29–50.

Stich, Klaus P. "Letting Go with the Mind: Dionysus and Medusa in Alice Munro's 'Meneseteung.'" *Canadian Literature* 169 (Summer 2001): 106–125.

Thacker, Robert. "Alice Munro's Willa Cather." *Canadian Literature* 134 (Fall 1992): 42–57.

———. "What's 'Material': The Progress of Munro Criticism, II." *Journal of Canadian Studies/Revue d'Etudes Canadiennes* 33, no. 2 (Summer 1998): 196–210.

———, ed. *The Rest of the Story: Critical Essays on Alice Munro*. Toronto, ON: ECW, 1999.

Ventura, Héliane. "The Ordinary as Subterfuge: Alice Munro's 'Pictures Of The Ice.'" *Journal of the Short Story in English* 38 (Spring 2002): 73–84.

Wachtel, Eleanor. "Alice Munro: A Life in Writing." *Queen's Quarterly* 112, no. 2 (Summer 2005): 267–80.

Wall, Kathleen. "Representing the Other Body: Frame Narratives in Margaret Atwood's 'Giving Birth' and Alice Munro's 'Meneseteung.'" *Canadian Literature* 154 (Autumn 1997): 74–90.

Ware, Tracy. "Tricks with 'a Sad Ring': The Endings of Alice Munro's 'The Ottawa Valley.'" *Studies in Canadian Literature/Etudes en Littérature Canadienne* 31, no. 2 (2006): 126–41.

Weinhouse, Linda. "Alice Munro: Hard-Luck Stories or There Is No Sexual Tension." *Critique* 36, no. 2 (Winter 1995): 121–129.

# *Acknowledgments*

Magdalene Redekop, *"Dance of the Happy Shades*: Reading the Signs of Invasion." From *Mothers and Other Clowns: The Stories of Alice Munro*, pp. 37–59. © 1992 by Magdalene Redekop. Reprinted by permission.

Katherine J. Mayberry, "'Every Last Thing . . . Everlasting': Alice Munro and the Limits of Narrative." From *Studies in Short Fiction* 29, no. 4 (Fall 1992): 531–41. © 1992 by Newberry College. Reprinted by permission.

Georgeann Murphy, "The Art of Alice Munro: Memory, Identity, and the Aesthetics of Connection. pp. 12–27, 155–56 " From *Canadian Women: Writing Fiction*, edited by Mickey Pearlman. © 1993 by the University Press of Mississippi. Reprinted by permission.

Ajay Heble, "'It's What I Believe': Patterns of Complicity in The Progress of Love." From *The Tumble of Reason: Alice Munro's Discourse of Absence*, pp. 143–68, 198–99. © 1994 by the University of Toronto Press, Inc. Reprinted with permission of the publisher.

Mark Levene, "'It Was About Vanishing': A Glimpse of Alice Munro's Stories." From *University of Toronto Quarterly* 68, no. 4 (Fall 1999): 841–860. © 1999 by the University of Toronto Press and the Graduate Centre for the Study of Drama. Reprinted by permission of University of Toronto Press Incorporated (www.utpjournals.com).

Deborah Heller, "Getting Loose: Women and Narration in Alice Munro's *Friend of My Youth*." From *The Rest of the Story: Critical Essays on Alice Munro*, edited by Robert Thacker, pp. 60–80. © 1999 by ECW Press. Reprinted by permission.

Judith McCombs, "Searching Bluebeard's Chambers: Grimm, Gothic, and Bible Mysteries in Alice Munro's 'The Love of a Good Woman.'" From *American Review of Canadian Studies* 30, no. 3 (Autumn 2000): 327–48. © 2000 by *American Review of Canadian Studies*. Reprinted by permission.

Janet Beer, "Short Fiction with Attitude: The Lives of Boys and Men in the *Lives of Girls and Women*." From *The Yearbook of English Studies*, vol. 31, North American Short Stories and Short Fictions (2001): 125–32. © Modern Humanities Research Association, 2001. Reproduced by permission of the publisher.'

Rowland Smith, "Rewriting the Frontier: Wilderness and Social Code in the Fiction of Alice Munro." From *Telling Stories: Postcolonial Short Fiction in English*, edited by Jacqueline Bardolph, pp. 77–90. © 2001 by Rodopi. Reprinted by permission.

Coral Ann Howells, "Intimate Dislocations: Alice Munro, *Hateship, Friendship, Courtship, Loveship, Marriage*." From *Contemporary Canadian Women's Fiction: Refiguring Identities*, pp. 53–78, 210–12. © 2003 by Coral Ann Howells. Reproduced with permission of Palgrave Macmillan.

Every effort has been made to contact the owners of copyrighted material and secure copyright permission. Articles appearing in this volume generally appear much as they did in their original publication with few or no editorial changes. In some cases, foreign language text has been removed from the original essay. Those interested in locating the original source will find the information cited above.

# Index

Abish, Walter, 1
"Accident"
    connections in, 47
    France in, 47, 89
    Ted in, 47
"Age of Faith," 44
Agnon, Shmuel Yosef, 1
"Albanian Virgin, The," 95–96
    travel writing, 94
"Among School Children" (Yeats),
    27
Andreyev, Leonid, 1
Atwood, Margaret, 84, 134, 186
    *Strange Things*, 154–156, 159
Austen, Jane, 2

Babel, Isaac, 1
"Babtizing," 183
"Bardon Bus," 49
    Dennis in, 48
    fantasies in, 184
    narrator in, 30, 36, 45, 163
Barthelme, Donald, 1
"Bear Came over the Mountain,
    The"
    Aubrey in, 187–189
    dementia in, 172, 175, 187–190
    Fiona in, 167, 172–175, 187–190
    Grant in, 172, 175, 187–190
    jokes in, 175, 188–189
    narrative, 187–188, 190

Beer, Janet
    on the subsidiary role of male
        characters in Munro's stories,
        143–151
Benveniste, Emile, 59, 61, 63, 65
Bloom, Harold
    introduction, 1–3
"Boarding House" (Joyce), 137
Borges, Jorge Luis, 1
Bowen, Elizabeth, 1
Brontë, Charlotte
    *Jane Eyre*, 133, 135–137
Bunin, Ivan, 1

Calvino, Italo, 1, 83
"Carried Away," 81, 97
    Arthur in, 95
    charting of one's real life in, 86
    Jack Agnew in, 95
    Louisa in, 95–96, 98, 184
    mystery of, 92, 96
    narrative, 94–95
Carrington, Ildikó de Papp, 65, 67,
    69
Chekhov, Anton, 1, 3
Chesterton, G.K., 2
"Circle of Prayer," 49
    connections in, 46
"Comfort," 173
"Connection," 26, 163
Conrad, Joseph

*Heart of Darkness*, 12–13, 15–17
*Lord Jim*, 137
Cortázar, Julio, 1

*Dance of the Happy Shades*, 41
    on compassion and ironic
        distancing in, 5–28
    setting, 42, 168
    stories in, 5–28, 104
    unstable landscapes of, 86
"Dance of the Happy Shades"
    compassion in, 26
    Dolores Boyle in, 27
    Miss Marsalles in, 26–28
    narrator of, 27
"Day of the Butterfly"
    connections in, 46
    Helen in, 46
"Differently," 50
    Georgia in, 112
Dinesen, Isak, 1
"Directive" (Frost), 26
division of women and men themes,
    1–3
    complex relations, 167–192
    marriages, 2
*Dubliners* (Joyce), 86, 137
Duffy, Dennis, 130, 172
"Dulse"
    Lydia in, 30, 36–37, 44, 77

Eliot, George, 15
"Epilogue: The Photographer," 44,
    150
"Eskimo"
    Mary Jo of, 45
"Executioners"
    connections in, 46
    Helena in, 46

"Family Furnishings," 173
Faulkner, William, 1
"Fitcher's Bird" (Grimm), 124, 126
"Fits," 49, 95
    patterns of complicity in, 65

Peg Kuiper in, 65–69, 89–92
Robert Kuiper in, 65–67, 91–92
self-interest in, 66–67
Weebles' murder-suicide in,
    65–67, 91
Fitzgerald, F. Scott, 1
"Five Points"
    Brenda in, 111–112
    Maria in, 48, 111–112
    narrative, 111
    Neil in, 111–112
"Flat Roads, The"
    connections in, 46
"Floating Bridge," 167
    Helen in, 180–183
    Jinny in, 171, 178–182
    jokes in, 179–181
    landscape of, 171, 178, 182
    Matt in, 182
    narrative, 175, 180
    Neal in, 180–183
    Ricky in, 171, 182–183
"Flowering Judas" (Porter), 2
Foy, Nathalie, 94, 96–97, 178
Freud, Sigmund, 85, 172, 189
    *Jokes and Their Relation to the
        Unconscious*, 179
Friedman, Norman, 82
Friedman, Thomas, 71
*Friend of My Youth*, 41
    characterization in, 42
    loose women in, 103
    narrators in, 36, 94, 103, 111
    stories in, 103–119, 164
"Friend of My Youth"
    codas in, 106–108
    dreams in, 104–106, 109–110,
        116, 118
    Ellie Grieves in, 48, 108, 110
    Flora in, 106–109, 111, 164
    husband-hunting nurses in, 42
    loose women in, 104–105, 107
    mother-daughter relation in,
        104–111, 117–118, 164
    narrative, 30, 43, 105–111, 113, 118

Robert in, 106, 164
Frost, Robert
    "Directive," 26
Frye, Northrop, 157

Gadamer, Hans-Georg, 68–70
Gallant, Mavis, 83–84, 88
Garson, Marjorie, 84
Godard, Barbara
    '"Heirs of the Living Body":
        Alice Munro and the Question
        of a Female Aesthetic,' 149
"Goodness and Mercy"
    Averill in, 118–119
    mother-daughter relation in, 111,
        117
Gordimer, Nadine, 1, 83–84
Greene, Gayle, 33
Grimm fairy tales
    Bluebeard's tales, 124–128, 130,
        132–133, 138
    "Fitcher's Bird," 124, 126
    "Hansel and Gretel," 125
    "The Robber Bridegroom," 124–
        128, 132, 134
Gurr, Andrew
    "Short Fictions and Whole
        Books," 143
Gzowksi, Peter, 94, 168, 179, 184

"Half a Grapefruit"
    Rose in, 48
Hall, Stuart, 170
Hanly, Charles, 67
"Hansel and Gretel" (Grimm), 125
"Hard-Luck Stories"
    Douglas Reider in, 30–31, 33–36
    Julie in, 30–36
    middle-aged love wars in, 161
    narrator in, 30–37, 161–162
Hardy, Thomas, 1
*Hateship, Friendship, Courtship,*
    *Loveship, Marriage*
    memory and imagination in, 169
    stories in, 168, 170–190

"Hateship, Friendship, Courtship,
    Loveship, Marriage," 181
    Edith in, 176, 178
    Johanna Parry in, 170, 173,
        176–178
    Ken Bourdreau in, 176–177
    letters in, 176–178
    narrative, 173, 175–178
    Sabitha in, 176
    schoolgirls' game in, 173, 176,
        178
*Heart of Darkness* (Conrad)
    the "Intended" in, 12–13, 15–17
Heble, Ajay, 88, 90, 188
    on Munro's poetics of surprise,
        57–80
"Heirs of the Living Body," 51, 146
    connections in, 46–47
    Del Jordan in, 44, 46
'"Heirs of the Living Body": Alice
    Munro and the Question of a
    Female Aesthetic' (Godard), 149
Heller, Deborah
    on Munro's irony, 103–121
Hemingway, Ernest, 1, 3
    "Hills Like White Elephants," 2
Herk, Aritha van, 182
"Hills Like White Elephants"
    (Hemingway), 2
"Hold Me Fast, Don't Let Me Pass"
    Antoinette in, 112
    Brenda in, 112
    Hazel in, 112
    irresponsible sex in, 42, 111–112
    Judy in, 111–112
    Tania in, 111
"Home"
    self-consciousness in, 57
Howells, Coral Ann, 84, 133, 143,
    149–150
    on the complex relations of
        women and men in Munro's
        work, 167–192
"How I Met My Husband"
    Edie in, 49

irresponsible sex in, 42
Hunter, Lynette, 150
Hutcheon, Linda, 74

*Idylls of the King* (Tennyson), 132
"Images," 133
  husband-hunting nurses in, 42
  Joe Phippen in, 15–17
  Mary McQuade in, 12–14, 16–17,
    20
  mock mother in, 12
  narrator in, 14–16
  practical jokes in, 13–14
  quest in, 11–12, 15–17, 19
  secrets in, 8
  structure of, 12
irony, 2, 103–121
Irvine, Lorna, 12

"Jack Randa Hotel, The," 184
James, Henry, 1, 24
*Jane Eyre* (Brontë), 133, 135–137
"Jesse and Meribeth," 66
  connections in, 47–48
  Mr. Cryderman in, 61
  Jessie in, 61–62
  Marybeth in, 61
  narrative, 61–62
  notion of truth in, 62
*Jokes and Their Relation to the
  Unconscious* (Gzowski), 179
Joyce, James, 1–3, 81
  "Boarding House," 137
  *Dubliners*, 86, 137
  "A Painful Case," 136
  *Portrait of the Artist as a Young
    Man*, 8

Kafka, Franz, 1
Keats, John, 37
Kemp, Peter, 41
Kipling, Rudyard, 1

"Labor Day Dinner"
  narrator in, 49

Roberta in, 49
Laidlaw, Ann Chamney, 41–43
Laidlaw, Robert Eric, 41, 43
Landolfi, 1
Lawrence, D.H., 1–3, 82
Lefebvre, Henri, 172
  *The Production of Space*, 169
Lessing, Doris, 83
Levene, Mark, 58, 60
  on Munro's womenfolk's survival,
    81–101
"Lichen," 49, 94
  David in, 90
  Stella in, 8, 89, 96
*Lives of Girls and Women*, 12, 15, 41,
  44, 84, 123
  Ada Johnson in, 43, 48, 145, 149
  Addie in, 7
  autobiographical, 144
  Benny in, 58, 86, 97, 144, 146–
    148
  Bobby Sherriff in, 9, 87, 150,
    174–175
  body language in, 9
  Mr. Chamberlain in, 47, 62, 87,
    144, 146–147
  Craig, 144–147
  Del in, 30, 34, 36, 47–49, 62, 87,
    143, 145–149, 151, 174–175,
    178, 183
  Garnet French in, 87, 144, 146,
    148–149
  Jerry Storey in, 144, 147–148
  Moria in, 146
  narrative in, 30, 36, 87–88, 143–
    145, 147, 149–151
  setting, 42, 155–156
  sexuality in, 96
  unstable landscapes of, 86–87
*Lord Jim* (Conrad), 137
*Love of a Good Woman, The*, 81, 89
  charting of one's real life in, 86,
    168
  mystery of, 92
  setting, 168

stories in, 86, 94–95
"Love of a Good Woman, The"
   D.M. Willens in, 97, 123–124,
      126–131, 134–135, 138
   Enid in, 97–98, 126–127, 130–138
   murder in, 123, 126–129, 137–138
   narrative, 98, 127
   Mrs. Quinn in, 97–98, 126–138
   Rupert Quinn in, 97–98, 126–
      127, 129–133, 135–138
   setting of, 123
   sexuality in, 132
*Love Labour's Lost* (Shakespeare), 2
Lynch, Gerald, 168–169

Malamud, Bernard, 1
"Man with the Blue Guitar, The"
   (Stevens), 57
Mann, Thomas, 1
Mansfield, Katherine, 127
"Mariana" (Tennyson), 146
"Marrakesh"
   Dorothy in, 44
Martin, W.R., 24
"Material," 18
   Dotty in, 48
   Hugo in, 44, 87–88–88
   narrative of, 81–82, 87
Maugham, W. Somerset, 1
Mayberry, Katherine J.
   on Munro's storytellers'
      limitations, 29–39
McCarthy, Dermot, 114
McCombs, Judith
   on mythic origins in Munro's
      work, 123–142
"Memorial," 50
   autobiographical, 104
"Meneseteung," 51, 97, 107
   Almeda Joynt Roth in, 113–117,
      156–159, 161
   Jarvis Poulter in, 113–115, 157–
      159, 161
   mother-daughter relation in, 111,
      118

   narrator in, 113, 116–117, 156–
      159
   Queen Aggie in, 158
   *Vidette* in, 113–116, 157–158
*Midnight's Children* (Rushdie), 57
"Miles City, Montana," 66, 89
   Andrew in, 63
   Cynthia in, 63–64
   Meg in, 63–65
   memory in, 63–64
   narrator, 63–65
   notion of truth in, 62
   Steve Gauley in, 63–64
"Mischief"
   Clifford in, 49
   Rose in, 49
"Moon in the Orange Street Skating
   Rink, The"
   Callie in, 48, 91
   Edgar in, 91
   narrator in, 86
   Sam in, 91
*Moons of Jupiter, The*
   connections in, 162–163
   self-corrective moments in, 65
   somberness of, 89
   stories in, 30–37, 78, 162–163,
      172, 184
"Moons of Jupiter, The," 22
   narrator in, 43
*Mothers and Other Clowns* (Redekop),
   174
"Mrs. Cross and Mrs. Kidd"
   connections in, 46
   Mrs. Cross in, 30
   narrative in, 30
Munro, Alice
   awards, 41
   birth, 41
   childhood, 41–42, 85, 168
Munro, H.H., 1
Munro, James, 42
Murphy, Georgeann
   on issues of memory in Munro's
      work, 41–56

"My Mother's Dream"
    narrative, 99
mythic origins, 123–142

Nabokov, Vladimir, 1
narrative, 175
    connections, 81, 83–84
    exuberance, 1–3
    geographically specific, 168–171
    limitations, 29–39, 87
    open-ended, 104, 109
    spatial character of, 81, 91
naturalism, 3
"Nettles," 173, 175, 184
New, W.H., 88

O'Brien, Edna, 1
O'Connor, Flannery, 1
O'Connor, Frank, 1
"Office, The"
    Malley in, 17–19
    mother and writing in, 17–18
    narrator in, 17–18, 43
    self-reproduction in, 18–19
"Oh, What Avails"
    Joan in, 112, 164
    Matilda in, 49
Ondaatje, Michael, 89
*Open Secrets*, 89
    stories in, 94–95, 184
    supernatural in 168
"Oranges and Apples," 179
    Barbara in, 110, 112
    loose women in, 103
"Ottawa Valley," 18
    autobiographical, 104
    mother in, 110
    narrator of, 43, 88, 108–109
    self-consciousness in, 57
"Ounce of Cure, An," 48
"Our Gothic Mother," 133
Ozick, Cynthia, 1

"Painful Case, A" (Joyce), 136

"Passing of the Old Forest, The,"
    156–157
"Peace of Utrecht, The"
    Arthurian legends in, 25
    Aunt Annie in, 22–23
    autobiographical, 85, 104, 133
    connections in, 46
    daughters in, 117
    dead mother in, 19–23, 43
    dream in, 104
    Fred in, 23
    Helen in, 19–25
    Maddy in, 20–26, 46
    symbolism in, 25
Peretz, I.L., 1
Poe, Edgar Allan, 82
Porter, Katherine Anne, 1
    "Flowering Judas," 2
*Portrait of the Artist as a Young Man*
    (Joyce), 8
"Post and Beam," 173
"Princess Ida"
    Ada Jordan in, 48, 50
    Miss Rush in, 48
"Privilege"
    Rose in, 47
*Production of Space, The* (Lefebvre), 169
*Progress of Love, The*
    narrators in, 36, 88
    stories in, 2, 57, 79, 86, 94
    storytelling in, 89, 94
"Progress of Love," 21
    Beryl in, 58–60
    compassion in storytelling in, 17,
      58
    grandmother in, 58–59
    Marietta in, 59
    marriage in, 2
    narrative in, 49–50, 58, 60–61, 92
    notion of truth in, 59–62
    Phemie in, 58–63, 69, 71
Proulx, E. Annie, 84
"Providence," 25
    Rose in, 43

"Prue"
     Prue in, 32–34, 48

*Queenie: A Story*, 173
"Queer Streak, A"
     Dane in, 69
     Dawn Rose in, 48, 69–70
     father's past in, 68–70
     Heather and Gillian in, 69–70
     narrative, 68
     the past and memory in, 67–70
     structure of, 68
     Violet in, 68–70

Rasporich, Beverly, 85
realism, 57, 84, 123, 170, 177
"Real Life, A"
     Millicent in, 51
"Red Dress–1946"
     daughter in, 5
     narrator in, 48
Redekop, Magdalene
     on compassion and ironic
          distancing in *Dance of the
          Happy Shades*, 5–28
     *Mothers and Other Clowns*, 174
Rich, Adrienne, 176
"Rich as Stink"
     Derek in, 98
     Karin in, 86, 98
"Robber Bridegroom, The"
     (Grimm), 124–128, 132, 134
Rorty, Richard, 63
Ross, Catherine Sheldrick, 11–12,
     16, 24
"Royal Beatings"
     Rose in, 43, 68
     narrators of, 43
*Runaway*
Rushdie, Salman
     *Midnight's Children*, 57

Said, Edward, 154
Sansom, William, 83

Schor, Naomi, 25
*Selected Stories*, 1
     stories in, 85
Shakespeare, William
     *Love Labour's Lost*, 2
Shields, Carol, 110, 175
"Shining Hours, The"
     Mary in, 44
"Short Fictions and Whole Books"
     (Gurr), 143
"Simon's Luck"
     fantasies in, 183
     Rose in, 48
     Simon in, 48
Singer, Shelley, 1
Smith, Rowland
     on the frontier code, 153–165
*Something I've Been Meaning to Tell
You*
     narratives, 87–88
     setting, 42
     stories in, 81, 104, 108
"Something I've Been Meaning to
Tell You"
     Arthur in, 25
     sexual jealousy in, 49
"Spanish Lady, The"
     narrator of, 45
Sparshott, Francis, 9
"Spelling"
     Flo in, 50
Stevens, Wallace
     "The Man with the Blue Guitar,"
     57
"Stone in the Field, The"
     Fleming in, 43
     narrator of, 44, 89
Stone, Robert, 82
*Strange Things* (Atwood), 154–156,
159
Struthers, Tim, 12

"Tell Me Yes or No"
     narrator in, 49

Tennyson, Lord Alfred
   *Idylls of the King*, 132
   "Mariana," 146
Thacker, Robert, 168
Thomson, David, 72
Tolstoy, Leo, 2
"Trip to the Coast, A," 51
Turgenev, Ivan, 2–3
   *Fathers and Sons*, 186

"Vandals"
   coda in, 96
   Kenny in, 96
   Ladner in, 96–98
   Liza in, 96–98
*View from Castle Rock, The*
*Vintage Munro*
"Visitors"
   Wilfred in, 32–34

"Walker Brothers Cowboy," 18, 51
   daughter in, 5–9, 11, 19, 85
   father Ben Jordan in, 5–9, 11,
      15–17, 19, 43, 50, 85–86, 97
   irony, 19
   "I Spy" game in, 7–8, 10
   mask of, 6
   miming in, 9
   mother in, 5–8, 10–12, 16, 19, 27
   narrator in, 7–9, 11, 14, 85–86
   Nora in, 6–11, 13, 20
   secrets in, 8, 10–11, 19
Walser, Robert, 1
Welty, Eudora, 1–2, 45
Wharton, Edith, 1
"What Is Remembered?" 173, 179
   bush doctor in, 183–185
   Jonas in, 184–185
   Meriel in, 183–186
   narrative, 175
   Pierre in, 184–186
   woman's escape into fantasy in,
      183–186
"White Dump," 81, 96

Bastille Day in, 71–72, 79
Denise in, 70–74, 76–79, 92–93,
   98
individual points of view in,
   70–79, 92, 94
irresponsible sex in, 42
Isabel in, 71, 73–74, 77–79,
   93–94, 98
Sophie in, 71, 74–77, 93–94, 98
*Who Do You Think You Are?*
   memory and imagination in,
      168–169
   setting, 42
   sexuality in, 96
   stories in, 9, 88
"Who Do You Think You Are?"
   daughter in, 21
   mimicry in, 9
   Ralph Gillespie in, 9
   Rose Gillespie in, 9, 42, 49, 88
   storytelling in, 88
"Wigtime"
   Anita in, 47–48, 112
   connections in, 47
   Margot in, 47–48, 112
   Reuel in, 47
   Teresa in, 47–48
"Wilderness Station, A"
   Annie Herron in, 128, 160–161
   James Mullen in, 161
   murder in, 94, 123
   Reverend McBain in, 160
   setting, 123, 159–161
"Wild Swans"
   Rose Jordan in, 45
"Winter Wind"
   autobiographical, 104
   mother-daughter relation in, 110
   narrator in, 50
   self-consciousness in, 57
Woolf, Virginia, 2, 113, 127

Yeats, William Butler
   "Among School Children," 27